The Public Voice WSIS Sourcebook: Perspectives on the World Summit on the Information Society

The Public Voice
thepublicvoice.org

Printed in the United States of America

ISBN: 1-893044-21-1

About the Public Voice

The Public Voice is a project of the Electronic Privacy Information Center (EPIC), http://www.epic.org. The Public Voice project was established to promote public participation in Internet policy making on issues ranging from privacy and free expression to consumer protection and Internet governance. Through international conferences, reports and funding for travel, the Public Voice project seeks to increase the presence of NGOs at meetings across the globe.

In cooperation with the OECD, UNESCO, and other international organizations, the Public Voice project brings civil society leaders face to face with government officials for constructive engagement about current policy issues. Public Voice events have been held in Buenos Aires, Dubai, Hong Kong, Honolulu, Kuala Lumpur, Ottawa, Paris, and Washington, DC.

The Public Voice project is made possible, in part, by the Knowledge, Creativity, and Freedom program of the Ford Foundation and by the Open Society Institute.

The Public Voice WSIS Sourcebook: Perspectives on the World Summit on the Information Society

Foreward

"We are going through a historic transformation in the way we live, learn, work, communicate and do business. We must do so not passively, but as makers of our own destiny. Technology has produced the information age. Now it is up to all of us to build an information society." – Secretary-General Kofi Annan

The United Nations has launched a crtical discussion about the futue of the information society. This is far more than a debate about the governance of the Internet or the role of regulation in the context of new technology. Fundamentally, it is an effort to answer the question, posed by the inventor Thomas Edison, whether we can control with our heads what we create with our hands. How do we ensure that the benefits of information technology are widely disseminated? How do we promote education and science and address the great challenges facing us in the twenty-first century? How do we preserve core human rights, such as freedom of expression and privacy, as new technology creates both opportunities and risks? How do we learn more about one anothers cultural heritage, social concerns, and economic aspirations?

The collection of materials contained in this volume is our effort to further the dialogue. Some of the materials are provided as basic documents that will help those who are new to the World Summit on the Information Society learn more about the role of various institutions, including the International Telecommunications Union, the various meetings, such as the recent summit in Geneva, and the future activities that will take place in the run-up to Tunisia in 2005

Other materials provide more opinionated perspectives on the challenges that the United Nations faces as it pursues work in this field. While our sympathies are clearly with those in the civil society community who have urged the UN to carry forward its commitment to fundamental human rights into the Information Society, it is also clear that there are a range of views about how this might best be accomplished. On the question, for example, of whether to hold the 2005 meeting in Tunis, some organizations concerned about the protection of free expression and human rights have questioned whether Tunis is the appropriate setting for the next summit. Still others urge ongoing engagement with governments precisely to build support for the principles set out in the Universal Declaration of Human Rights. This is an important discussion and should continue through the summit and beyond.

There is also a debate concerning the future of the Internet than tends to focus too narrowly on whether the Internet is to be "governed," "managed," or simply left alone. A broader understanding of the emerging communications infrastructure might consider instead how best to promote the extraordinary cultural heritage of the peoples around the world, how to address the enormous educational challenges facing many societies, and simply how access to communications technology is itself a critical transformative opportunity. Many of the articles in this collection point to these larger questions.

The Public Voice WSIS Sourcebook also provides a useful list of resources and contacts for individuals and organizations that wish to become more involbed in this processs. In the first phase of the WSIS it was clear that few NGOs in the United States were aware of this process or its possible significance. We hope that the publication of the Sourcebook will enable more organizations in the US and around the world to learn about the WSIS, the perspectives of various organizations, and to participate in this discussion.

Marc Rotenberg
Frannie Wellings
Thepublicvoice.org
May 2004

Table of Contents

WSIS Background

Basic Information: About WSIS[1]

Document of the ITU

The World Summit on the Information Society will be held in two phases. The first phase of WSIS will take place in Geneva hosted by the Government of Switzerland from 10 to 12 December 2003. The second phase will take place in Tunis hosted by the Government of Tunisia, from 16 to 18 November 2005.

Background

Resolution 73 of the International Telecommunication Union (Minneapolis, 1998) resolved to instruct the ITU Secretary-General to place the question of the holding of a World Summit on the Information Society (WSIS) on the agenda of the United Nations Administrative Committee on Coordination (ACC now the United Nations System Chief Executive Board - CEB) and to report to the ITU governing body, the Council, on the results of that consultation. In his report to the 1999 session of the Council on that consultation, the Secretary- General indicated that the ACC had reacted positively and that a majority of other organizations and agencies had expressed interest in being associated with the preparation and holding of the Summit. It was decided that the Summit would be held under the high patronage of the UN Secretary-General, with ITU taking the lead role in preparations.

In 2001, the ITU Council decided to hold a Summit in two phases with the first phase to be held from 10 to 12 December 2003, in Geneva, Switzerland and the second from 16 to 18 November 2005 in Tunis, Tunisia.

The UN General Assembly Resolution 56/183 endorsed the framework for the Summit adopted by the ITU Council. The Resolution also endorses the leading role of the Union in the Summit and its preparation, in cooperation with other interested organizations and partners.

The UN General Assembly Resolution 56/183 further recommended that preparations for the Summit take place through an open-ended intergovernmental Preparatory Committee that would define the agenda of the Summit, decide on the modalities of

[1] http://www.itu.int/wsis/basic/about.html

the participation of other stakeholders in the Summit, and finalize both the draft declaration and the draft plan of action. It invited the ITU to assume the leading managerial role in the Executive Secretariat of the Summit and invited Governments to participate actively in the preparatory process of the Summit and to be represented in the Summit at the highest possible level.

In Resolution 56/183 the General Assembly also encouraged contributions from all relevant UN bodies and other intergovernmental organizations, including international and regional institutions, non-governmental organizations, civil society and the private sector to actively participate in the intergovernmental preparatory process of the Summit and the Summit itself.

The Challenge

The global information society is evolving at breakneck speed. The accelerating convergence between telecommunications, broadcasting multimedia and information and communication technologies (ICTs) is driving new products and services, as well as ways of conducting business and commerce. At the same time, commercial, social and professional opportunities are exploding as new markets open to competition and foreign investment and participation. The modern world is undergoing a fundamental transformation as the industrial society that marked the 20th century rapidly gives way to the information society of the 21st century. This dynamic process promises a fundamental change in all aspects of our lives, including knowledge dissemination, social interaction, economic and business practices, political engagement, media, education, health, leisure and entertainment. We are indeed in the midst of a revolution, perhaps the greatest that humanity has ever experienced. To benefit the world community, the successful and continued growth of this new dynamic requires global discussion.

The Opportunity

The World Summit on the Information Society will provide a unique opportunity for all key stakeholders to assemble at a high-level gathering and to develop a better understanding of this revolution and its impact on the international community. It aims to bring together Heads of State, Executive Heads of United Nations agencies, industry leaders, non-governmental organizations, media representatives and civil society in a single high-level event. The roles of the various partners (Member States, UN specialized agencies, private sector and civil society) in ensuring smooth coordination of the practical establishment of the information society around the globe will also be at the heart of the Summit and its preparation.

Outcome

The anticipated outcome of the Summit is to develop and foster a clear statement of political will and a concrete plan of action for achieving the goals of the Information Society, while fully reflecting all the different interests at stake. The scope and nature of this ambitious project will require partnerships with public and private entities, and such partnerships will be actively sought in the coming months.

High Level Summit Organizing Committee (HLSOC)

A High-Level Summit Organizing Committee (HLSOC) has been established under the patronage of Kofi Annan, UN Secretary-General and Chairman of the United Nations System Chief Executive Board for Coordination (CEB formally ACC).

Its purpose is to coordinate the efforts of the international United Nations family in the preparation, organization and holding of WSIS. All the members of the HLSOC have engaged to provide specific information about their work that will help develop the Summit themes. The HLSOC reports directly to the CEB and oversees the work of the Executive Secretariat

Composition
The HLSOC is composed of a Representative of the United Nations Secretary-General and Executive Heads of the following UN specialized agencies: FAO, IAEA, ICAO, ILO, IMO, ITU, UNCTAD, UNDP, UNEP, UNESCO, UNHCR, UNIDO, UPU, WHO, WIPO, WMO. It comprises also the Director General of WTO, the Executive Director of UNITAR, the Executive Secretaries of the UN Regional Economic Commissions and the President of the World Bank. The Secretary-General of the International Telecommunication Union serves as Chairman of the HLSOC.

Executive Secretariat

Executive Director: Mr. Pierre Gagné
Deputy Executive Director: Mr. Art Levin

The Executive Secretariat of the World Summit on the Information Society (WSIS/ES) was established under the authority of the HLSOC to assist in the preparation of the Summit. It is based at the ITU headquarters in Geneva, with the following mandate and terms of reference:

Mandate

The mandate of the ES is as follows :

- Advise on all aspects of Summit preparation
- Prepare progress reports on the preparation if the Summit
- Develop an operation plan and a timetable for preparation of the Summit
- Obtain sponsorship and funding

Composition

A number of different organizations, including government ministries, private companies, UN agencies and NGOs have sent experts to the WSIS Executive Secretariat on a full or part-time basis. The composition of the ES is as follows:

- Staff from Member States
- Staff from the UN specialized agencies participating in the HLSOC
- Staff from the private sector
- Staff from NGOs and Civil Society

Host Countries Executive Secretariats

Switzerland and Tunisia have created working secretariats under the direction of their respective Ambassadors to the World Summit.

Who will participate?

Governments

All governments have a stake in the Information Society, whatever their level of national income or their infrastructure facilities. Governments are key for bringing the benefits of the Information Society to everyone through the development of national and global policies and frameworks to meet the challenges of the Information Society. In their pursuit of the public interest, governments can raise awareness, facilitate access to information for the public, and they also can lay the foundations for all citizens to benefit from Information and Communication Technologies in terms of improved quality of life, social services and economic growth

Private Sector

The private sector will play an active role, in conjunction with governments and civil society, by offering an economically viable model to achieve the development objectives on the world agenda. The contribution of the private sector is instrumental in creating the material conditions for universal access to information and value-added ICT services. Its involvement in the Summit will promote economic growth and new partnerships, technology transfer, increase awareness of new technologies, and motivate the creation of local content development and skilled employment opportunities.

The private sector input to the Summit is being facilitated by the Coordinating Committee of Business Interlocutors (CCBI), chaired by the International Chamber of Commerce (ICC). For more information about the mobilization, contributions and participation of the global business community, please click here.

Civil Society
Civil society is playing an active role in identifying the social and cultural consequences of current trends and in drawing attention to the need to introduce democratic accountability on the strategic options taken at all levels. Its diversity and, often, hands-on approach to issues, make civil society a key player in the renewed international partnership called for by the UN Secretary-General.

United Nations Family
The Summit offers a unique opportunity for the global community to reflect, discuss and give shape to our common destiny in an era when countries and peoples are interconnected as never before. The UN family of organizations serves as a catalyst for change by bringing together state governments, as well as the private sector, international institutions and civil society in pursuit of common goals. The United Nations system and its specialized agencies will be deeply involved in the organization and holding of the Summit, with the International Telecommunication Union (ITU) taking a lead role.

How to Contribute?

The key opportunity to contribute and be part of the World Summit is to actively participate in the preparatory process of the World Summit. This can be done is the following suggested ways:

- Build a constructive network
- Stimulate multi-actor cooperation
- Submit substantive inputs
- Organize meetings
- Organize training sessions
- Formulate operational proposals
- Provide funding and support

When and Where?

The Summit is being held under the high patronage of Kofi Annan, UN Secretary-General, with the International Telecommunication Union taking the lead role, in cooperation with other interested UN agencies, and will occur in two phases:

Geneva 2003: First Phase
The first phase of the World Summit will take place in Geneva hosted by the Government of Switzerland from 10 to 12 December 2003. It will address the broad range of themes concerning the Information Society and adopt a Declaration of Principles and plan of action, addressing the whole range of issues related to the Information Society.

Tunis 2005: Second Phase
The second phase of the World Summit will take place in Tunis hosted by the Government of Tunisia, from 16 to 18 November 2005. Development themes will be a key focus in this phase, and it will assess progress that has been made and adopt any further plan of action to be taken.

Report on the Preparatory Process for the First Phase of the Summit[2]

Adama Samassékou, President of the WSIS Preparatory Committee

Introduction

On 21 December 2001, the United Nations General Assembly adopted Resolution 56/183 concerning the organization of a World Summit on the Information Society (WSIS). The resolution recommended creating an open-ended intergovernmental Preparatory Committee which would be responsible for the preparations for WSIS. Its tasks would include drawing up an agenda for the Summit, finalizing a draft Declaration and a draft Action Plan, and deciding on the arrangements for participation by other stakeholders. The resolution further invited governments to participate actively in the WSIS preparatory process and encouraged other intergovernmental organizations, including international and regional institutions, non-governmental organizations, civil society and the private sector to contribute to, and actively participate in, the intergovernmental preparatory process of the Summit and the Summit itself.

Preparatory process: meetings of the Preparatory Committee (PrepCom)

First meeting of the Preparatory Committee - PrepCom-1

The first meeting of the intergovernmental WSIS Preparatory Committee, convened by the Secretary-General of the International Telecommunication Union (ITU), took place in Geneva from 1 to 5 July 2002, and took the following decisions:

President of PrepCom
A total of 969 delegates, representing 142 governments, numerous international organizations and groups from the private sector and civil society, elected as President of the Preparatory Committee Mr Adama Samassékou of Mali. Mr Samassékou, who served for seven years (from 1993 to 2000) as Mali's Minister of Education, is currently the President of the African Academy of Languages. He is very active in the work of volunteer organizations, being the Founding President of the People's Movement for Human Rights Education.

[2] On the web at http://www.itu.int/wsis/documents/listing-all-en-s|1.asp

Participation arrangements, accreditation arrangements and Rules of Procedure

The arrangements governing participation1 and the arrangements governing accreditation2 for the WSIS preparatory process for stakeholders other than governments were determined at PrepCom-1, having been drawn up by Subcommittee 1 under the chairmanship of Ambassador Daniel Stauffacher of Switzerland. The Plenary Meeting also adopted the Rules of Procedure3 for the Preparatory Committee, also drawn up by Subcommittee 1.

Work on content

Subcommittee 2, chaired by Ambassador Pablo Macedo of Mexico, was entrusted with consideration of the proposed themes for the Summit.
On the basis of the discussions, the Chairman of Subcommittee 2 submitted a document4 to the Plenary containing the principles governing the preparatory work and WSIS itself and the proposed themes for the Summit. The Plenary Meeting took note of the report of the Chairman of Subcommittee 2 and adopted the document on principles. The document on themes was considered in informal consultations that took place from 16 to 18 September 2002 in Geneva.

Election of the members of the PrepCom Bureau

On the basis of consultations carried out with the regional groups of the United Nations system, the Preparatory Committee elected the 16 members of the Bureau by acclamation: South Africa, Brunei Darussalam, Brazil, Dominican Republic, United States, Finland, France, Latvia, Libya, Mexico, Romania, Japan, Pakistan, Russian Federation, Switzerland (host country for the first phase), Tunisia (host country for the second phase).

Preparation of the second meeting of PrepCom

At a meeting on 19 September 2002, the members of the Bureau agreed that work on the substance of the Summit should continue after the informal consultations on 16 to 18 September 2002, under the authority of President Samassékou, in order to prepare effectively the second meeting of the PrepCom. They therefore requested the President to prepare, with the assistance of an informal drafting group, a preliminary draft WSIS Declaration and Plan of Action to serve as a basis for discussion on the content of the Summit at PrepCom-2 in February 2003. On reflection, the President considered that it was the prerogative of PrepCom-2 to prepare the draft Declaration and Plan of Action, in a participative and effective manner, and he accordingly opted to prepare an orientation document (or non-paper) which, drawn up under his authority, would enjoy only informal status and would in no way constitute a result of prior negotiations between the various stakeholders in the Summit.

The informal drafting group met on 13 to 16 December 2002 in Glion sur Montreux. In their discussions, the experts also referred to the Bamako and Bucharest Declarations, the outcome document of the informal consultations of Subcommittee 2 of PrepCom-1 held on 16 to 18 September 2002[5] and the written contributions from the various stakeholders in the information society received by the WSIS Executive Secretariat before 7 December 2002. The outcome of the discussions of the informal drafting group was posted on the WSIS website in January 2003 under the title: "Proposal of an Orientation Document for PrepCom-2, Information and Communication for All"[6]. The Glion meeting was organized and financed by Switzerland.

Second meeting of the Preparatory Committee - PrepCom-2

PrepCom-2 was held from 17 to 28 February 2003 in Geneva. Three days were devoted to contributions from visionaries at the highest level and to thematic round tables. The PrepCom-2 participants then examined, within Subcommittee 2 on content, the draft Declaration of Principles and draft Action Plan for WSIS. Subcommittee 2, chaired by Ambassador Yasuaki Nogawa of Japan, set up a working group under the chairmanship of Ms Lyndall Shope-Mafole of South Africa and a small working group chaired by Adama Samassékou.

Ms Shope-Mafole's working group was open to all States and was entrusted with preparing the draft Declaration of Principles and draft Action Plan for the Summit. During a 30-minute timeslot each day, Subcommittee 2 listened to statements by observers.

Mr Samassékou's working group was responsible for outlining the overall structure of the draft Declaration and draft Action Plan of the Summit. The overall structure was approved as a working basis by the subcommittee on Friday 21 February.

At its last Plenary Meeting, on Friday 28 February 2003, after taking note of the report by Subcommittee 2, the Preparatory Committee adopted a proposal by the Bureau to the effect that the work on content be pursued in the period between PrepCom-2 and PrepCom-3.

Decision concerning continuation of the work on content
At the end of the meeting, and with the aim of ensuring continuity in the work on content, PrepCom-2 requested the Chairman of the Working Group of Subcommittee 2 to prepare, by 21 March 2003, a consolidation of the written contributions received

at 28 February 2003, and to draw up basic working documents for the future negotiations.

PrepCom-2 mandated the President of PrepCom to oversee the intersessional work and, inter alia, to bring together a formal intergovernmental drafting group for a five-day meeting in July 2003, so as to advance negotiations on the content.
PrepCom-2 further decided to set up an intersessional mechanism to refine further the documents for the meeting of the aforementioned drafting group.

Finally, PrepCom-2 mandated the WSIS Executive Secretariat to prepare a reference document containing written contributions from participants, for publication on the WSIS website.

Second phase of the Summit
The participants in the third Plenary Meeting were informed by the President of PrepCom of consultations held on the articulation between Geneva and Tunis, including in particular the establishment of a coordination group comprising representatives of the host countries, the ITU Secretary-General, the Executive Director of the WSIS Executive Secretariat and the President of PrepCom. The members of the group would work in close collaboration until 2005.

The President of PrepCom said that the outcome of the first phase would be a Declaration of Principles and a Plan of Action setting forth a vision and covering the essential issues associated with the information society. The second phase of the Summit, on the basis of the results of the Geneva phase, would address the transition to a knowledge society. The outcome could take the form of the adoption of an instrument, such as a charter, and a Tunis agenda enshrining digital solidarity at the global level, and regional action plans. The second phase would be prepared in a structured manner during 2004 and 2005, including through the organization of PrepComs.

The Tunisian Government announced that the second phase of the Summit would take place from 16 to 18 November 2005 in Tunis.

Implementation of PrepCom-2 decisions
Under the supervision of the President of PrepCom, acting in liaison with the PrepCom Bureau, the basic working documents were drawn up and posted on the WSIS website on 21 March 2003, together with the reference document setting out all contributions received by 31 May 2003, namely from governments, intergovernmental organizations, the private sector and civil society.

Through the good offices of the Director-General of UNESCO, a meeting of the formal intergovernmental drafting group was organized from 15 to 18 July 2003 at UNESCO headquarters in Paris. The dates were set on the basis of UNESCO availabilities and to avoid a clash with the Asia-Pacific Telecommunity (APT) meeting on information society initiatives organized in Bangalore from 21 to 25 July 2003.

PrepCom-2's decision to put in place an intersessional mechanism gave rise to lengthy and arduous discussion within the PrepCom Bureau, which was torn between a desire to adhere to the letter of the decision and the need to reflect the spirit of the decision in order to make significant progress in work on refining the documents during the intersessional period.

After several Bureau meetings and following bilateral consultations conducted by the PrepCom President with each member country of the Bureau and each regional group, the members of the Bureau decided merely to refine the documents without altering the content, so as not to prejudge the negotiations in July. The refined documents were posted on the WSIS website on 5 June 2003.

In view of the enormous quantity of written contributions on the draft Declaration and draft Action Plan received by the Executive Secretariat up to the end of May, the President of PrepCom and the members of the Bureau both considered that it was necessary to carry out some consolidation work in order to make the basic working documents easier to use at the July intersessional meeting. Under a mandate from the Bureau, the President of PrepCom therefore prepared, with the assistance of the Executive Secretariat, working documents for the intersessional meeting, in which all the contributions from governments were incorporated. These documents were posted on the WSIS website in mid-June.

Again with the same aim of preparing the July 2003 meeting effectively, the members of the Bureau also agreed to the proposal by the President of PrepCom to draw up, with the assistance of the WSIS Executive Secretariat, a reader's guide, as suggested by a member of the Bureau, for use by participants as a handy tool for rapidly identifying points of convergence and divergence and new points in the contributions on the draft Declaration and draft Action Plan. In the preparation of the guide, which was published on the WSIS website in early July 2003, account was also taken of the inputs from observers.

Intersessional meeting in Paris

The meeting of the open-ended intergovernmental drafting group took place from 15 to 18 July 2003 in UNESCO (Paris), with the mandate to advance negotiations on the draft Declaration and draft Action Plan. The drafting group meeting was attended by 750 delegates.

The opening session of the meeting, at the proposal of the PrepCom Bureau, elected Ms Lyndall Shope-Mafole (South Africa) by acclamation as Chairman of the drafting group. The work began with a discussion of the draft Declaration of Principles and the draft Action Plan, as refined since PrepCom-2. To advance the work, the Chairman established small groups to consider the following difficult issues: right to communicate, Internet management, good governance and network security.

The meeting was open to observers. At the beginning of the deliberations, two hours were set aside for observers to express their priorities in relation to the basic documents; on subsequent days, observers were given the floor for one hour at the beginning of the meeting.

The meeting reviewed and revised the draft Declaration of Principles (DT/4)[7]. The meeting also exchanged views on the draft of the Action Plan. At its meeting on 18 July, the PrepCom Bureau decided to send the revised text of the draft Declaration direct to PrepCom-3, without amendment, and mandated the Chairman of the drafting group to carry out, on the basis of the comments formulated at the intersessional meeting, a further revision of the Action Plan during the intersessional period until PrepCom-3, with the assistance of the Executive Secretariat and under the supervision of the President of PrepCom. This decision of the Bureau was announced at the closure of the Paris meeting and distributed as a note by the President of PrepCom[8].

This task was completed within the set time-frame and the revised text of the draft Action Plan was published on the WSIS website on 26 August 2003[9].

Third meeting of the Preparatory Committee - PrepCom-3

The third meeting of PrepCom was held in Geneva from 15 to 26 September 2003. It was attended by some 1 600 delegates representing Member States of the United Nations, intergovernmental organizations, civil society and the business sector. The committee's work focused in particular on the Rules of Procedure of the Summit and on the draft Declaration of Principles and draft Plan of Action.

Rules of Procedure of the Summit

The Rules of Procedure of the Summit were drawn up by Subcommittee 1 under the chairmanship of Ambassador Daniel Stauffacher (Switzerland) and adopted by the Plenary10.

Work on the content and suspension of the meeting
Subcommittee 2, chaired by Ambassador Asko Numminen (Finland), reviewed the draft Declaration of Principles and draft Plan of Action. It also established a working group, under the chairmanship of Ms Lyndall Shope-Mafole (South Africa), on the draft Declaration of Principles, while maintaining the work on the draft Plan of Action under its own responsibility. In order to advance work on the two documents, it was also decided to set up ad hoc groups on specific topics under the guidance of different countries. In addition, the draft text of the Declaration of Principles was examined at a special meeting of heads of delegation.

Observers were able to attend the discussion in the Plenary and working group meetings and were invited by the chairmen to make brief statements. Observers were also invited to make brief statements at the start of each ad hoc group meeting.

At its third Plenary Meeting, on 26 September 2003, the Preparatory Committee heard the report of the Chairman of Subcommittee 2 and considered the revised versions of the draft Declaration of Principles and draft Action Plan. It was decided that both documents should be considered as the basis for future negotiations.

In view of the lack of consensus on several paragraphs, the Plenary decided to suspend the meeting of PrepCom-3 and to resume negotiations in Geneva from 10 to 14 November 2003. It also decided that the President of PrepCom should supervise the informal consultations in order to facilitate work when the negotiations were resumed in November, and that, on the basis of the discussions during PrepCom-3 and his own consultations, he should prepare a non-paper on the Declaration for possible consideration by the reconvened PrepCom-3. The matters remaining to be resolved following PrepCom-3's September meeting were those relating to funding, security, intellectual property, human rights and media and Internet governance.

The non-governmental partners were authorized to express their priorities at all meetings of the Plenary, Subcommittee 2 and the working group.

Resumed PrepCom-3 negotiations, 10 to 14 November 2003
During the opening meeting, the Plenary accepted the proposal by the President of PrepCom to amend the decision made in September and to use as a basis for negotiation the non-paper by the President of PrepCom. In preparing that document, the President of PrepCom had organized a series of informal open-ended consultation

meetings, which had been held on 20, 30 and 31 October 2003 under the chairmanship of Ambassador Asko Numminen of Finland.

On the basis of a participatory working method intended to build a consensus on the draft Declaration of Principles, the inputs from government delegations had been taken into account in a balanced manner in the preparation of the non-paper by the President of PrepCom that was presented to the resumed PrepCom-3. The President of PrepCom had also solicited the remarks of observers on the document. Comments received from the CCBI and Civil Society Bureau had been posted on the Summit website before 10 November 2003.

During the resumed session of PrepCom-3 in November 2003, Ambassador Asko Numminen, Chairman of Subcommittee 2, led the negotiations aimed at reducing the points on which views among governments diverged on the Declaration of Principles and Plan of Action.

In the interests of eliminating those divergences, he established a number of working groups which met with bilateral and multilateral ad hoc groups. Each of those small groups focused on specific areas in which views diverged, particularly security, Internet governance, intellectual property rights, the financing of a global and inclusive information society, the role of the media and human rights issues.

The negotiations ended on 14 November 2003 with agreement having been reached on the great majority of the paragraphs in the two draft texts. Nevertheless, a number of points on which views diverged remained open, calling for further negotiations:

Security - protection of privacy, of the consumer and of data, including the fight against spam, and the integrity and protection of networks.
Internet governance - role of all stakeholders in the management of the Internet, both at the technical level and by public authorities, and the balance between these two levels.
Intellectual property rights - striking a balance between the interests of the holders of intellectual property rights and the interests of users in the information society.
Funding for ICTs in the interests of development, with the creation of a digital solidarity fund.
Role of the media and human rights issues - importance of the role played by the media in the information society, particularly the question as to whether the media are to be considered as specific players within civil society and whether the references to freedom of opinion and expression in Article 19 of the Universal Declaration of Human Rights should be linked to the references in Article 29 in regard to the rights and freedoms of others.

During the final Plenary on 14 November 2003, the participants took note of the proposal for a decision concerning the Tunis phase which would be submitted to the Summit in December 2003: "We decided to hold a preparatory meeting in first half of 2004 to review those issues of the information society which should form the focus of the Tunis phase of the WSIS and to agree on the structure of the process for the second phase on the basis of contribution from delegations. The Bureau of the Tunis phase of the WSIS under the leadership of its Chairman should commence preparation of this preparatory meeting".

At the closure of the meeting, the President of PrepCom proposed to the Plenary that PrepCom-3 be suspended a second time in order to allow for the finalization, at a high-level meeting to be held on 5 and 6 December 2003, of the negotiations on the points on which views diverged. The participants approved that proposal, as well as a proposal to entrust Switzerland, the host country for the first phase of the Summit, with the task of holding informal consultations in the intervening period, with a view to preparing those final negotiations ahead of the Summit.

Finalization of the PrepCom-3 negotiations on 5 and 6 December 2003

At the first Plenary Meeting of the resumed PrepCom-3 on 5 December 2003 the participants agreed to follow the recommendations of the PrepCom Bureau and limit negotiations to those points on which the diverging views had not been reconciled on 14 November, taking for a basis the compromise text submitted by Switzerland as facilitator of the informal consultations. The participants also agreed to set up a working group to conduct negotiations, under the chairmanship of Switzerland. At the end of that Plenary Meeting observers were invited to share their observations. While excluded from the working group, they were regularly informed of the progress made in its work. As the financing question remained unresolved on 6 December, it was decided to continue on 9 December. On that day, an agreement was reached on the point in question, and the working group made its report to the PrepCom-3 plenary. This final Plenary Meeting adopted the draft Declaration of Principles and Action Plan to be submitted to the Summit.

Regional conferences

The following regional conferences have been held:

- African Regional Conference, Bamako (Mali), 28-30 May 2002[11]
- Pan-European Regional Conference, Bucharest (Romania), 7-9 September 2002[12]
- Asia-Pacific Regional Conference, Tokyo (Japan), 13-15 January 2003[13]

- Latin America and the Caribbean Regional Conference, Bávaro (Dominican Republic), 29-31 January 200314
- Western Asia Preparatory Conference, Beirut (Lebanon), 4-6 February 200315

The results of these regional conferences are posted on the WSIS website and were distributed to PrepCom-2 participants as a compilation so that they could be taken into account in the work of Subcommittee 2 on the content of the Summit.

Activities undertaken to enhance the visibility of WSIS

Mr Samassékou took the initiative of meeting with Heads of State interested in the Summit and with United Nations authorities and agencies, as well as with key figures from international organizations and other bodies and institutions from the public sector, the private sector and civil society, in order to enhance the visibility of WSIS and obtain the best possible participation in the preparatory process and the Summit itself. The details of his meetings and visits are provided in his reports to PrepCom-216 and PrepCom-317, it being particularly significant that he had the honour of being received by the authorities, on several occasions at the very highest level, of the following countries: Germany, Brazil, Brunei Darussalam, Dominican Republic, Egypt, United States, France, Greece, Italy, Japan, Mali, Morocco, Mexico, Mozambique, Romania, Switzerland and Tunisia. He was also received by the United Nations Secretary-General in New York and by his undersecretaries, as well as the Directors-General of the United Nations agencies and international organizations in Geneva; by the Commission for Enterprise and the Information Society, the commission responsible for external relations and the Directorate-General for Development of the European Communities; by the Secretary-General of the African, Caribbean and Pacific Group of States; by the Secretary-General of Francophonie; by the Secretary-General of the Commonwealth; as well as by a large number of heads of permanent missions to the international organizations at Geneva with responsibility for WSIS.

Mr Samassékou has also participated, in his capacity as President of the Preparatory Committee for WSIS, in a series of events and conferences in order to inform participants of the preparatory work for the Summit and share with them his personal vision:

- 23rd University Summer Course in Communication, 26-30 August 2002, Hourtin

- World Summit on Sustainable Development, 26 August - 4 September 2002, Johannesburg
- GlobalCN 2002, III Global Congress on Community Networking in the Digital Era, 9-13 October 2002, Montreal
- United Nations General Assembly, Commission II, 16 October 2002, New York
- Bishkek-Moscow Conference on the Information Society (WSIS preparatory conference for CIS countries), 22-24 October 2002, Moscow
- G77 High Level Conference on Science and Technology, 27-30 October 2002, Dubai
- Civil Society Consultative Meeting in preparation for WSIS, UNESCO, 27-28 November 2002, Paris
- Ministerial meeting of Francophone countries, 12-13 December 2002, Lausanne
- Asia-Pacific Regional Conference for WSIS, 13-15 January 2003, Tokyo
- Latin America and Caribbean Regional Conference for WSIS, 29-31 January 2003, Bávaro, Dominican Republic
- OECD/UN/World Bank, "Forum on the knowledge economy. Integration of ICTs in development programmes", 4-5 March 2003, Paris, France
- 2nd Symposium on Francophonie, "Three dimensions of language: Cooperation, Diversity and Peace", 2-4 April 2003, Mexico City, Mexico
- EU/Greek Government, Symposium on e-inclusion, "Towards an information society in Europe for citizens", 11 April 2003, Heraklion, Crete, Greece
- Global Business Dialogue on e-commerce (GBDe), workshop on WSIS, 20 May 2003, Brussels, Belgium
- European Internet Foundation, Dinner debate, "Preparing for WSIS", 21 May 2003, Brussels, Belgium
- Global Knowledge Partnership (GKP), Annual Conference, "Knowledge for development initiatives", 21-23 May 2003, Rome, Italy
- UN ICT Task Force, Regional conference for Latin America and the Caribbean, "Towards WSIS - renewed roles for the private sector", 12-13 June 2003, Rio de Janeiro, Brazil
- Arab League/Arab Republic of Egypt, Regional Pan-Arab Conference on WSIS, 16-18 June 2003, Cairo, Egypt
- EU/Italian Government, Conference on "e-government", 7-8 July 2003, Como, Italy
- African Union, Second ordinary assembly of Heads of State and Government, 10-12 July 2003, Maputo, Mozambique

- International Federation of Libraries Associations and Institutions (IFLA), World Congress of Libraries and Information and General Assembly, 1-9 August 2003, Berlin, Germany
- Pacific Economic Cooperation Council (PECC), 15th session "Securing the future: a strategic path for the next decade", 1-3 September 2003, Brunei Darussalam
- OIF/Government of Morocco, Conference of French-speaking Ministers on the Information Society, 4-5 September 2003, Rabat, Morocco
- Ministerial round table "Towards knowledge societies", UNESCO, 9-10 October 2003, Paris
- ITU TELECOM WORLD 2003, 12-18 October 2003, Geneva

Overview of Civil Society Elements and how to get involved: the Plenary, the Content and Themes Group, and the Bureau[3]

Seán Ó Siochrú and Wolfgang Kleinwaechter

The following describes in summary the basic structures that civil society has developed over the preparatory process of the WSIS.

A key principle underlying the structures of civil society is that there must be multiple avenues and means for participation, and that all civil society entities can select the nature, level and extent of participation according to their needs and interests.

Civil Society can constitute itself into a Plenary (CSP) at every official convening of the WSIS process, such as Regional Conferences, PrepComs, Intersessional meetings and Summits. The CSP is open to the participation of all civil society participants. When convened, it is the ultimate civil society authority in the WSIS process, in relation to the mandate and scope of the specific event. At PrepCom II, CSP endorsed the existence and terms of the Civil Society Content & Themes Group and the Civil Society Bureau.

The Civil Society Content and Themes Group (CS C&T) coordinates the work of numerous self-constituting civil society Caucuses, Working Groups and other content related entities. It is charged with facilitating agreement on and taking decisions on content-related issues, while respecting the domain expertise and competence of Caucuses and Content Groups. It reports regularly to the CS plenary on decisions taken.

The Civil Society Bureau (CSB) functions as an interlinkage between civil society participants and the intergovernmental Bureau and process, with regard to operational and logistical needs, procedures and interactions. It does not concern itself with content-related issues. The Bureau is constituted by 21 'family nodal points', that enable any civil society entity to find a 'home', and it enhances interaction between all sections of civil society and between civil society and others. The Civil Society Division of the WSIS Secretariat provides the Secretariat for the CS Bureau. The Bureau reports regularly to the CS Plenary on decisions taken.

---

[3] On the web at http://www.wsis-cs.org/cs-overview.html

The Civil Society Division of the WSIS Secretariat (CSD) supports the activities of all civil society participants and entities in the Summit, including the above. It may also provide support to participants who chose not to associate with some or all of the above entities, in a manner that respects the functions and authority of the above.

The CSP approved a Virtual CS Plenary group as an electronic forum between physical meetings of the CSP, to promote debate and greater transparency in the organisation of civil society during the Summit preparatory process, including between the various entities above. It is not a decision making entity, but decisions of other entities will be circulated there. It is open to all accredited entities, to registered bodies at WSIS meetings, and to all civil society entities with an active interest in the WSIS.

All the above entities will take action to ensure that, within the available resources, key decisions are taken only after consideration of the issues in the working languages of the Summit: English, French and Spanish.

Overview and Composition of the Civil Society Bureau[4]

Document of the FdD, Executive Secretariat, Civil Society Division

Overview

Global civil society has created an international civil society Bureau. This decision was taken during the second session of he PrepCom (17-28 February 2003) after intense consultations organised by the civil society division with numerous civil society representatives that lasted more than a year. The international civil society Bureau represents a "turning point" in the history of the United Nations and international negotiations, insofar as, for the first time, civil society has mechanisms that facilitate the dialogue with governments and insures its effective participation at the heart of the decisive structure of a United Nations Summit.

In the context of the WSIS, the Bureau offers new perspectives to raise all questions that are being asked to solve the concrete preoccupations of our citizens. The Bureau is composed of larges "families" of global civil society: unions, media, creators and actors of culture, towns and local authorities, NGOs, youth, gender, indigenous people, handicapped people, etc. It also includes the regional contact points in order to establish links with all continents.

Composition of the Bureau

The CSB Civil Society Bureau has been put forward to respond to the need of setting up a civil society mechanism that can ensure optimum participation of all constituencies of civil society in all aspects of the WSIS process. This was required because of the great diversity of civil society, the large number of organizations it comprises and the vast array of interests and perspectives it holds.

The CSB is composed of various 'families' that represent the different constituencies within the civil society. Each family has some common characteristics: an homogeneous institutional culture, established or informal consultation mechanisms, a coordinator organization of international character that cluster a large number of members under the same reference structure. Thus with communication mechanisms the family allows information dissemination and exchanges between members of the same group. The family offers the opportunity to discuss the different ways in which

[4] On the web at http://www.wsis2005.org/wsis/main_c01_08.htm

information can be provided to all interested members of this family. The family also provides a channel to disseminate to all these interested members of each family the relevant information on the negotiation process.

Address by Secretary-General Kofi Annan to the World Summit on the Information Society[5]

Document of the United Nations

I would like to thank the Government of Switzerland for the extraordinary support it has provided for this Summit -- not just the warm hospitality and the typical Swiss efficiency, but also the steadfast political commitment to making this Summit a success.

I would also like to thank Mr. Utsumi and the International Telecommunication Union for the openness with which they have managed the Summit process, and for working so effectively with the entire UN system.

We are going through a historic transformation in the way we live, learn, work, communicate and do business. We must do so not passively, but as makers of our own destiny. Technology has produced the information age. Now it is up to all of us to build an information society.

This Summit is unique. Where most global conferences focus on global threats, this one will consider how best to use a new global asset.

We are all familiar with the extraordinary power of information and communications technologies.

From trade to telemedicine, from education to environmental protection, we have in our hands, on our desktops and in the skies above, the ability to improve standards of living for millions of people on this planet.

We have tools that can propel us toward the Millennium Development Goals; instruments with which to advance the cause of freedom and democracy; vehicles with which to propagate knowledge and mutual understanding.

We have all of this potential. The challenge before this Summit is what to do with it.

The so-called digital divide is actually several gaps in one.

---

[5] Press Release SG/SM/9070 PI/1535, http://www.un.org/News/Press/docs/2003/sgsm9070.doc.htm

There is a technological divide — great gaps in infrastructure.

There is a content divide. A lot of web-based information is simply not relevant to the real needs of people. And nearly 70 percent of the world's web sites are in English, at times crowding out local voices and views.

There is a gender divide, with women and girls enjoying less access to information technology than men and boys. This can be true of rich and poor countries alike: some developing countries are among those offering the most digital opportunities for women, while some developed countries have done considerably less well.

There is a commercial divide. E-commerce is linking some countries and companies ever more closely together. But others run the risk of further marginalization. Some experts describe the digital divide as one of the biggest non-tariff barriers to world trade.

And there are obvious social, economic and other disparities and obstacles that affect a country's ability to take advantage of digital opportunities.

We cannot assume that such gaps will disappear on their own, over time, as the diffusion of technology naturally spreads its wealth. An open, inclusive information society that benefits all people will not emerge without sustained commitment and investment. We look to you, the leaders assembled here, to produce those acts of political will.

We also look to the business community, which I am glad to say is represented here in impressive numbers. The future of the IT industry lies not so much in the developed world, where markets are getting saturated, as in reaching the billions of people in the developing world who remain untouched by the information revolution. E-health, e-school and other applications can offer the new dynamic of growth for which the industry has been looking.

We look to civil society groups, in particular for their rich knowledge of hopes and concerns at the local level, among communities that are eager to join in the global exchange of ideas and information, but may also feel their identities are threatened by a pre-packaged global culture.

And we look to media organizations, which are both creators of content and essential watchdogs. At yesterday's World Electronic Media Forum, broadcasting leaders from all the world's regions adopted a declaration in which they pledged to do their part for development and social cohesion. It is vital that they retain their freedom to do so, as spelt out in Article 19 of the Universal Declaration of Human Rights. Indeed, the right to freedom of opinion and expression is fundamental to development, democracy and peace, and must remain a touchstone for our work ahead.

Information and communication technologies are not a panacea or magic formula. But they can improve the lives of everyone on this planet.

Yet even as we talk about the power of technology, let us remember who is in charge. While technology shapes the future, it is people who shape technology, and decide what it can and should be used for.

So let us embrace these new technologies. But let us recognize that we are embarked on an endeavour that transcends technology. Building an open, empowering information society is a social, economic and ultimately political challenge.

There is no comparison between the technologies of the atomic age and those of the information age. Nonetheless, something written half a century ago by the American nuclear scientist J. Robert Oppenheimer seems strangely prescient and applicable today. And I quote:

"The open society, the unrestricted access to knowledge, the unplanned and uninhibited association of men for its furtherance -- these are what may make a vast, complex, ever growing, ever changing, ever more specialized and expert technological world, nevertheless a world of human community."

We must remember that.

Official Outcomes

Declaration of Principles

Building the Information Society: a Global Challenge in the New Millennium[6]

Document of the ITU

A. Our Common Vision of the Information Society

1. We, the representatives of the peoples of the world, assembled in Geneva from 10-12 December 2003 for the first phase of the World Summit on the Information Society, declare our common desire and commitment to build a people-centred, inclusive and development-oriented Information Society, where everyone can create, access, utilize and share information and knowledge, enabling individuals, communities and peoples to achieve their full potential in promoting their sustainable development and improving their quality of life, premised on the purposes and principles of the Charter of the United Nations and respecting fully and upholding the Universal Declaration of Human Rights.

2. Our challenge is to harness the potential of information and communication technology to promote the development goals of the Millennium Declaration, namely the eradication of extreme poverty and hunger; achievement of universal primary education; promotion of gender equality and empowerment of women; reduction of child mortality; improvement of maternal health; to combat HIV/AIDS, malaria and other diseases; ensuring environmental sustainability; and development of global partnerships for development for the attainment of a more peaceful, just and prosperous world. We also reiterate our commitment to the achievement of sustainable development and agreed development goals, as contained in the Johannesburg Declaration and Plan of Implementation and the Monterrey Consensus, and other outcomes of relevant United Nations Summits.

3. We reaffirm the universality, indivisibility, interdependence and interrelation of all human rights and fundamental freedoms, including the right to development, as enshrined in the Vienna Declaration. We also reaffirm that democracy, sustainable development, and respect for human rights and fundamental freedoms as well as good governance at all levels are interdependent

---

[6] WSIS-03/GENEVA/DOC/4-E, 12 December 2003, Original: English, http://www.itu.int/wsis/documents/listing-all-en-s|1.asp

and mutually reinforcing. We further resolve to strengthen respect for the rule of law in international as in national affairs.

4. We reaffirm, as an essential foundation of the Information Society, and as outlined in Article 19 of the Universal Declaration of Human Rights, that everyone has the right to freedom of opinion and expression; that this right includes freedom to hold opinions without interference and to seek, receive and impart information and ideas through any media and regardless of frontiers. Communication is a fundamental social process, a basic human need and the foundation of all social organization. It is central to the Information Society. Everyone, everywhere should have the opportunity to participate and no one should be excluded from the benefits the Information Society offers.

5. We further reaffirm our commitment to the provisions of Article 29 of the Universal Declaration of Human Rights, that everyone has duties to the community in which alone the free and full development of their personality is possible, and that, in the exercise of their rights and freedoms, everyone shall be subject only to such limitations as are determined by law solely for the purpose of securing due recognition and respect for the rights and freedoms of others and of meeting the just requirements of morality, public order and the general welfare in a democratic society. These rights and freedoms may in no case be exercised contrary to the purposes and principles of the United Nations. In this way, we shall promote an Information Society where human dignity is respected.

6. In keeping with the spirit of this declaration, we rededicate ourselves to upholding the principle of the sovereign equality of all States.

7. We recognize that science has a central role in the development of the Information Society. Many of the building blocks of the Information Society are the result of scientific and technical advances made possible by the sharing of research results.

8. We recognize that education, knowledge, information and communication are at the core of human progress, endeavour and well-being. Further, Information and Communication Technologies (ICTs) have an immense impact on virtually all aspects of our lives. The rapid progress of these technologies opens completely new opportunities to attain higher levels of development. The capacity of these technologies to reduce many traditional obstacles, especially those of time and distance, for the first time in history makes it possible to use the potential of these technologies for the benefit of millions of people in all corners of the world.

9. We are aware that ICTs should be regarded as tools and not as an end in themselves. Under favourable conditions, these technologies can be a powerful instrument, increasing productivity, generating economic growth, job creation and employability and improving the quality of life of all. They can also promote dialogue among people, nations and civilizations.

10. We are also fully aware that the benefits of the information technology revolution are today unevenly distributed between the developed and developing countries and within societies. We are fully committed to turning this digital divide into a digital opportunity for all, particularly for those who risk being left behind and being further marginalized.

11. We are committed to realizing our common vision of the Information Society for ourselves and for future generations. We recognize that young people are the future workforce and leading creators and earliest adopters of ICTs. They must therefore be empowered as learners, developers, contributors, entrepreneurs and decision-makers. We must focus especially on young people who have not yet been able to benefit fully from the opportunities provided by ICTs. We are also committed to ensuring that the development of ICT applications and operation of services respects the rights of children as well as their protection and well-being.

12. We affirm that development of ICTs provides enormous opportunities for women, who should be an integral part of, and key actors, in the Information Society. We are committed to ensuring that the Information Society enables women's empowerment and their full participation on the basis on equality in all spheres of society and in all decision-making processes. To this end, we should mainstream a gender equality perspective and use ICTs as a tool to that end.

13. In building the Information Society, we shall pay particular attention to the special needs of marginalized and vulnerable groups of society, including migrants, internally displaced persons and refugees, unemployed and underprivileged people, minorities and nomadic people. We shall also recognize the special needs of older persons and persons with disabilities.

14. We are resolute to empower the poor, particularly those living in remote, rural and marginalized urban areas, to access information and to use ICTs as a tool to support their efforts to lift themselves out of poverty.

15. In the evolution of the Information Society, particular attention must be given to the special situation of indigenous peoples, as well as to the preservation of their heritage and their cultural legacy.

16. We continue to pay special attention to the particular needs of people of developing countries, countries with economies in transition, Least Developed Countries, Small Island Developing States, Landlocked Developing Countries, Highly Indebted Poor Countries, countries and territories under occupation, countries recovering from conflict and countries and regions with special needs as well as to conditions that pose severe threats to development, such as natural disasters.

17. We recognize that building an inclusive Information Society requires new forms of solidarity, partnership and cooperation among governments and other stakeholders, i.e. the private sector, civil society and international organizations. Realizing that the ambitious goal of this Declaration—bridging the digital divide

and ensuring harmonious, fair and equitable development for all—will require strong commitment by all stakeholders, we call for digital solidarity, both at national and international levels.

18. Nothing in this Declaration shall be construed as impairing, contradicting, restricting or derogating from the provisions of the Charter of the United Nations and the Universal Declaration of Human Rights, any other international instrument or national laws adopted in furtherance of these instruments.

B. An Information Society for All: Key Principles

19. We are resolute in our quest to ensure that everyone can benefit from the opportunities that ICTs can offer. We agree that to meet these challenges, all stakeholders should work together to: improve access to information and communication infrastructure and technologies as well as to information and knowledge; build capacity; increase confidence and security in the use of ICTs; create an enabling environment at all levels; develop and widen ICT applications; foster and respect cultural diversity; recognize the role of the media; address the ethical dimensions of the Information Society; and encourage international and regional cooperation. We agree that these are the key principles for building an inclusive Information Society.

1) The role of governments and all stakeholders in the promotion of ICTs for development

20. Governments, as well as private sector, civil society and the United Nations and other international organizations have an important role and responsibility in the development of the Information Society and, as appropriate, in decision-making processes. Building a people-centred Information Society is a joint effort which requires cooperation and partnership among all stakeholders.
2) Information and communication infrastructure: an essential foundation for an inclusive information society

21. Connectivity is a central enabling agent in building the Information Society. Universal, ubiquitous, equitable and affordable access to ICT infrastructure and services, constitutes one of the challenges of the Information Society and should be an objective of all stakeholders involved in building it. Connectivity also involves access to energy and postal services, which should be assured in conformity with the domestic legislation of each country.

22. A well-developed information and communication network infrastructure and applications, adapted to regional, national and local conditions, easily-accessible and affordable, and making greater use of broadband and other innovative technologies where possible, can accelerate the social and economic progress of countries, and the well-being of all individuals, communities and peoples.

23. Policies that create a favourable climate for stability, predictability and fair competition at all levels should be developed and implemented in a manner that not only attracts more private investment for ICT infrastructure development but also enables universal service obligations to be met in areas where traditional market conditions fail to work. In disadvantaged areas, the establishment of ICT public access points in places such as post offices, schools, libraries and archives, can provide effective means for ensuring universal access to the infrastructure and services of the Information Society.

3) Access to information and knowledge

24. The ability for all to access and contribute information, ideas and knowledge is essential in an inclusive Information Society.

25. The sharing and strengthening of global knowledge for development can be enhanced by removing barriers to equitable access to information for economic, social, political, health, cultural, educational, and scientific activities and by facilitating access to public domain information, including by universal design and the use of assistive technologies.

26. A rich public domain is an essential element for the growth of the Information Society, creating multiple benefits such as an educated public, new jobs, innovation, business opportunities, and the advancement of sciences. Information in the public domain should be easily accessible to support the Information Society, and protected from misappropriation. Public institutions such as libraries and archives, museums, cultural collections and other community-based access points should be strengthened so as to promote the preservation of documentary records and free and equitable access to information.

27. Access to information and knowledge can be promoted by increasing awareness among all stakeholders of the possibilities offered by different software models, including proprietary, open-source and free software, in order to increase competition, access by users, diversity of choice, and to enable all users to develop solutions which best meet their requirements. Affordable access to software should be considered as an important component of a truly inclusive Information Society.

28. We strive to promote universal access with equal opportunities for all to scientific knowledge and the creation and dissemination of scientific and technical information, including open access initiatives for scientific publishing.

4) Capacity building

29. Each person should have the opportunity to acquire the necessary skills and knowledge in order to understand, participate actively in, and benefit fully from, the Information Society and the knowledge economy. Literacy and universal primary education are key factors for building a fully inclusive information society, paying particular attention to the special needs of girls and women.

Given the wide range of ICT and information specialists required at all levels, building institutional capacity deserves special attention.

30. The use of ICTs in all stages of education, training and human resource development should be promoted, taking into account the special needs of persons with disabilities and disadvantaged and vulnerable groups.

31. Continuous and adult education, re-training, life-long learning, distance-learning and other special services, such as telemedicine, can make an essential contribution to employability and help people benefit from the new opportunities offered by ICTs for traditional jobs, self-employment and new professions. Awareness and literacy in ICTs are an essential foundation in this regard.

32. Content creators, publishers, and producers, as well as teachers, trainers, archivists, librarians and learners, should play an active role in promoting the Information Society, particularly in the Least Developed Countries.

33. To achieve a sustainable development of the Information Society, national capability in ICT research and development should be enhanced. Furthermore, partnerships, in particular between and among developed and developing countries, including countries with economies in transition, in research and development, technology transfer, manufacturing and utilization of ICT products and services are crucial for promoting capacity building and global participation in the Information Society. The manufacture of ICTs presents a significant opportunity for creation of wealth.

34. The attainment of our shared aspirations, in particular for developing countries and countries with economies in transition, to become fully-fledged members of the Information Society, and their positive integration into the knowledge economy, depends largely on increased capacity building in the areas of education, technology know-how and access to information, which are major factors in determining development and competitiveness.

5) Building confidence and security in the use of ICTs

35. Strengthening the trust framework, including information security and network security, authentication, privacy and consumer protection, is a prerequisite for the development of the Information Society and for building confidence among users of ICTs. A global culture of cyber-security needs to be promoted, developed and implemented in cooperation with all stakeholders and international expert bodies. These efforts should be supported by increased international cooperation. Within this global culture of cyber-security, it is important to enhance security and to ensure the protection of data and privacy, while enhancing access and trade. In addition, it must take into account the level of social and economic development of each country and respect the development-oriented aspects of the Information Society.

36. While recognizing the principles of universal and non-discriminatory access to ICTs for all nations, we support the activities of the United Nations to prevent

the potential use of ICTs for purposes that are inconsistent with the objectives of maintaining international stability and security, and may adversely affect the integrity of the infrastructure within States, to the detriment of their security. It is necessary to prevent the use of information resources and technologies for criminal and terrorist purposes, while respecting human rights.

37. Spam is a significant and growing problem for users, networks and the Internet as a whole. Spam and cyber-security should be dealt with at appropriate national and international levels.

6) Enabling environment

38. An enabling environment at national and international levels is essential for the Information Society. ICTs should be used as an important tool for good governance.

39. The rule of law, accompanied by a supportive, transparent, pro-competitive, technologically neutral and predictable policy and regulatory framework reflecting national realities, is essential for building a people-centred Information Society. Governments should intervene, as appropriate, to correct market failures, to maintain fair competition, to attract investment, to enhance the development of the ICT infrastructure and applications, to maximize economic and social benefits, and to serve national priorities.

40. A dynamic and enabling international environment, supportive of foreign direct investment, transfer of technology, and international cooperation, particularly in the areas of finance, debt and trade, as well as full and effective participation of developing countries in global decision-making, are vital complements to national development efforts related to ICTs. Improving global affordable connectivity would contribute significantly to the effectiveness of these development efforts.

41. ICTs are an important enabler of growth through efficiency gains and increased productivity, in particular by small and medium sized enterprises (SMEs). In this regard, the development of the Information Society is important for broadly-based economic growth in both developed and developing economies. ICT-supported productivity gains and applied innovations across economic sectors should be fostered. Equitable distribution of the benefits contributes to poverty eradication and social development. Policies that foster productive investment and enable firms, notably SMEs, to make the changes needed to seize the benefits from ICTs, are likely to be the most beneficial.

42. Intellectual Property protection is important to encourage innovation and creativity in the Information Society; similarly, the wide dissemination, diffusion, and sharing of knowledge is important to encourage innovation and creativity. Facilitating meaningful participation by all in intellectual property issues and knowledge sharing through full awareness and capacity building is a fundamental part of an inclusive Information Society.

43. Sustainable development can best be advanced in the Information Society when ICT-related efforts and programmes are fully integrated in national and regional development strategies. We welcome the New Partnership for Africa's Development (NEPAD) and encourage the international community to support the ICT-related measures of this initiative as well as those belonging to similar efforts in other regions. Distribution of the benefits of ICT-driven growth contributes to poverty eradication and sustainable development.

44. Standardization is one of the essential building blocks of the Information Society. There should be particular emphasis on the development and adoption of international standards. The development and use of open, interoperable, non-discriminatory and demand-driven standards that take into account needs of users and consumers is a basic element for the development and greater diffusion of ICTs and more affordable access to them, particularly in developing countries. International standards aim to create an environment where consumers can access services worldwide regardless of underlying technology.

45. The radio frequency spectrum should be managed in the public interest and in accordance with principle of legality, with full observance of national laws and regulation as well as relevant international agreements.

46. In building the Information Society, States are strongly urged to take steps with a view to the avoidance of, and refrain from, any unilateral measure not in accordance with international law and the Charter of the United Nations that impedes the full achievement of economic and social development by the population of the affected countries, and that hinders the well-being of their population.

47. Recognizing that ICTs are progressively changing our working practices, the creation of a secure, safe and healthy working environment, appropriate to the utilisation of ICTs, respecting all relevant international norms, is fundamental.

48. The Internet has evolved into a global facility available to the public and its governance should constitute a core issue of the Information Society agenda. The international management of the Internet should be multilateral, transparent and democratic, with the full involvement of governments, the private sector, civil society and international organizations. It should ensure an equitable distribution of resources, facilitate access for all and ensure a stable and secure functioning of the Internet, taking into account multilingualism.

49. The management of the Internet encompasses both technical and public policy issues and should involve all stakeholders and relevant intergovernmental and international organizations. In this respect it is recognized that:

a) Policy authority for Internet-related public policy issues is the sovereign right of States. They have rights and responsibilities for international Internet-related public policy issues;

b) The private sector has had and should continue to have an important role in the development of the Internet, both in the technical and economic fields;

c) Civil society has also played an important role on Internet matters, especially at community level, and should continue to play such a role;

d) Intergovernmental organizations have had and should continue to have a facilitating role in the coordination of Internet-related public policy issues;

e) International organizations have also had and should continue to have an important role in the development of Internet-related technical standards and relevant policies.

50. International Internet governance issues should be addressed in a coordinated manner. We ask the Secretary-General of the United Nations to set up a working group on Internet governance, in an open and inclusive process that ensures a mechanism for the full and active participation of governments, the private sector and civil society from both developing and developed countries, involving relevant intergovernmental and international organizations and forums, to investigate and make proposals for action, as appropriate, on the governance of Internet by 2005.

7) ICT applications: benefits in all aspects of life

51. The usage and deployment of ICTs should seek to create benefits in all aspects of our daily life. ICT applications are potentially important in government operations and services, health care and health information, education and training, employment, job creation, business, agriculture, transport, protection of environment and management of natural resources, disaster prevention, and culture, and to promote eradication of poverty and other agreed development goals. ICTs should also contribute to sustainable production and consumption patterns and reduce traditional barriers, providing an opportunity for all to access local and global markets in a more equitable manner. Applications should be user-friendly, accessible to all, affordable, adapted to local needs in languages and cultures, and support sustainable development. To this effect, local authorities should play a major role in the provision of ICT services for the benefit of their populations.

8) Cultural diversity and identity, linguistic diversity and local content

52. Cultural diversity is the common heritage of humankind. The Information Society should be founded on and stimulate respect for cultural identity, cultural and linguistic diversity, traditions and religions, and foster dialogue among cultures and civilizations. The promotion, affirmation and preservation of diverse cultural identities and languages as reflected in relevant agreed United Nations documents including UNESCO's Universal Declaration on Cultural Diversity, will further enrich the Information Society.

53. The creation, dissemination and preservation of content in diverse languages and formats must be accorded high priority in building an inclusive Information Society, paying particular attention to the diversity of supply of creative work and due recognition of the rights of authors and artists. It is essential to promote the production of and accessibility to all content—educational, scientific, cultural or recreational—in diverse languages and formats. The development of local content suited to domestic or regional needs will encourage social and economic development and will stimulate participation of all stakeholders, including people living in rural, remote and marginal areas.
54. The preservation of cultural heritage is a crucial component of identity and self–understanding of individuals that links a community to its past. The Information Society should harness and preserve cultural heritage for the future by all appropriate methods, including digitisation.

9) Media

55. We reaffirm our commitment to the principles of freedom of the press and freedom of information, as well as those of the independence, pluralism and diversity of media, which are essential to the Information Society. Freedom to seek, receive, impart and use information for the creation, accumulation and dissemination of knowledge are important to the Information Society. We call for the responsible use and treatment of information by the media in accordance with the highest ethical and professional standards. Traditional media in all their forms have an important role in the Information Society and ICTs should play a supportive role in this regard. Diversity of media ownership should be encouraged, in conformity with national law, and taking into account relevant international conventions. We reaffirm the necessity of reducing international imbalances affecting the media, particularly as regards infrastructure, technical resources and the development of human skills.

10) Ethical dimensions of the information society

56. The Information Society should respect peace and uphold the fundamental values of freedom, equality, solidarity, tolerance, shared responsibility, and respect for nature.
57. We acknowledge the importance of ethics for the Information Society, which should foster justice, and the dignity and worth of the human person. The widest possible protection should be accorded to the family and to enable it to play its crucial role in society.
58. The use of ICTs and content creation should respect human rights and fundamental freedoms of others, including personal privacy, and the right to freedom of thought, conscience, and religion in conformity with relevant international instruments.

59. All actors in the Information Society should take appropriate actions and preventive measures, as determined by law, against abusive uses of ICTs, such as illegal and other acts motivated by racism, racial discrimination, xenophobia, and related intolerance, hatred, violence, all forms of child abuse, including paedophilia and child pornography, and trafficking in, and exploitation of, human beings.

11) International and regional cooperation

60. We aim at making full use of the opportunities offered by ICTs in our efforts to reach the internationally agreed development goals, including those contained in the Millennium Declaration, and to uphold the key principles set forth in this Declaration. The Information Society is intrinsically global in nature and national efforts need to be supported by effective international and regional cooperation among governments, the private sector, civil society and other stakeholders, including the international financial institutions.

61. In order to build an inclusive global Information Society, we will seek and effectively implement concrete international approaches and mechanisms, including financial and technical assistance. Therefore, while appreciating ongoing ICT cooperation through various mechanisms, we invite all stakeholders to commit to the "Digital Solidarity Agenda" set forth in the Plan of Action. We are convinced that the worldwide agreed objective is to contribute to bridge the digital divide, promote access to ICTs, create digital opportunities, and benefit from the potential offered by ICTs for development. We recognize the will expressed by some to create an international voluntary "Digital Solidarity Fund", and by others to undertake studies concerning existing mechanisms and the efficiency and feasibility of such a Fund.

62. Regional integration contributes to the development of the global Information Society and makes strong cooperation within and among regions indispensable. Regional dialogue should contribute to national capacity building and to the alignment of national strategies with the goals of this Declaration of Principles in a compatible way, while respecting national and regional particularities. In this context, we welcome and encourage the international community to support the ICT-related measures of such initiatives.

63. We resolve to assist developing countries, LDCs and countries with economies in transition through the mobilization from all sources of financing, the provision of financial and technical assistance and by creating an environment conducive to technology transfer, consistent with the purposes of this Declaration and the Plan of Action.

64. The core competences of the International Telecommunication Union (ITU) in the fields of ICTs—assistance in bridging the digital divide, international and regional cooperation, radio spectrum management, standards development and

the dissemination of information—are of crucial importance for building the Information Society.

C. Towards an Information Society for All Based on Shared Knowledge

65. We commit ourselves to strengthening cooperation to seek common responses to the challenges and to the implementation of the Plan of Action, which will realize the vision of an inclusive Information Society based on the Key Principles incorporated in this Declaration.

66. We further commit ourselves to evaluate and follow-up progress in bridging the digital divide, taking into account different levels of development, so as to reach internationally agreed development goals, including those contained in the Millennium Declaration, and to assess the effectiveness of investment and international cooperation efforts in building the Information Society.

67. We are firmly convinced that we are collectively entering a new era of enormous potential, that of the Information Society and expanded human communication. In this emerging society, information and knowledge can be produced, exchanged, shared and communicated through all the networks of the world. All individuals can soon, if we take the necessary actions, together build a new Information Society based on shared knowledge and founded on global solidarity and a better mutual understanding between peoples and nations. We trust that these measures will open the way to the future development of a true knowledge society.

Plan of Action[7]

Document of the ITU

A. Introduction

1. The common vision and guiding principles of the Declaration are translated in this Plan of Action into concrete action lines to advance the achievement of the internationally-agreed development goals, including those in the Millennium Declaration, the Monterrey Consensus and the Johannesburg Declaration and Plan of Implementation, by promoting the use of ICT-based products, networks, services and applications, and to help countries overcome the digital divide. The Information Society envisaged in the Declaration of Principles will be realized in cooperation and solidarity by governments and all other stakeholders.

2. The Information Society is an evolving concept that has reached different levels across the world, reflecting the different stages of development. Technological and other change is rapidly transforming the environment in which the Information Society is developed. The Plan of Action is thus an evolving platform to promote the Information Society at the national, regional and international levels. The unique two-phase structure of the World Summit on the Information Society (WSIS) provides an opportunity to take this evolution into account.

3. All stakeholders have an important role to play in the Information Society, especially through partnerships:

a) Governments have a leading role in developing and implementing comprehensive, forward looking and sustainable national e-strategies. The private sector and civil society, in dialogue with governments, have an important consultative role to play in devising national e-strategies.

b) The commitment of the private sector is important in developing and diffusing information and communication technologies (ICTs), for infrastructure, content and applications. The private sector is not only a market player but also plays a role in a wider sustainable development context.

c) The commitment and involvement of civil society is equally important in creating an equitable Information Society, and in implementing ICT-related initiatives for development.

---

[7] WSIS-03/GENEVA/DOC/5-E, Original: English, 12 December 2003, http://www.itu.int/wsis/documents/listing-all-en-s|1.asp

d) International and regional institutions, including international financial institutions, have a key role in integrating the use of ICTs in the development process and making available necessary resources for building the Information Society and for the evaluation of the progress made.

B. Objectives, goals and targets

4. The objectives of the Plan of Action are to build an inclusive Information Society; to put the potential of knowledge and ICTs at the service of development; to promote the use of information and knowledge for the achievement of internationally agreed development goals, including those contained in the Millennium Declaration; and to address new challenges of the Information Society, at the national, regional and international levels. Opportunity shall be taken in phase two of the WSIS to evaluate and assess progress made towards bridging the digital divide.

5. Specific targets for the Information Society will be established as appropriate, at the national level in the framework of national e-strategies and in accordance with national development policies, taking into account the different national circumstances. Such targets can serve as useful benchmarks for actions and for the evaluation of the progress made towards the attainment of the overall objectives of the Information Society.

6. Based on internationally agreed development goals, including those in the Millennium Declaration, which are premised on international cooperation, indicative targets may serve as global references for improving connectivity and access in the use of ICTs in promoting the objectives of the Plan of Action, to be achieved by 2015. These targets may be taken into account in the establishment of the national targets, considering the different national circumstances:

to connect villages with ICTs and establish community access points;

to connect universities, colleges, secondary schools and primary schools with ICTs;

to connect scientific and research centres with ICTs;

to connect public libraries, cultural centres, museums, post offices and archives with ICTs;

to connect health centres and hospitals with ICTs;

to connect all local and central government departments and establish websites and email addresses;

to adapt all primary and secondary school curricula to meet the challenges of the Information Society, taking into account national circumstances;

to ensure that all of the world's population have access to television and radio services;

to encourage the development of content and to put in place technical conditions in order to facilitate the presence and use of all world languages on the Internet;
to ensure that more than half the world's inhabitants have access to ICTs within their reach.

7. In giving effect to these objectives, goals and targets, special attention will be paid to the needs of developing countries, and in particular to countries, peoples and groups cited in paragraphs 11-16 of the Declaration of Principles.

C. Action Lines

C1. The role of governments and all stakeholders in the promotion of ICTs for development

8. The effective participation of governments and all stakeholders is vital in developing the Information Society requiring cooperation and partnerships among all of them.

a) Development of national e-strategies, including the necessary human capacity building, should be encouraged by all countries by 2005, taking into account different national circumstances.

b) Initiate at the national level a structured dialogue involving all relevant stakeholders, including through public/private partnerships, in devising e-strategies for the Information Society and for the exchange of best practices.

c) In developing and implementing national e-strategies, stakeholders should take into consideration local, regional and national needs and concerns. To maximize the benefits of initiatives undertaken, these should include the concept of sustainability. The private sector should be engaged in concrete projects to develop the Information Society at local, regional and national levels.

d) Each country is encouraged to establish at least one functioning Public/Private Partnership (PPP) or Multi-Sector Partnership (MSP), by 2005 as a showcase for future action.

e) Identify mechanisms, at the national, regional and international levels, for the initiation and promotion of partnerships among stakeholders of the Information Society.

f) Explore the viability of establishing multi-stakeholder portals for indigenous peoples at the national level.

g) By 2005, relevant international organizations and financial institutions should develop their own strategies for the use of ICTs for sustainable development, including sustainable production and consumption patterns and as an effective instrument to help achieve the goals expressed in the United Nations Millennium Declaration.

h) International organizations should publish, in their areas of competence, including on their website, reliable information submitted by relevant stakeholders on successful experiences of mainstreaming ICTs.

i) Encourage a series of related measures, including, among other things: incubator schemes, venture capital investments (national and international), government investment funds (including micro-finance for Small, Medium-sized and Micro Enterprises (SMMEs), investment promotion strategies, software export support activities (trade counseling), support of research and development networks and software parks.

C2. Information and communication infrastructure: an essential foundation for the Information Society

9. Infrastructure is central in achieving the goal of digital inclusion, enabling universal, sustainable, ubiquitous and affordable access to ICTs by all, taking into account relevant solutions already in place in developing countries and countries with economies in transition, to provide sustainable connectivity and access to remote and marginalized areas at national and regional levels.

a) Governments should take action, in the framework of national development policies, in order to support an enabling and competitive environment for the necessary investment in ICT infrastructure and for the development of new services.

b) In the context of national e-strategies, devise appropriate universal access policies and strategies, and their means of implementation, in line with the indicative targets, and develop ICT connectivity indicators.

c) In the context of national e-strategies, provide and improve ICT connectivity for all schools, universities, health institutions, libraries, post offices, community centres, museums and other institutions accessible to the public, in line with the indicative targets.

d) Develop and strengthen national, regional and international broadband network infrastructure, including delivery by satellite and other systems, to help in providing the capacity to match the needs of countries and their citizens and for the delivery of new ICT-based services. Support technical, regulatory and operational studies by the International Telecommunication Union (ITU) and, as appropriate, other relevant international organizations in order to:

broaden access to orbital resources, global frequency harmonization and global systems standardization;

encourage public/private partnership;

promote the provision of global high-speed satellite services for underserved areas such as remote and sparsely populated areas;

explore other systems that can provide high-speed connectivity.

e) In the context of national e-strategies, address the special requirements of older people, persons with disabilities, children, especially marginalized children and other disadvantaged and vulnerable groups, including by appropriate educational administrative and legislative measures to ensure their full inclusion in the Information Society.

f) Encourage the design and production of ICT equipment and services so that everyone, has easy and affordable access to them including older people, persons with disabilities, children, especially marginalized children, and other disadvantaged and vulnerable groups, and promote the development of technologies, applications, and content suited to their needs, guided by the Universal Design Principle and further enhanced by the use of assistive technologies.

g) In order to alleviate the challenges of illiteracy, develop affordable technologies and non-text based computer interfaces to facilitate people's access to ICT,

h) Undertake international research and development efforts aimed at making available adequate and affordable ICT equipment for end users.

i) Encourage the use of unused wireless capacity, including satellite, in developed countries and in particular in developing countries, to provide access in remote areas, especially in developing countries and countries with economies in transition, and to improve low-cost connectivity in developing countries. Special concern should be given to the Least Developed Countries in their efforts in establishing telecommunication infrastructure.

j) Optimize connectivity among major information networks by encouraging the creation and development of regional ICT backbones and Internet exchange points, to reduce interconnection costs and broaden network access.

k) Develop strategies for increasing affordable global connectivity, thereby facilitating improved access. Commercially negotiated Internet transit and interconnection costs should be oriented towards objective, transparent and non-discriminatory parameters, taking into account ongoing work on this subject.

l) Encourage and promote joint use of traditional media and new technologies.

C3. Access to information and knowledge

10. ICTs allow people, anywhere in the world, to access information and knowledge almost instantaneously. Individuals, organizations and communities should benefit from access to knowledge and information.

a) Develop policy guidelines for the development and promotion of public domain information as an important international instrument promoting public access to information.

b) Governments are encouraged to provide adequate access through various communication resources, notably the Internet, to public official information.

Establishing legislation on access to information and the preservation of public data, notably in the area of the new technologies, is encouraged.

c) Promote research and development to facilitate accessibility of ICTs for all, including disadvantaged, marginalized and vulnerable groups.

d) Governments, and other stakeholders, should establish sustainable multi-purpose community public access points, providing affordable or free-of-charge access for their citizens to the various communication resources, notably the Internet. These access points should, to the extent possible, have sufficient capacity to provide assistance to users, in libraries, educational institutions, public administrations, post offices or other public places, with special emphasis on rural and underserved areas, while respecting intellectual property rights (IPRs) and encouraging the use of information and sharing of knowledge.

e) Encourage research and promote awareness among all stakeholders of the possibilities offered by different software models, and the means of their creation, including proprietary, open-source and free software, in order to increase competition, freedom of choice and affordability, and to enable all stakeholders to evaluate which solution best meets their requirements.

f) Governments should actively promote the use of ICTs as a fundamental working tool by their citizens and local authorities. In this respect, the international community and other stakeholders should support capacity building for local authorities in the widespread use of ICTs as a means of improving local governance.

g) Encourage research on the Information Society, including on innovative forms of networking, adaptation of ICT infrastructure, tools and applications that facilitate accessibility of ICTs for all, and disadvantaged groups in particular.

h) Support the creation and development of a digital public library and archive services, adapted to the Information Society, including reviewing national library strategies and legislation, developing a global understanding of the need for "hybrid libraries", and fostering worldwide cooperation between libraries.

i) Encourage initiatives to facilitate access, including free and affordable access to open access journals and books, and open archives for scientific information.

j) Support research and development of the design of useful instruments for all stakeholders to foster increased awareness, assessment, and evaluation of different software models and licences, so as to ensure an optimal choice of appropriate software that will best contribute to achieving development goals within local conditions.

C4. Capacity building

11. Everyone should have the necessary skills to benefit fully from the Information Society. Therefore capacity building and ICT literacy are essential. ICTs can contribute to achieving universal education worldwide, through

delivery of education and training of teachers, and offering improved conditions for lifelong learning, encompassing people that are outside the formal education process, and improving professional skills.

a) Develop domestic policies to ensure that ICTs are fully integrated in education and training at all levels, including in curriculum development, teacher training, institutional administration and management, and in support of the concept of lifelong learning.

b) Develop and promote programmes to eradicate illiteracy using ICTs at national, regional and international levels.

c) Promote e-literacy skills for all, for example by designing and offering courses for public administration, taking advantage of existing facilities such as libraries, multipurpose community centres, public access points and by establishing local ICT training centres with the cooperation of all stakeholders. Special attention should be paid to disadvantaged and vulnerable groups.

d) In the context of national educational policies, and taking into account the need to eradicate adult illiteracy, ensure that young people are equipped with knowledge and skills to use ICTs, including the capacity to analyse and treat information in creative and innovative ways, share their expertise and participate fully in the Information Society.

e) Governments, in cooperation with other stakeholders, should create programmes for capacity building with an emphasis on creating a critical mass of qualified and skilled ICT professionals and experts.

f) Develop pilot projects to demonstrate the impact of ICT-based alternative educational delivery systems, notably for achieving Education for All targets, including basic literacy targets.

g) Work on removing the gender barriers to ICT education and training and promoting equal training opportunities in ICT-related fields for women and girls. Early intervention programmes in science and technology should target young girls with the aim of increasing the number of women in ICT careers. Promote the exchange of best practices on the integration of gender perspectives in ICT education.

h) Empower local communities, especially those in rural and underserved areas, in ICT use and promote the production of useful and socially meaningful content for the benefit of all.

i) Launch education and training programmes, where possible using information networks of traditional nomadic and indigenous peoples, which provide opportunities to fully participate in the Information Society.

j) Design and implement regional and international cooperation activities to enhance the capacity, notably, of leaders and operational staff in developing countries and LDCs, to apply ICTs effectively in the whole range of educational activities. This should include delivery of education outside the educational structure, such as the workplace and at home.

k) Design specific training programmes in the use of ICTs in order to meet the educational needs of information professionals, such as archivists, librarians, museum professionals, scientists, teachers, journalists, postal workers and other relevant professional groups. Training of information professionals should focus not only on new methods and techniques for the development and provision of information and communication services, but also on relevant management skills to ensure the best use of technologies. Training of teachers should focus on the technical aspects of ICTs, on development of content, and on the potential possibilities and challenges of ICTs.

l) Develop distance learning, training and other forms of education and training as part of capacity building programmes. Give special attention to developing countries and especially LDCs in different levels of human resources development.

m) Promote international and regional cooperation in the field of capacity building, including country programmes developed by the United Nations and its Specialized Agencies

n) Launch pilot projects to design new forms of ICT-based networking, linking education, training and research institutions between and among developed and developing countries and countries with economies in transition.

o) Volunteering, if conducted in harmony with national policies and local cultures, can be a valuable asset for raising human capacity to make productive use of ICT tools and build a more inclusive Information Society. Activate volunteer programmes to provide capacity building on ICT for development, particularly in developing countries.

p) Design programmes to train users to develop self-learning and self-development capacities.

C5. Building confidence and security in the use of ICTs

12. Confidence and security are among the main pillars of the Information Society.

a) Promote cooperation among the governments at the United Nations and with all stakeholders at other appropriate fora to enhance user confidence, build trust, and protect both data and network integrity; consider existing and potential threats to ICTs; and address other information security and network security issues.

b) Governments, in cooperation with the private sector, should prevent, detect and respond to cyber-crime and misuse of ICTs by: developing guidelines that take into account ongoing efforts in these areas; considering legislation that allows for effective investigation and prosecution of misuse; promoting effective mutual assistance efforts; strengthening institutional support at the international level for preventing, detecting and recovering from such incidents; and encouraging education and raising awareness.

c) Governments, and other stakeholders, should actively promote user education and awareness about online privacy and the means of protecting privacy.

d) Take appropriate action on spam at national and international levels.

e) Encourage the domestic assessment of national law with a view to overcoming any obstacles to the effective use of electronic documents and transactions including electronic means of authentication.

f) Further strengthen the trust and security framework with complementary and mutually reinforcing initiatives in the fields of security in the use of ICTs, with initiatives or guidelines with respect to rights to privacy, data and consumer protection.

g) Share good practices in the field of information security and network security and encourage their use by all parties concerned.

h) Invite interested countries to set up focal points for real-time incident handling and response, and develop a cooperative network between these focal points for sharing information and technologies on incident response.

i) Encourage further development of secure and reliable applications to facilitate online transactions.

j) Encourage interested countries to contribute actively to the ongoing United Nations activities to build confidence and security in the use of ICTs.

C6. Enabling environment

13. To maximize the social, economic and environmental benefits of the Information Society, governments need to create a trustworthy, transparent and non-discriminatory legal, regulatory and policy environment. Actions include:

a) Governments should foster a supportive, transparent, pro-competitive and predictable policy, legal and regulatory framework, which provides the appropriate incentives to investment and community development in the Information Society.

b) We ask the Secretary General of the United Nations to set up a working group on Internet governance, in an open and inclusive process that ensures a mechanism for the full and active participation of governments, the private sector and civil society from both developing and developed countries, involving relevant intergovernmental and international organizations and forums, to investigate and make proposals for action, as appropriate, on the governance of Internet by 2005. The group should, *inter alia*:

i) develop a working definition of Internet governance;

ii) identify the public policy issues that are relevant to Internet governance;

iii) develop a common understanding of the respective roles and responsibilities of governments, existing intergovernmental and international organisations and other forums as well as the private sector and civil society from both developing and developed countries;
iv) prepare a report on the results of this activity to be presented for consideration and appropriate action for the second phase of WSIS in Tunis in 2005.
c) Governments are invited to:
i) facilitate the establishment of national and regional Internet Exchange Centres;
ii) manage or supervise, as appropriate, their respective country code top-level domain name (ccTLD);
iii) promote awareness of the Internet.
d) In cooperation with the relevant stakeholders, promote regional root servers and the use of internationalized domain names in order to overcome barriers to access.
e) Governments should continue to update their domestic consumer protection laws to respond to the new requirements of the Information Society.
f) Promote effective participation by developing countries and countries with economies in transition in international ICT forums and create opportunities for exchange of experience.
g) Governments need to formulate national strategies, which include e-government strategies, to make public administration more transparent, efficient and democratic.
h) Develop a framework for the secure storage and archival of documents and other electronic records of information.
i) Governments and stakeholders should actively promote user education and awareness about online privacy and the means of protecting privacy.
j) Invite stakeholders to ensure that practices designed to facilitate electronic commerce also permit consumers to have a choice as to whether or not to use electronic communication.
k) Encourage the ongoing work in the area of effective dispute settlement systems, notably alternative dispute resolution (ADR), which can promote settlement of disputes.
l) Governments, in collaboration with stakeholders, are encouraged to formulate conducive ICT policies that foster entrepreneurship, innovation and investment, and with particular reference to the promotion of participation by women.
m) Recognising the economic potential of ICTs for Small and Medium-Sized Enterprises (SMEs), they should be assisted in increasing their competitiveness by streamlining administrative procedures, facilitating their access to capital and enhancing their capacity to participate in ICT-related projects.

n) Governments should act as model users and early adopters of e-commerce in accordance with their level of socio-economic development.
o) Governments, in cooperation with other stakeholders, should raise awareness of the importance of international interoperability standards for global e-commerce.
p) Governments, in cooperation with other stakeholders, should promote the development and use of open, interoperable, non-discriminatory and demand-driven standards.
q) ITU, pursuant to its treaty capacity, coordinates and allocates frequencies with the goal of facilitating ubiquitous and affordable access.
r) Additional steps should be taken in ITU and other regional organisations to ensure rational, efficient and economical use of, and equitable access to, the radio-frequency spectrum by all countries, based on relevant international agreements.

C7. ICT applications: benefits in all aspects of life
14. ICT applications can support sustainable development, in the fields of public administration, business, education and training, health, employment, environment, agriculture and science within the framework of national e-strategies. This would include actions within the following sectors:
15. E-government
a) Implement e-government strategies focusing on applications aimed at innovating and promoting transparency in public administrations and democratic processes, improving efficiency and strengthening relations with citizens.
b) Develop national e-government initiatives and services, at all levels, adapted to the needs of citizens and business, to achieve a more efficient allocation of resources and public goods.
c) Support international cooperation initiatives in the field of e-government, in order to enhance transparency, accountability and efficiency at all levels of government.
16. E-business
a) Governments, international organizations and the private sector, are encouraged to promote the benefits of international trade and the use of e-business, and promote the use of e-business models in developing countries and countries with economies in transition.
b) Through the adoption of an enabling environment, and based on widely available Internet access, governments should seek to stimulate private sector investment, foster new applications, content development and public/private partnerships.
c) Government policies should favour assistance to, and growth of SMMEs, in the ICT industry, as well as their entry into e-business, to stimulate economic

growth and job creation as an element of a strategy for poverty reduction through wealth creation.

17. E-learning (see section C4)

18. E-health

a) Promote collaborative efforts of governments, planners, health professionals, and other agencies along with the participation of international organizations for creating a reliable, timely, high quality and affordable health care and health information systems and for promoting continuous medical training, education, and research through the use of ICTs, while respecting and protecting citizens' right to privacy.

b) Facilitate access to the world's medical knowledge and locally-relevant content resources for strengthening public health research and prevention programmes and promoting women's and men's health, such as content on sexual and reproductive health and sexually transmitted infections, and for diseases that attract full attention of the world including HIV/AIDS, malaria and tuberculosis.

c) Alert, monitor and control the spread of communicable diseases, through the improvement of common information systems.

d) Promote the development of international standards for the exchange of health data, taking due account of privacy concerns.

e) Encourage the adoption of ICTs to improve and extend health care and health information systems to remote and underserved areas and vulnerable populations, recognising women's roles as health providers in their families and communities.

f) Strengthen and expand ICT-based initiatives for providing medical and humanitarian assistance in disasters and emergencies.

19. E-employment

a) Encourage the development of best practices for e-workers and e-employers built, at the national level, on principles of fairness and gender equality, respecting all relevant international norms.

b) Promote new ways of organizing work and business with the aim of raising productivity, growth and well-being through investment in ICTs and human resources.

c) Promote teleworking to allow citizens, particularly in the developing countries, LDCs, and small economies, to live in their societies and work anywhere, and to increase employment opportunities for women, and for those with disabilities. In promoting teleworking, special attention should be given to strategies promoting job creation and the retention of the skilled working force.

d) Promote early intervention programmes in science and technology that should target young girls to increase the number of women in ICT carriers.

20. E-environment

a) Governments, in cooperation with other stakeholders are encouraged to use and promote ICTs as an instrument for environmental protection and the sustainable use of natural resources.
b) Government, civil society and the private sector are encouraged to initiate actions and implement projects and programmes for sustainable production and consumption and the environmentally safe disposal and recycling of discarded hardware and components used in ICTs.
c) Establish monitoring systems, using ICTs, to forecast and monitor the impact of natural and man-made disasters, particularly in developing countries, LDCs and small economies.
21. E-agriculture
a) Ensure the systematic dissemination of information using ICTs on agriculture, animal husbandry, fisheries, forestry and food, in order to provide ready access to comprehensive, up-to-date and detailed knowledge and information, particularly in rural areas.
b) Public-private partnerships should seek to maximize the use of ICTs as an instrument to improve production (quantity and quality).
22. E-science
a) Promote affordable and reliable high-speed Internet connection for all universities and research institutions to support their critical role in information and knowledge production, education and training, and to support the establishment of partnerships, cooperation and networking between these institutions.
b) Promote electronic publishing, differential pricing and open access initiatives to make scientific information affordable and accessible in all countries on an equitable basis.
c) Promote the use of peer-to-peer technology to share scientific knowledge and pre-prints and reprints written by scientific authors who have waived their right to payment.
d) Promote the long-term systematic and efficient collection, dissemination and preservation of essential scientific digital data, for example, population and meteorological data in all countries.
e) Promote principles and metadata standards to facilitate cooperation and effective use of collected scientific information and data as appropriate to conduct scientific research.

C8. Cultural diversity and identity, linguistic diversity and local content
23. Cultural and linguistic diversity, while stimulating respect for cultural identity, traditions and religions, is essential to the development of an Information Society based on the dialogue among cultures and regional and international cooperation. It is an important factor for sustainable development.

a) Create policies that support the respect, preservation, promotion and enhancement of cultural and linguistic diversity and cultural heritage within the Information Society, as reflected in relevant agreed United Nations documents, including UNESCO's Universal Declaration on Cultural Diversity. This includes encouraging governments to design cultural policies to promote the production of cultural, educational and scientific content and the development of local cultural industries suited to the linguistic and cultural context of the users.

b) Develop national policies and laws to ensure that libraries, archives, museums and other cultural institutions can play their full role of content—including traditional knowledge—providers in the Information Society, more particularly by providing continued access to recorded information.

c) Support efforts to develop and use ICTs for the preservation of natural and, cultural heritage, keeping it accessible as a living part of today's culture. This includes developing systems for ensuring continued access to archived digital information and multimedia content in digital repositories, and support archives, cultural collections and libraries as the memory of humankind.

d) Develop and implement policies that preserve, affirm, respect and promote diversity of cultural expression and indigenous knowledge and traditions through the creation of varied information content and the use of different methods, including the digitization of the educational, scientific and cultural heritage.

e) Support local content development, translation and adaptation, digital archives, and diverse forms of digital and traditional media by local authorities. These activities can also strengthen local and indigenous communities.

f) Provide content that is relevant to the cultures and languages of individuals in the Information Society, through access to traditional and digital media services.

g) Through public/private partnerships, foster the creation of varied local and national content, including that available in the language of users, and give recognition and support to ICT-based work in all artistic fields.

h) Strengthen programmes focused on gender-sensitive curricula in formal and non-formal education for all and enhancing communication and media literacy for women with a view to building the capacity of girls and women to understand and to develop ICT content.

i) Nurture the local capacity for the creation and distribution of software in local languages, as well as content that is relevant to different segments of population, including non-literate, persons with disabilities, disadvantaged and vulnerable groups especially in developing countries and countries with economies in transition.

j) Give support to media based in local communities and support projects combining the use of traditional media and new technologies for their role in facilitating the use of local languages, for documenting and preserving local heritage, including landscape and biological diversity, and as a means to reach rural and isolated and nomadic communities.

k) Enhance the capacity of indigenous peoples to develop content in their own languages.

l) Cooperate with indigenous peoples and traditional communities to enable them to more effectively use and benefit from the use of their traditional knowledge in the Information Society.

m) Exchange knowledge, experiences and best practices on policies and tools designed to promote cultural and linguistic diversity at regional and sub-regional levels. This can be achieved by establishing regional, and sub-regional working groups on specific issues of this Plan of Action to foster integration efforts.

n) Assess at the regional level the contribution of ICT to cultural exchange and interaction, and based on the outcome of this assessment, design relevant programmes.

o) Governments, through public/private partnerships, should promote technologies and R&D programmes in such areas as translation, iconographies, voice-assisted services and the development of necessary hardware and a variety of software models, including proprietary, open source software and free software, such as standard character sets, language codes, electronic dictionaries, terminology and thesauri, multilingual search engines, machine translation tools, internationalized domain names, content referencing as well as general and application software.

C9. Media

24. The media—in their various forms and with a diversity of ownership—as an actor, have an essential role in the development of the Information Society and are recognized as an important contributor to freedom of expression and plurality of information.

a) Encourage the media—print and broadcast as well as new media—to continue to play an important role in the Information Society.

b) Encourage the development of domestic legislation that guarantees the independence and plurality of the media.

c) Take appropriate measures—consistent with freedom of expression—to combat illegal and harmful content in media content.

d) Encourage media professionals in developed countries to establish partnerships and networks with the media in developing ones, especially in the field of training.

e) Promote balanced and diverse portrayals of women and men by the media.

f) Reduce international imbalances affecting the media, particularly as regards infrastructure, technical resources and the development of human skills, taking full advantage of ICT tools in this regard.

g) Encourage traditional media to bridge the knowledge divide and to facilitate the flow of cultural content, particularly in rural areas.

C10. Ethical dimensions of the Information Society

25. The Information Society should be subject to universally held values and promote the common good and to prevent abusive uses of ICTs.

a) Take steps to promote respect for peace and to uphold the fundamental values of freedom, equality, solidarity, tolerance, shared responsibility, and respect for nature.

b) All stakeholders should increase their awareness of the ethical dimension of their use of ICTs.

c) All actors in the Information Society should promote the common good, protect privacy and personal data and take appropriate actions and preventive measures, as determined by law, against abusive uses of ICTs such as illegal and other acts motivated by racism, racial discrimination, xenophobia, and related intolerance, hatred, violence, all forms of child abuse, including paedophilia and child pornography, and trafficking in, and exploitation of, human beings.

d) Invite relevant stakeholders, especially the academia, to continue research on ethical dimensions of ICTs.

C11. International and regional cooperation

26. International cooperation among all stakeholders is vital in implementation of this plan of action and needs to be strengthened with a view to promoting universal access and bridging the digital divide, *inter alia*, by provision of means of implementation.

a) Governments of developing countries should raise the relative priority of ICT projects in requests for international cooperation and assistance on infrastructure development projects from developed countries and international financial organizations.

b) Within the context of the UN's Global Compact and building upon the United Nations Millennium Declaration, build on and accelerate public-private partnerships, focusing on the use of ICT in development.

c) Invite international and regional organizations to mainstream ICTs in their work programmes and to assist all levels of developing countries, to be involved in the preparation and implementation of national action plans to support the fulfilment of the goals indicated in the declaration of principles and in this Plan of Action, taking into account the importance of regional initiatives.

D. Digital Solidarity Agenda

27. The Digital Solidarity Agenda aims at putting in place the conditions for mobilizing human, financial and technological resources for inclusion of all men and women in the emerging Information Society. Close national, regional and international cooperation among all stakeholders in the implementation of this Agenda is vital. To overcome the digital divide, we need to use more efficiently existing approaches and mechanisms and fully explore new ones, in order to provide financing for the development of infrastructure, equipment, capacity building and content, which are essential for participation in the Information Society.

D1. Priorities and strategies

a) National e-strategies should be made an integral part of national development plans, including Poverty Reduction Strategies.

b) ICTs should be fully mainstreamed into strategies for Official Development Assistance (ODA) through more effective donor information-sharing and co-ordination, and through analysis and sharing of best practices and lessons learned from experience with ICT-for-development programmes.

D2. Mobilizing resources

a) All countries and international organizations should act to create conditions conducive to increasing the availability and effective mobilization of resources for financing development as elaborated in the Monterrey Consensus.

b) Developed countries should make concrete efforts to fulfil their international commitments to financing development including the Monterrey Consensus, in which developed countries that have not done so are urged to make concrete efforts towards the target of 0.7 per cent of gross national product (GNP) as ODA to developing countries and 0.15 to 0.20 per cent of GNP of developed countries to least developed countries.

c) For those developing countries facing unsustainable debt burdens, we welcome initiatives that have been undertaken to reduce outstanding indebtedness and invite further national and international measures in that regard, including, as appropriate, debt cancellation and other arrangements. Particular attention should be given to enhancing the Heavily Indebted Poor Countries initiative. These initiatives would release more resources that may be used for financing ICT for development projects.

d) Recognizing the potential of ICT for development we furthermore advocate:

developing countries to increase their efforts to attract major private national and foreign investments for ICTs through the creation of a transparent, stable and predictable enabling investment environment;

developed countries and international financial organisations to be responsive to the strategies and priorities of ICTs for development, mainstream ICTs in their work programmes, and assist developing countries and countries with economies in transition to prepare and implement their national e-strategies. Based on the priorities of national development plans and implementation of the above commitments, developed countries should increase their efforts to provide more financial resources to developing countries in harnessing ICTs for development;

the private sector to contribute to the implementation of this Digital Solidarity Agenda.

e) In our efforts to bridge the digital divide, we should promote, within our development cooperation, technical and financial assistance directed towards national and regional capacity building, technology transfer on mutually agreed terms, cooperation in R&D programmes and exchange of know-how.

f) While all existing financial mechanisms should be fully exploited, a thorough review of their adequacy in meeting the challenges of ICT for development should be completed by the end of December 2004. This review shall be conducted by a Task Force under the auspices of the Secretary-General of the United Nations and submitted for consideration to the second phase of this summit. Based on the conclusion of the review, improvements and innovations of financing mechanisms will be considered including the effectiveness, the feasibility and the creation of a voluntary Digital Solidarity Fund, as mentioned in the Declaration of Principles.

g) Countries should consider establishing national mechanisms to achieve universal access in both underserved rural and urban areas, in order to bridge the digital divide.

E) Follow-up and evaluation

28. A realistic international performance evaluation and benchmarking (both qualitative and quantitative), through comparable statistical indicators and research results, should be developed to follow up the implementation of the objectives, goals and targets in the Plan of Action, taking into account different national circumstances.

a) In cooperation with each country concerned, develop and launch a composite ICT Development (Digital Opportunity) Index. It could be published annually, or every two years, in an ICT Development Report. The index could show the statistics while the report would present analytical work on policies and their implementation, depending on national circumstances, including gender analysis.

b) Appropriate indicators and benchmarking, including community connectivity indicators, should clarify the magnitude of the digital divide, in both its domestic and international dimensions, and keep it under regular assessment, and tracking global progress in the use of ICTs to achieve internationally agreed development goals, including those of the Millennium Declaration.

c) International and regional organizations should assess and report regularly on universal accessibility of nations to ICTs, with the aim of creating equitable opportunities for the growth of ICT sectors of developing countries.

d) Gender-specific indicators on ICT use and needs should be developed, and measurable performance indicators should be identified to assess the impact of funded ICT projects on the lives of women and girls.

e) Develop and launch a website on best practices and success stories, based on a compilation of contributions from all stakeholders, in a concise, accessible and compelling format, following the internationally-recognized web accessibility standards. The website could be periodically updated and turned into a permanent experience-sharing exercise.

f) All countries and regions should develop tools so as to provide statistical information on the Information Society, with basic indicators and analysis of its key dimensions. Priority should be given to setting up coherent and internationally comparable indicator systems, taking into account different levels of development.

F) Towards WSIS phase 2 (Tunis)

29. Recalling General Assembly Resolution 56/183 and taking into account the outcome of the Geneva phase of the WSIS, a preparatory meeting will be held in the first half of 2004 to review those issues of the Information Society which should form the focus of the Tunis phase of the WSIS and to agree on the structure of the preparatory process for the second phase. In line with the decision of this Summit concerning its Tunis phase, the second phase of the WSIS should consider, *inter alia*:

a) Elaboration of final appropriate documents based on the outcome of the Geneva phase of the WSIS with a view to consolidating the process of building a global Information Society, and reducing the Digital Divide and transforming it into digital opportunities.

b) Follow-up and implementation of the Geneva Plan of Action at national, regional and international levels, including the United Nations system, as part of an integrated and coordinated approach, calling upon the participation of all relevant stakeholders. This should take place, *inter alia*, through partnerships among stakeholders.

Global Information Society Summit Spurs Solidarity, Alliances But Hard Work, Action Ahead[8]

Document of the ITU

The World Summit on the Information Society closed on an optimistic note of consensus and commitment, but Yoshio Utsumi, Secretary-General of the International Telecommunication Union and Summit cautioned that the meeting was only the start of a long and complex process.

"Telephones will not feed the poor, and computers will not replace textbooks. But ICTs can be used effectively as part of the toolbox for addressing global problems. The Summit's successes now give us the necessary momentum to achieve this," he said.

"Building the inclusive information society requires a multi-stakeholder approach. The challenges raised — in areas like Internet governance, access, investment, security, the development of applications, intellectual property rights and privacy — require a new commitment to work together if we are to realize the benefits of the information society.

"Seeing the fruits of today's powerful knowledge-based tools in the most impoverished economies will be the true test of an engaged, empowered and egalitarian information society, he added.

Over 54 Heads of State, Prime Ministers, Presidents, Vice-Presidents and 83 ministers and vice-ministers from 176 countries came together in Geneva to endorse a Declaration of Principles — or a common vision of an information society's values – and a Plan of Action which sets forth a road map to build on that vision and to bring the benefits of ICTs to underserved economies.

The three-day Summit is the first multi-stakeholder global effort to share and shape the use of information and communications technologies (ICTs) for a better world.

But the Summit was groundbreaking in other ways too. It offered a genuine "venue of opportunity" in a unique meeting of leaders, policy-makers, ICT business people,

---

[8] SUMMIT NEWSROOM: PRESS RELEASES, Geneva, 12 December 2003
http://www.itu.int/wsis/geneva/newsroom/press_releases/wsisclosing.html

voluntary and non-governmental organizations of every possible kind, and top-level thinkers and speakers. Alongside the three-days of Plenary meetings and high-level roundtables, nearly 300 side-events helped bring the dream of an inclusive information society one-step closer to becoming reality.

Partnership announcements included a USD 400,000 grant by the US Government for ICT development in low-income countries. Cisco and ITU also signed a Memorandum of Understanding to open 20 more Internet Training Centres in developing countries. As well, Hewlett-Packard will provide low-cost products that will help overcome the illiteracy barrier to ICT. Handwritten texts for example will be recognized for e-mail transmission. Microsoft, working with UNDP, will provide a billion dollar programme over 5 years to bring ICT skills to underserved communities. One innovative initiative announced to bridge the digital divide is the Bhutan E-Post project. For faster, cheaper and more reliable communication to remote, mountainous areas of Bhutan, the Government of India will deliver e-post services to the Bhutanese Postal Service via a USD 400,000 a V-satellite network and solar panels power system. The partners include ITU, Bhutan Telecom and Post, Worldspace and Encore India. And at the very close of the Summit, the cities of Geneva and Lyon and the Government of Senegal have announced contributions totalling about 1 million euros to fund information technology in developing countries. The contributions will represent the first three payments towards the Digital Solidarity Fund, the creation of which is to be considered by a UN working group for the Tunis phase.

The second phase of the Summit takes place in Tunis in 2005 and will measure ambitious goals set this week. With WSIS phase I over, the hard work begins and hard work lies ahead in the two years before Tunis, to show that the information society is on the right path.

The overarching goal of the Summit has been to gain the will and commitment of policy-makers to make ICTs a top priority, and to bring together public and private sector players to forge an inclusive dialogue based on the interests of all. In these two respects, the Summit has been heralded a success.

United Nations Secretary-General Kofi Annan told delegates "technology has given birth to the information age. Now it is up to all of us to build an information society from trade to telemedicine, from education to environmental protection, we have in our hands, on our desktops and in the skies above, the ability to improve standards of living for millions upon millions of people.

Top Summit targets now remain to be achieved, including connecting all schools, villages, governments and hospitals, and bringing half the world's population within ICT reach, all by the year 2015.

The Summit has clearly identified national e-strategies as the key vehicle to meet the targets. Connecting public places, revising school curricula, extending the reach of TV and radio broadcasting services and fostering rich multilingual content are all recognized as needing strong national-level governmental commitments. To encourage and assist national and local governments in this work, the Summit also foresees the development of international statistical indicators to provide yardsticks of progress; exchanges of experience to help develop "best practice" models, and the fostering of public-private partnerships internationally in the interests of sustainable ICT development.

Indeed, collaboration across the complex information society chain — from the scientists that create powerful ICT tools, to the governments that foster a culture of investment and rule of law, to the businesses that build infrastructure and supply services, to the media that create and disseminate content and — above all —human society which ultimately employs such tools and shapes their use —lays the foundation for an inclusive knowledge-based world on which the riches of an information society can flourish.

The Summit's most notable achievement was across-the-board consensus earned for a Declaration of Principles and Plan of Action wording around several contentious issues, and the spirit of cooperation that permeated the Summit.

Internet governance, and financing ICT investments in underserved economies were two of the issues which called for long negotiations. On the issue of Internet management, the involvement of all stakeholders and intergovernmental organizations to address both technical and public policy issues has been underscored although global Internet governance is set to be the subject of deeper talks up to Tunis in 2005. An open and inclusive working group will be set up on the topic, in order to review and make proposals for action by the 2005 Summit.

Similarly on the issue of financing for underserved economies, a task force will be established to undertake a review of existing ICT funding mechanisms and will also study the feasibility of an international voluntary Digital Solidarity Fund.

On the areas of intellectual property rights and the need for enabling environments, universal access policies, and multilingual, diverse and culturally appropriate content to speed ICT adoption and use — particularly in the world's most underserved economies — government-level commitment to follow a set of common values and principles has been attained.

Although these achievements fuel hope and may stoke further collaboration, Mr. Utsumi, together with many world leaders, appealed to all stakeholders keep the spirit of cooperation alive well beyond the two years to Tunis, and to back up universally agreed principles with concrete actions to spark more peace and prosperity across the planet.

"The realization of the Plan of Action is crucial to the long-term success of the Summit. We need imagination and creativity to develop projects and programmes that can really make a difference. We need commitment — on the part of governments, the private sector and civil society — to realistic targets and concrete actions. We need the mobilization of resources and investment," he said.

"With the unique occasion of a World Summit, we have the chance to scale up our ambitions to the global level, which is equal to the size of the challenge. Let us not miss this opportunity."

Civil Society Outcomes

Shaping Information Societies for Human Needs: Civil Society Declaration to the World Summit on the Information Society[9]

WSIS Civil Society Plenary

We, women and men from different continents, cultural backgrounds, perspectives, experience and expertise, acting as members of different constituencies of an emerging global civil society, considering civil society participation as fundamental to the first ever held UN Summit on Information and Communication issues, the World Summit on the Information Society, have been working for two years inside the process, devoting our efforts to shaping people-centred, inclusive and equitable concept of information and communication societies.[10]

Working together both on-line and off-line as civil society entities, practising an inclusive and participatory use of information and communication technologies, has allowed us to share views and shape common positions, and to collectively develop a vision of information and communication societies.

At this step of the process, the first phase of the Summit, Geneva, December 2003, our voices and the general interest we collectively expressed are not adequately reflected in the Summit documents. We propose this document as part of the official outcomes of the Summit. Convinced that this vision can become reality through the actions and lives of women and men, communities and people, we hereby present our own vision to all, as an invitation to participate in this ongoing dialogue and to join forces in shaping our common future.

This declaration is divided into four Core Principles: Social Justice and People-Centred Sustainable Development; the Centrality of Human Rights; Culture, Knowledge and Public Domain; and Enabling Environment.

---

[9] Unanimously Adopted by the WSIS Civil Society Plenary on 8 December 2003. Endorsements of this declaration are being compiled at ct-endorse@wsis-cs.org and archived on http://www.wsis-cs.org.

[10] There is no single information, communication or knowledge society: there are, at the local, national and global levels, possible future societies; moreover, considering communication is a critical aspect of any information society, we use in this document the phrase "information and communication societies." For consistency with previous WSIS language, we retain the use of the phrase "Information Society" when directly referencing WSIS.

A Visionary Society

At the heart of our vision of information and communications societies is the human being. The dignity and rights of all peoples and each person must be promoted, respected, protected and affirmed. Redressing the inexcusable gulf between levels of development and between opulence and extreme poverty must therefore be our prime concern.

We are committed to building information and communication societies that are people-centred, inclusive and equitable. Societies in which everyone can freely create, access, utilise, share and disseminate information and knowledge, so that individuals, communities and peoples are empowered to improve their quality of life and to achieve their full potential. Societies founded on the principles of social, political, and economic justice, and peoples' full participation and empowerment, and thus societies that truly address the key development challenges facing the world today. Societies that pursue the objectives of sustainable development, democracy, and gender equality, for the attainment of a more peaceful, just, egalitarian and thus sustainable world, premised on the principles enshrined in the Charter of the United Nations and in the Universal Declaration of Human Rights.

We aspire to build information and communication societies where development is framed by fundamental human rights and oriented to achieving a more equitable distribution of resources, leading to the elimination of poverty in a way that is non-exploitative and environmentally sustainable. To this end we believe technologies can be engaged as fundamental means, rather than becoming ends in themselves, thus recognising that bridging the Digital Divide is only one step on the road to achieving development for all. We recognise the tremendous potential of information and communications technologies (ICTs) in overcoming the devastation of famine, natural catastrophes, new pandemics such as HIV/AIDS, as well as the proliferation of arms.

We reaffirm that communication is a fundamental social process, a basic human need and a foundation of all social organisations. Everyone, everywhere, at any time should have the opportunity to participate in communication processes and no one should be excluded from their benefits. This implies that every person must have access to the means of communication and must be able to exercise their right to freedom of opinion and expression, which includes the right to hold opinions and to seek, receive and impart information and ideas through any media and regardless of frontiers. Similarly, the right to privacy, the right to access public information and the public domain of knowledge, and many other universal human rights of specific relevance to information and communication processes, must also be upheld. Together with access, all these communication rights and freedoms must be actively guaranteed for all in clearly written national laws and enforced with adequate technical requirements.

Building such societies implies involving individuals in their capacity as citizens, as well as their organisations and communities, as participants and decision-makers in shaping frameworks, policies and governing mechanisms. This means creating an enabling environment for the engagement and commitment of all generations, both women and men, and ensuring the involvement of diverse social and linguistic groups, cultures and peoples, rural and urban populations without exclusion. In addition, governments should maintain and promote public services where required by citizens and establish accountability to citizens as a pillar of public policy, in order to ensure that models of information and communication societies are open to continuing correction and improvement.

We recognise that no technology is neutral with respect to its social impacts and, therefore, the possibility of having so-called "technology-neutral" decision-making processes is a fallacy. It is critical to make careful social and technical choices concerning the introduction of new technologies from the inception of their design through to their deployment and operational phases. Negative social and technical impacts of information and communications systems that are discovered late in the design process are usually extremely difficult to correct and, therefore, can cause lasting harm. We envision an information and communication society in which technologies are designed in a participatory manner with and by their end-users so as to prevent or minimise their negative impacts.

We envision societies where human knowledge, creativity, cooperation and solidarity are considered core elements; where not only individual creativity, but also collective innovation, based on cooperative work are promoted. Societies where knowledge, information and communication resources are recognised and protected as the common heritage of humankind; societies that guarantee and foster cultural and linguistic diversity and intercultural dialogue, in environments that are free from discrimination, violence and hatred.

We are conscious that information, knowledge and the means of communication are available on a magnitude that humankind has never dreamt of in the past; but we are also aware that exclusion from access to the means of communication, from information and from the skills that are needed to participate in the public sphere, is still a major constraint, especially in developing countries. At the same time information and knowledge are increasingly being transformed into private resources which can be controlled, sold and bought, as if they were simple commodities and not the founding elements of social organisation and development. Thus, as one of the main challenges of information and communication societies, we recognise the urgency of seeking solutions to these contradictions.

We are convinced that with the sufficient political will to mobilise this wealth of human knowledge and the appropriate resources, humanity could certainly achieve the goals of the Millennium Declaration, and even surpass them. As civil society organisations, we accept our part of responsibility in making this goal and our vision a reality.

Core Principles and Challenges

In accordance with this vision, it is essential that the development of information and communication societies be grounded in core principles that reflect a full awareness of the challenges to be met and the responsibility of different stakeholders. This includes the full recognition of the need to address gender concerns and to make a fundamental commitment to gender equality, non-discrimination and women's empowerment, and recognise these as non-negotiable and essential prerequisites to an equitable and people-centred development within information and communication societies. Such a commitment means consciously redressing the effects of the intersection of unequal power relations in the social, economic and political spheres, which manifests in differential access, choice, opportunity, participation, status and control over resources between women and men as well as communities in terms of class, ethnicity, age, religion, race, geographical location and development status.

We have identified the following as key areas of concern. We recognise and uphold the following principles; and we have identified certain priority areas for action by the international community.

2.1 Social Justice and People-Centred Sustainable Development

Within a social justice framework, human development implies cultural, social, economic, political and environmental living conditions that fulfill and empower individuals and communities. Despite the enormous advancements in knowledge and technology achieved by humanity, a majority of people continue to live in appalling conditions.

Social justice in the information and communication societies can only be pursued by taking into account geo-political and historical injustices along economic, social, political and cultural lines. Current global dynamics are characterised by tensions resulting from the inter-linkages of global economic liberalisation, cultural globalisation, increased militarism, rising fundamentalisms, racism and the suspension and violation of basic human rights.

The unequal distribution of ICTs and the lack of information access for a large majority of the world's population, often referred to as the digital divide, is in fact a mapping of new asymmetries onto the existing grid of social divides. These include the divide between the North and South, rich and poor, men and women, urban and rural populations, those with access to information and those without. Such disparities are found not only between different cultures, but also within national borders. The international community must exercise its collective power to ensure action on the part of individual states in order to bridge domestic digital divides.

Redressing all forms of discrimination, exclusion and isolation that different marginalised and vulnerable groups and communities experience will require more than the deployment of technology alone. Their full participation in information and communication societies requires us to reject at a fundamental level, the solely profit-motivated and market-propelled promotion of ICTs for development. Conscious and purposeful actions need to be taken in order to ensure that new ICTs are not deployed to further perpetuate existing negative trends of economic globalisation and market monopolisation. Instead, ICT development and applications should be oriented to advance the social, economic and cultural progress of the world's peoples and contribute to transforming the development paradigm.

Technological decisions should be taken with the goal of meeting the life-critical needs of people, not with goal of enriching companies or enabling undemocratic control by governments. Therefore, fundamental decisions concerning the design and use of technologies must be made in cooperation with Civil Society, including individual end-users, engineers, and scientists. In particular, where community-based technologies are concerned the study and practice of community informatics must be applied in order to respond adequately to the particular characteristics and needs of communities in design processes.

2.1.1 Poverty Eradication

Poverty Eradication must be a key priority on the WSIS agenda. Without challenging existing inequalities, no sustainable development embracing the new ICTs can be achieved. People living in extreme poverty must be enabled to contribute their experiences and knowledge in a dialogue involving all parties. Challenging poverty requires more than setting `development agendas'. It requires a fundamental commitment to examine the current frameworks, to improve local access to information that is of relevance for the specific context, to improve training in ICT-related skills, and to allocate significant financial and other resources. Also, because volunteers are working at the grassroots level, they play an important role in social inclusion.

Financial resources, linked with social and digital solidarity, need to be channelled through existing and new financial mechanisms that are managed transparently and inclusively by all sectors of society. Among the frameworks that need to be examined in terms of their potentially adverse effects on equitable development are the current arrangements for recognition and governance of monopolised knowledge and information, including the work of WIPO and the functioning of the TRIPS agreement.

2.1.2 Global Citizenship

Information and communication societies have the potential to catalyse and help release the enormous financial, technical, human and moral resources required for sustainable development. These resources will only be freed up as the peoples of the world develop a profound sense of responsibility for the fate of the planet and the well-being of the entire human family. In this regard, there is a need for the development in the individual and in communities, as well as governments, of a global consciousness, and a sense of world citizenship. Since the body of humankind is one and indivisible, each member of the human race is born into the world as a trust of the whole and is best served by ensuring the equal importance of each member through the proactive exercise and application of international human rights standards.

2.1.3 Gender Justice

Equitable, open and inclusive information and communication societies must be based on gender justice and be particularly guided by the interpretation of principles of gender equality, non-discrimination and women's empowerment as contained in the Beijing Declaration and Platform for Action (Fifth World Conference on Women) and the Convention on the Elimination of All Forms of Discrimination Against Women (CEDAW). Actions must demonstrate not only a strong commitment but also a high level of consciousness to an intersectional approach to redressing discrimination resulting from unequal power relations at all levels of society. Proactive policies and programmes across all sectors must be developed for women as active and primary agents of change in owning, designing, using and adapting ICT. To empower girls and women throughout their life cycle, as shapers and leaders of society, gender responsive educational programs and appropriate learning environments need to be promoted. Gender analysis and the development of both quantitative and qualitative indicators in measuring gender equality through an extensive and integrated national system of monitoring and evaluation are "musts."

2.1.4 Importance of Youth

We recognise also that young people are the future workforce and leading creators and earliest adopters of ICTs. They must therefore be empowered as learners, developers, contributors, entrepreneurs and decision-makers. We must focus especially on young people who have not yet been able to benefit fully from the opportunities provided by information and communication societies. In particular, we must seek to assist and empower youth from disadvantaged backgrounds, especially young people in developing countries. Equality of opportunity for girls and young women must be integral to our efforts, and we must create a greater awareness of their specific needs and potential in the field of ICT. Issues facing young workers in ICT industries, such as low pay, poor working conditions, and a lack of job stability and collective representation, must also be addressed. As main users of ICTs, young people are most affected and vulnerable to the health risks exposed by their use. Therefore we commit to develop and use only those ICTs that ensure the well-being, protection, and harmonious development of all children.

2.1.5 Access to Information and the Means of Communication

Access to information and the means of communication as a public and global commons should be participatory, universal, inclusive and democratic. Inequalities in access must be addressed in terms of the North/South divide as well as in terms of enduring inequalities within developed and less developed nations. Barriers that need to be overcome are of an economic, educational, technical, political, social, ethnic, and age nature, and inequitable gender relations are embedded into all of these and need to be specifically addressed.

Universal access to information that is essential for human development must be ensured. Infrastructure and the most appropriate forms of information and communication technologies must be accessible for all in their different social context, and the social appropriation of these technologies must be encouraged. This implies addressing diverse realities experienced by distinct social groups such as indigenous peoples, diasporas and migrants, and privileging local or targeted solutions. Traditional media and community-based information and communication initiatives have a vital role to play in these respects, and so does the effective use of the new ICTs. The regulatory and legal framework in all information and communication societies must be strengthened to support broad-based sharing of technologies, information, and knowledge, and to foster community control, respectful of human rights and freedoms.

Specific needs and requirements of all stakeholders, including those with disabilities, must be considered in ICT development. Accessibility and inclusiveness of ICTs is best done at an early stage of design, development and production, so that the information and communication society becomes the society for all, at minimum cost.

The need to access, send and receive information represents a particularly vital challenge to vulnerable people such as refugees, those displaced by war, and asylum seekers who often do not know their rights, which are frequently violated. Access to means of communication for these groups is necessary for the defence and promotion of their rights, in order to make legitimate claims in conformity with international law.

2.1.6 Access to Health Information

The delivery of life-critical mental and physical health information can be facilitated and improved through ICT-based solutions. Lack of access to information and communication has been identified as a critical factor in the public mental and physical health crises around the world. Experts have suggested that providing citizens of developing countries with community level points of access to mental and physical health information would be a critical starting point for addressing the mental and physical health care crises. However, such access points should support more than one-way flows of information (for example, from expert to community or patient). Communities must be allowed to participate in the selection and creation of communication flows that they find useful and necessary to address the prevention, treatment, and promotion of mental and physical health care for all people. Open access to medical information is absolutely essential so that all known data are available to medical doctors and practitioners.

2.1.7 Basic Literacy

Literacy and free universal access to education is a key principle. Knowledge societies require an informed and educated citizenry. Capacity-building needs to include skills to use ICTs, media and information literacy, and the skills needed for active citizenship including the ability to find, appraise, use and create information and technology. Approaches that are local, horizontal, gender-responsive and socially driven and mediated should be prioritised. A combination of traditional and new media as well as open access to knowledge and information should be encouraged. Libraries €ê both real and virtual -€ê have an important role to play to ensure access to knowledge and information available to everyone. At the international and multilateral level, the public domain of knowledge and culture needs to be protected. People-centred information technologies can foster eradication of illnesses and epidemics, can help give everyone food, shelter, freedom and peace.

Literacy, education and research are fundamental components of information, communication and knowledge societies. Knowledge creation and acquisition should be nurtured as a participatory and collective process and not considered a one-way flow or confined to one section of capacity building. Education (formal, informal, and lifelong) builds democracy both by creating a literate citizenry and a skilled workforce. But only an informed and educated citizenry with access to the means and outputs of pluralistic research can fully participate in and effectively contribute to knowledge societies.

Urgent attention should be paid to the potential positive and negative impacts of ICTs on the issues of illiteracy in regional, national and international languages of the great majority of the world€ïs peoples. Literacy, education, and research efforts in the information and communication societies must include a focus on the needs of people who have physical impairments and all means of transcending those impairments (for example, voice recognition, e-learning, and open university training) must be promoted.

2.1.8 Development of Sustainable and Community-based ICT Solutions

In order that communities and individuals may fully enjoy the benefits of the information and communication society, ICTs must be designed and manufactured according to environmentally sustainable principles. Technological solutions must also be sustainable in the sense that communities are able to support their use and evolution.

Equipment recycling must meet environmental standards. The production of technologies must not consume an unsustainable amount of energy or natural resources.

It is essential to develop concrete proposals and policies to improve resource efficiency and develop renewable energy resources. This involves 'dematerialising' (for example, using less paper) and reducing ICT-related waste; increasing the useful life of hardware; improving recycling conditions; ensuring safe disposal of discarded ICT hardware and parts; and encouraging the development of alternatives to toxic ICT components. This also implies giving the highest priority to creating and using renewable energy resources to address the basic needs of populations living in developing countries. Renewable energy resources should be used for ICT-based dissemination of information and communications, including radio and television. Africa can particularly benefit from solar power due to its high level of exposure to direct solar radiation. By mobilising regional synergies, complemented by the necessary technical and financial cooperation, Africa could play a leading role in this strategic domain in the next decade.

Communities must have the ability to participate directly in the development and maintenance of ICT-based solutions to their own problems. In order that communities may create and sustain their own solutions using ICTs, they must be empowered to develop their own productive forces and control the means of production within information societies. This must include the right to participate fully in the development and sustenance of ICT-based projects through democratic processes, including decision making with respect to economic, cultural, environmental, and other issues. ICTs should be used as an instrument for the creation of genuine and sustainable sources of work, thus providing new labour opportunities.

In order that communities and individuals may create economically and technically sustainable solutions, they must have the right to use Free Software. This makes software more affordable, and, allows people to participate in its development and maintenance[11]. ICT-based innovation should adhere to the use of international technical standards for hardware, software, and processes, which are open, freely implementable, publicly documented, interoperable, non-discriminatory and demand-driven.

It is important to support community-based communications using both traditional and new media and communication technologies. There is a need for the development and nurturing of the discipline of community informatics, which focuses on the particular characteristics and needs of communities, in relation to design, development, deployment, and operation of ICTs, as well as local content production.

2.1.9 Conflict Situations

We recognise that the use of media can be both positive and negative in conflict situations, including post-conflict peace building. We therefore insist that the rights of journalists and of all people to gather and communicate information, using any media, be especially respected during conflicts. These rights should be inviolate at all times but are crucial during war, violent conflict, and non-violent protest.

---

[11] The authors write: "In this document, we use the term "Free Software" to refer to the specific concept defined by the Free Software Foundation. Free Software is software that is licensed in such a way that people have the freedom to run, copy, distribute, study, change and improve it. Free Software implies access to source code as does "open source software"; however, open source software as the term is popularly used is not necessarily Free Software in our definition. Some organisations release open source software without permitting all of these actions. See http://www.fsf.org and http://www.fsfeurope.org for in-depth discussions of this concept."

We are particularly concerned about the deployment of "information warfare" technologies and techniques, including the purposeful jamming, blocking, or destruction of civilian communication systems during conflict situations; the use of 'embedded' journalists coupled with the targeting of non-embedded journalists; the use of media and communication systems to promote hatred and genocide; by military, police, or other security forces, be they governmental, privately owned, or non-state actors, during conflict situations both international and domestic.

Information intervention in conflict situations should be bound by international law, and the WSIS should encourage work on a future convention against information warfare to address these concerns. At the same time, the WSIS should not only limit information warfare and the control of media in conflict situations, but also actively promote media and communications for peace. To that end, we encourage governments to decrease public subsidy for military communications technology, and instead spend money directly on developing peaceful communications tools and applications.

2.2 Centrality of Human Rights

An information and communication society should be based on human rights and human dignity. With the Charter of the United Nations and the Universal Declaration of Human Rights as its foundation, it must embody the universality, indivisibility, interrelation and interdependence of all human rights - civil, political, economic, social and cultural - including the right to development and linguistic rights. This implies the full integration, concrete application and enforcement of all rights and the recognition of their centrality to democracy and sustainable development. Information and communication societies must be inclusive, so that all people, without distinction of any kind, can achieve their full potential. The principles of non-discrimination and diversity must be mainstreamed in all ICT regulation, policies, and programmes.

2.2.1 Freedom of Expression

Article 19 of the Universal Declaration of Human Rights is of fundamental and specific importance, since it forms an essential condition for human rights-based information and communication societies. Article 19 requires that everyone has the right to freedom of opinion and expression and the right to seek, receive and impart information and ideas, through any media and regardless of frontiers. This implies free circulation of ideas, pluralism of the sources of information and the media, press freedom, and availability of the tools to access information and share knowledge. Freedom of expression on the Internet must be protected by the rule of law rather than through self-regulation and codes of conduct. There must be no prior censorship, arbitrary control of, or constraints on, participants in the communication process or on the content, transmission and dissemination of information. Pluralism of the sources of information and the media must be safeguarded and promoted.

2.2.2 Right to Privacy

The right to privacy, enshrined in Article 12 of the Universal Declaration of Human Rights, is essential for self-determined human development in regard to civic, political, social, economic and cultural activities. The right to privacy faces new challenges in information and communication societies, and must be protected in public spaces, online, offline, at home and in the workplace. Every person must have the right to decide freely whether and in what manner he or she wants to receive information and communicate with others. The possibility of communicating anonymously must be ensured for everyone. The power of the private sector and of governments over personal data increases the risk of abuse, including monitoring and surveillance. Such activities must be kept to a legally legitimised minimum in a democratic society, and must remain accountable. The collection, retention, processing, use and disclosure of personal data, no matter by whom, should remain under the control of and determined by the individual concerned.

2.2.3 Right to Participate in Public Affairs

Good government administration and justice in a democratic society implies openness, transparency, accountability, participation and compliance with the rule of law. Respect for these principles is needed to enforce the right to take part in the conduct of public affairs. Public access to information produced or maintained by governments should be enforced, ensuring that the information is timely, complete and accessible in a format and language the public can understand. This further applies to access to documents of corporations relating to their activities affecting the public interest, especially in situations where the government has not made such information public.

2.2.4 Workers√ï Rights

ICTs are progressively changing our way of working. The creation of fair, secure, safe and healthy working conditions, in the manufacture of equipment and software, and in the utilisation of ICTs in the workplace in general, which respect international labour standards, for instance through tripartite social dialogue, is fundamental. ICTs should be used to promote awareness of, respect for and enforcement of human rights standards and international labour standards. Human rights, such as privacy, freedom of expression, linguistic rights, the right for on-line workers to form and join trade unions and the right of trade unions to function freely, including communicating with employees, must be respected in the workplace.

2.2.5 Rights of Indigenous Peoples

The evolution of information and communication societies must be founded on the respect and promotion of the recognition of the Rights of Indigenous Peoples and their distinctiveness as outlined in international conventions. Indigenous Peoples have fundamental rights to protect, preserve and strengthen their own language, culture and identity. ICT's should be used to support and promote diversity and the rights and means of Indigenous Peoples to benefit fully and with priority from their cultural, intellectual and so-called natural resources.

2.2.6 Women√ïs Rights

In order to realise women's rights in the information and communication societies, as spelled out in the Convention on the Elimination of All Forms of Discrimination Against Women (CEDAW) and the Beijing Declaration and Platform for Action (Fifth World Conference on Women), it is crucial to acknowledge and address the differences, disparities and disadvantages that women experience. This means taking into account the ways in which women are different from men, and how these differences translate into differential levels of access, opportunity, participation and use of ICTs. It must be ensured that policy or legal interventions and programmes consciously address these differences. To ensure effective equality of women, and thereby enabling women's full ability to claim and exercise their human rights, it is necessary to adopt a substantive equality approach in the analysis, which informs the content of ICT policy and programmes. This approach implies that actions to promote women's rights must transform the unequal power relation between women and men. Women need not only equality of opportunity, but also equality of access to opportunities and the ability to fully participate in availing such opportunities.

2.2.7 Rights of the Child

Information and communication societies must respect and promote the principles of the Convention on the Rights of the Child. Every child is entitled to a happy childhood and to enjoy the rights and freedoms available to all persons under the Universal Declaration of Human Rights. All persons, civil society, private sector and governments should commit to uphold the Rights of the Child in information and communication societies.

2.2.8 Rights of Persons with Disabilities

In inclusive information and communication societies, the rights of persons with disabilities to have full and equal access to information and communications including ICTs, regardless of types and degree of disabilities, must be ensured by public policies, laws and regulations at all levels. In order to achieve this goal, a Universal Design principle and the use of assistive technologies must be seriously promoted and supported throughout the whole process of building and nurturing information and communication societies in which persons with disabilities and their organisations must be allowed to participate fully and on equal terms with non-disabled people.

2.2.9 Regulation and the Rule of Law

National regulation should be in full compliance with international human rights standards, adhering to the rule of law. Information and communication societies must not result in any discrimination or deprivation of human rights resulting from the acts or omission of governments or of non-state actors under their jurisdictions. Any restriction on the use of ICTs must pursue a legitimate aim under international law, be prescribed by law, be strictly proportionate to such an aim, and be necessary in a democratic society.

2.3 Culture, Knowledge and the Public Domain

Information and communication societies are enriched by their diversity of cultures and languages, retained and passed on through oral tradition or recorded and transmitted through a variety of media, and together contributing to the sum of human knowledge. Human knowledge is the heritage of all humankind and the reservoir from which all new knowledge is created. The preservation of cultural and linguistic diversity, the freedom of the media and the defence and extension of the public domain of global knowledge are as essential, for information and communication societies, as the diversity of our natural environment.

2.3.1 Cultural and Linguistic Diversity

Cultural and linguistic diversity is an essential dimension of people-centred information and communication societies. Every culture has dignity and value that must be respected and preserved. Cultural and linguistic diversity is based, among other things, on the freedom of information and expression and the right of everyone to freely participate in the cultural life of the community, at local, national and international levels. This participation includes activities both as users and producers of cultural content. ICTs including traditional communications media have a particularly important role to play in sustaining and developing the world's cultures and languages.

2.3.1.1 Capacity Building and Education

Cultural and linguistic diversity should not only be preserved; it needs to be fostered. This implies capacity to express oneself, in one's own language, at any time, by any means, including traditional media and new ICTs. In order to become a contributor and a creator in the information and communication societies, not only technical skills are needed, but critical and creative competence. Media education in the sense of the UNESCO Grunwald Declaration must be given specific attention in education and training programs. Cultural and linguistic diversity also implies equal access to the means of expression and of dissemination of cultural goods and services. Priority should be given to community-driven initiatives.

2.3.1.2 Language

Plurality of languages is at the core of vibrant information and communication societies. ICTs can be applied to bridge cultural and linguistic divides, given the right priorities. In the past, ICT development has too often reinforced inequalities, such as dominance of roman letter based languages (especially English) and marginalization of local, regional and minority languages. Priority should be given in ICT research and development to overcoming barriers and addressing inequalities between languages and cultures.

2.3.1.3 International Law and Regulation

International law and regulation should strengthen cultural, linguistic and media diversity, in accordance with existing international declarations and covenants, in particular Article 19 and Article 27 of the Universal Declaration of Human Rights; Articles 19 and 27 of the International Covenant on Civil and Political Rights; Articles 13 and 15 of the International Covenant on Economic, Social and Cultural Rights; and Articles 5 and 6 of the Universal Declaration of Cultural Diversity adopted by UNESCO in 2001. International trade agreements should treat culture, including audio-visual content and services, not simply as a commodity, but should take account of the need for cultural, linguistic and media diversity. The establishment of an International Convention on Cultural Diversity should be accelerated, with a view to achieving an effective and binding international agreement. Existing international copyright regulation instruments including TRIPS and WIPO should be reviewed to ensure that they promote cultural, linguistic and media diversity and contribute to the development of human knowledge.

2.3.2 Media

2.3.2.1 The Role of the Media

Freedom of Expression and Freedom of the Media are central to any conception of information and communication societies. The media is an integral enabling mechanism for a global communications vision. Its role in producing, gathering and distributing diverse content in which all citizens are included and can actively participate, is vital. Especially for the developing countries, broadcast radio and television will continue to be the most effective ways to deliver high-quality information. All forms of media can make crucial contributions to social cohesion and development in the digital era.

Article 19 is the foundation for five regional declarations on media freedom and plurality that must continue to frame the role of the media in all its means of delivery. These texts[12] have been unanimously endorsed by the member states of UNESCO.

Security and other considerations should not be allowed to compromise freedom of expression and media freedom. Media pluralism and diversity should be guaranteed through appropriate laws to avoid excessive media concentration.

Editorial independence of media professionals and creators must be protected and the formulation of professional and ethical standards in journalism and other media production must be the responsibility of media workers themselves. Online authors, journalists and editors should have the same contractual rights and social protections as other media workers.

Public service broadcasting has a specific and crucial role to play in ensuring the participation of all in the information and communication societies. State-controlled media should be transformed into editorially independent public service organisations.

2.3.2.2 Community Media

Community media, that is media which are independent, community-driven and civil society-based, have a particular role to play in enabling access to and participation for all in information and communication societies, especially the poorest and most marginalized communities. Community media can be vital enablers of information, voice and capacities for dialogue. Legal and regulatory frameworks that protect and enhance community media are especially critical for ensuring vulnerable groups access to information and communication.

Governments should ensure that legal frameworks for community media are non-discriminatory and provide for equitable allocation of frequencies through transparent and accountable mechanisms. Targets should be established for the opening up of broadcast licenses to allow for the operation of community broadcasting where this is not currently permitted. Spectrum planning and regulation should ensure sufficient spectrum and channel capacity, and appropriate technical standards, for community media to develop in both the analogue and the digital environment.

---

[12] The Windhoek Declaration on the Promotion of Free and Pluralistic African Press, 1991; the Declaration of Alma Ata on Promoting Independent and Pluralistic Asian Media, 1992; the Declaration of Sana€ïa on Promoting Independent and Pluralistic Media, 1994; the Sofia Declaration on Promoting European Pluralistic and Independent Media, 1997 (adopted in 95 and 97)

A Community Media Fund should be established through a donor civil society partnership to invest in and support community-driven media, information and communication initiatives using traditional media and new ICTs including projects that make provision for the poorest communities, for cultural and linguistic diversity and for the equal participation of women and girls. Community-based media and communication centres should be encouraged and assisted to combine traditional media technologies, including radio and television, with access to new ICTs.

2.3.3 The Public Domain of Global Knowledge

A rich public domain of knowledge available to all is essential to sustainable information societies, to bridge the digital divide and to provide the grounds for a positive development of intellectual creativity, technological innovation and effective use of that technology. In information societies, new digital forms of storing information mean that this can be copied and transmitted in innovative ways that challenge existing customs and laws. The increasing privatisation of knowledge production threatens to restrict the availability of research results. Attempts have been made to commercially exploit traditional indigenous knowledge without consulting the communities, who are the owners of that knowledge.

2.3.3.1 Indigenous Peoples' Knowledge

Indigenous peoples are the guardians of their traditional knowledge and have the right to protect and control that knowledge. Existing intellectual property regimes are insufficient for the protection of indigenous people's cultural and intellectual property rights.

Traditional knowledge should be protected from any attempt at patenting. Indigenous peoples should freely decide whether their heritage should become part of the public domain or not. They should decide whether or not it should be exploited commercially and in what way.

We should give particular attention to measures to maintain knowledge diversity and to protect the cultural, intellectual and so-called natural resources of indigenous peoples, especially botanical and agricultural knowledge, from commercial exploitation and appropriation.

We urge the United Nations to establish specific legal frameworks, in accordance with Article 26.4 of the Agenda 21 of the Earth Summit, to recognise indigenous peoples' rights to self-determination and ancestral territories, as a necessary prerequisite to ensure the protection, preservation and development of their traditional knowledge in information and communication societies.

2.3.3.2 Copyright, Patents and Trademarks

Limited intellectual monopolies, also known as intellectual property rights, are granted only for the benefit of society, most notably to encourage creativity and innovation. The benchmark against which they must be reviewed and adjusted regularly is how well they fulfill this purpose. Today, the vast majority of humankind has no access to the public domain of global knowledge, a situation that is contributing to the growth of inequality and exploitation of the poorest peoples and communities. Yet instead of extending and strengthening the global domain, recent developments are restricting information more and more to private hands. Patents are being extended to software (and even to ideas), with the consequent effect of limiting innovation and reinforcing monopolies. Drugs that could save millions of lives are denied to disease sufferers because pharmaceutical companies that hold the patents resist making them available to those countries that can not pay high prices. Copyright periods have been extended again and again, making them practically indefinite and defeating their original purpose.

2.3.3.3 Software

Software provides the medium and regulatory framework for digital information, and access to software determines who may participate. Equal access to software is fundamental for inclusive and empowering digital information and communication societies, and a diversity of platforms is essential to this.

We must recognise the political and regulatory impact of software on digital societies and build, through public policy and specific programs, awareness of the effects and benefits of different software models. In particular, Free Software, with its freedoms of use for any purpose, study, modification and redistribution should be promoted for its unique social, educational, scientific, political and economic benefits and opportunities. Its special advantages for developing countries, such as low cost, empowerment and the stimulation of sustainable local and regional economies, easier adaptation to local cultures and creation of local language versions, greater security, capacity building, etc, need to be recognised, publicised and taken advantage of. Governments should promote the use of Free Software in schools and higher education and in public administration.

The UN should carry out a fundamental review of the impact on poverty and human rights of current arrangements for recognition and governance of monopolised knowledge and information, including the work of WIPO and the functioning of the TRIPS agreement. Efforts should be made to ensure that limited intellectual monopolies stimulate innovation and reward initiative, rather than keeping knowledge in private hands until it is of little use to society.

2.3.3.4 Research

Increasing private sector participation in scientific research is leading to patents and scientific knowledge being held in private hands instead of being available in the public domain, and increasing competition among scientists and scientific teams sometimes results in poor scientific practices, secrecy and the patenting of discoveries that would previously have been available to all. Research should continue to be based on cooperation, openness and transparency.

Public bodies such as libraries, scientific research centres, universities, should be able to contribute to enrich the common good of culture and knowledge, by putting into the public domain the results of their publicly funded activities. The public domain of global knowledge should be defended and extended through public policy, awareness-building and investments in programmes. These should ensure that any work funded by public or philanthropic bodies enters the public domain and should increase accessibility of information in online and offline media by means of Free Documentation, public libraries and other initiatives to disseminate information, such as Open Access journals and Open Archives giving access to scientific and other public domain information. All scientific data, such as genomes of living beings, should be freely accessible to all in Open Access databases.

2.4 Enabling Environment

2.4.1 Ethical Dimensions

Information and communication societies are about how our societies create, share and utilise the information, cultural production and knowledge, which in turn shape the evolution of those societies. The value-base of the information society must be founded on the principles contained in the ensemble of internationally agreed-upon conventions, declarations, and charters.

More specifically, equal, fair and open access to knowledge and information resources, - whatever the technical means used to store and transmit them - must be established as fundamental principles of such societies. Technological, financial and regulatory considerations must conform to these principles.

Transparent and accountable governance, ethical business and accounting practices in communications sector firms and ethical media practice are of particular relevance in this context. Codes of ethics and standards should be adopted in these cases and mechanisms should be established to monitor their application as well as appropriate sanctions for their violation. Formulation of ethics and standards in journalism and other media production should be the responsibility of media workers themselves.

Respect for diversity must be a central criterion in establishing the principles and mechanisms for resolving conflicts that arise in information societies. Such societies, if they are built on values such as cooperation, equity, honesty, integrity, respect and solidarity, can have a significant impact on the quality of interaction between cultures and the promotion of meaningful dialogue among civilisations, and thus contribute to bringing about world peace.

2.4.2 Democratic and Accountable Governance

National and international regulations for information and communication societies should be in full compliance with international human rights standards. Openness, transparency, accountability and the rule of law should be the guiding principles for the democratic governance of societies at all levels, from the local to the national and international. Inclusive, participatory and peaceful information and communication societies rest on the responsiveness of governing bodies as well as on the commitment of all actors involved in governance, both of governmental and non governmental nature, to progressively implement greater political, social and economic equity.

A democratic perspective on information and communication societies, in which information is crucial for citizens, is necessary in order to make choices grounded on the awareness of alternatives and opportunities. Information and communication are the foundation for transparency, debate and decision-making. They can contribute to a culture and a practice of cooperation, basis for a renewal of democracy. Information and communication technologies offer potential benefits to the world's communities that will only be exploited if there is a political will to do so.

In this spirit, the aim of WSIS "to develop a common vision and understanding of the Information Society", and the methods to achieve such a vision, requires shared communication values and mechanisms including the right to communicate, respect for freedom of opinion and expression in all of its dimensions, and a commitment to transparency, accountability, and democracy.

2.4.3 Infrastructure and Access

The dramatic lack of a reliable infrastructure is the main physical obstacle for ICT-based services to be offered to populations living in Africa. Here, the fragmented and incomplete structure and the unreliability of the existing infrastructure and access networks constitute the underlying structure of the so-called Digital Divide.

(Tele) communications infrastructure is essential for disseminating ICT-based services and is central in achieving the goal of universal, sustainable, ubiquitous and affordable access to and usage of these technologies and services by all. Furthermore, energy is a prerequisite for infrastructure and access.

Most voice, data and Internet traffic between African countries is currently routed outside of the continent because of the lack of an efficient African backbone network, increasing the cost of this traffic. Increased cost always limits access. Existing efforts to build an African network infrastructure must be supported and expanded (e.g. Internet exchange points).

The implementation and roll-out of (tele)communications infrastructure and access in DCs will require financial investments consistent with the huge needs in this area. In order to reduce the amount of financial resources needed, investments should be optimised by consolidating projects nationally or (sub) regionally, and by technological (re-) designing and updating. Furthermore, synergy between different sectors should be systematically exploited from the project phase, particular attention being paid to the energy and transport sectors that show very close links. Finally, the particularly strong synergy and technological similarity between ICT and Radio-TV networks should lead governments and planning authorities to deploy and use a common infrastructure for both their services to be transported and disseminated.

Community telecentres (public access centres) have become spaces for the effective access and strategic use of information and communication technologies with emphasis on the democratisation of communications. Governments should guarantee policies for the development of telecentres, among others, to provide equitable and affordable access to infrastructure and ICTs; to encourage digital inclusion policies for the population, independently of gender, ethnic aspects, language, culture and geographical situation. This would promote the discussion and active participation of communities in public policy processes related to the implementation and role of telecentres for local development.

Orbital satellite paths should be recognised as a public resource and should be allocated to benefit the public interest through transparent and accountable frameworks. Moreover, spectrum planning and regulation should ensure equitable access among a plurality of media including sufficient satellite capacity reserved for community media. A fixed percentage of orbital resources, satellite capacity and radio frequency spectrum should be reserved for educational, humanitarian, community and other non-commercial use.

The expansion of the global information infrastructure should be based on principles of equality and partnership and guided by rules of fair competition and regulation at both national and international levels.

The integration of access, infrastructure and training of the citizenry and the generation of local content, in a framework of social networks and clear public or private policies, is a key basis for the development of egalitarian and inclusive information societies.

2.4.4 Financing and Infrastructure

Existing and new financing measures should be envisaged and appraised. The 'Digital Solidarity Fund' has been proposed by Africa. Such a fund could be a real hope for African peoples if it clearly states its goals, is transparently managed, and aims to foster primarily public services, especially for populations living in underserved and isolated areas. In addition, we stress the significant role that diaspora populations from all the world's regions can play in financing ICT programmes and projects.

In order to optimise scarce financial resources, appropriate cost-effective technological options should be used, while avoiding duplication of infrastructure. Additionally, synergies between different sectors and networks can be exploited to this end, with particular attention to the energy and transport sectors, given their close links with the telecommunications sector.

A Community Media Fund should be established through a donor civil society partnership to invest in and support community-driven and community-based media, and information and communication initiatives using both traditional media and new ITCs. Effort should be made to eliminate the duplication of infrastructures and to consolidate projects in a national or regional frame to encourage investment funding. Where possible, ICT and radio/TV networks should use common infrastructure for dissemination.

2.4.5 Human Development, Education and Training

Literacy, education and research are fundamental and interrelated components of the information exchanges necessary to build knowledge societies. Knowledge creation and acquisition should be nurtured as a participatory and collective process; it should not be considered a one-way flow or confined to one section of capacity building. Education, in its different components - formal, informal, and lifelong - is fundamental to building democratic societies both by creating a literate citizenry and a skilled workforce.

To utilise the full potential of e-learning and long-distance education, they must be complemented by traditional educational resources and methods, in a local context of media pluralism and linguistic diversity.

Only informed and educated citizens with access to empowering education, a plurality of means of information, and the outputs of research efforts can fully participate in and effectively contribute to knowledge societies. Therefore it is also essential to recognise the right to education as stated both in the Declaration on the Right to Development and the Universal Declaration of Human Rights

Capacity building initiatives designed to empower individuals and communities in the information society must include, in addition to basic literacy and ICT skills, media and information literacy, the ability to find, appraise, use and create information and technology. In particular, educators, students and researchers must be able to use and develop Free Software, which allows the unfettered ability to study, change, copy, distribute, and run software. Finally, capacity building initiatives should be designed to stimulate the desire for general learning and respond to specific as well as special needs: those of young and elderly people, of women, of people with impairments, of indigenous peoples, of migrant communities, of refugees and returnees in post-conflict situations, in a life-long perspective. Volunteers can help transmit knowledge and enhance capacity, in particular of marginalized groups not reached by government training institutions.

Capacity building in the information and communication societies requires people who are competent in teaching media and communication literacy. Therefore training of trainers and training of educators in every level is equal important in order to reach out to people at the limits of the information society.

Libraries are an important tool to fight digital divide and to ensure continuous, out-of-market-ruled access to information, by freeing the results of research funded by public support, by sharing content and educational materials to promote literacy, build capacities and bring autonomy to learners of all kinds, world wide. This also entails convincing content producers to be active participants in the open access paradigm of knowledge.

Global barriers to knowledge and education must be transparently evaluated by looking beyond technological obstacles at legal and institutional gridlocks (like Intellectual Property Laws and International standards) and promoting a new balance of intellectual properties as a common ground for creators to protect their works and for civil society to benefit from their contributions.

Civil society sees the need for alternative models for the production and exchange of knowledge and information. To secure and finance the global knowledge commons, civil society actors support new open and self-organised publishing models in science and software production and community-based communications, with in-built maintenance programs and upgrading capacities.

2.4.6 Information Generation and Knowledge Development

Research must be promoted in all fields related to the information and communication societies, and its development must be sensitive to the social uses of ICTs. In particular, research on community informatics must be supported[13]. This would include the development of a research agenda among practitioners, scholars, and communities; the cataloguing of community informatics projects and identification of both factors for failure and success; and support for research projects and systems trials. Fundamental research should be strengthened by expanding open access to primary scientific data and publications. Public bodies such as libraries, scientific research centres, universities should foster independent investigation, build a pluralistic body of knowledge and promote the results of activities which have been funded by public money. This body of knowledge should be made available in all public spaces, or spaces with public access (community centres, universities, schools, museums, libraries, media centres, and other dedicated entities), through appropriate and plural modes of access, avoiding the risk of high dependency on digital technology alone.

2.4.7 Global Governance of ICT and Communications

International "rules of the game" play an increasingly central role in the global information economy. In recent years, governments have liberalised traditional international regulatory regimes for telecommunications, radio frequency spectrum, and satellite services, and have created new multilateral arrangements for international trade in services, intellectual property, "information security," and electronic commerce. At the same time, business groups have established a variety of "self-regulatory" arrangements concerning Internet identifiers (names and numbers), infrastructure, and content.

It is not acceptable for these and related global governance frameworks to be designed by and for small groups of powerful governments and companies and then exported to the world as *faits accomplis*. Instead, they must reflect the diverse views and interests of the international community as a whole. This overarching principle has both procedural and substantive dimensions.

[13] Community informatics refers here to the interdisciplinary study and practice of the design, implementation, and management of information and communication technologies developed by communities to solve their own problems. This field takes into account social science research about the social impacts of ICTs -- also known as social informatics -- as well as information and communication systems analysis and design techniques.

Procedurally, decision-making processes must be based on such values as inclusive participation, transparency, and democratic accountability. In particular, institutional reforms are needed to facilitate the full and effective participation of marginalized stakeholders like developing and transitional countries, global civil society organisations, small and medium-sized enterprises, and individual users.

Substantively, global governance frameworks must promote a more equitable distribution of benefits across nations and social groups. To do so, they must strike a better balance between commercial considerations and other legitimate social objectives. For example, existing international arrangements should be reformed to promote: efficient management of network interconnections and traffic revenue distribution, subject to the mutual agreement of corresponding operators; equitable allocations of radio frequency spectrum and satellite orbital slots that fully support developmental and non-commercial applications; fair trade in electronic goods and services, taking into account the developing countries' need for special and differential treatment; an open public domain of information resources and ideas; and the protection of human rights, consumer safety, and personal privacy. In parallel, new diverse international arrangements are needed to promote: financial support for sustainable e-development, especially but not only in less affluent nations; linguistic, cultural, and informational diversity; and the curtailment of concentrated market power in ICT and mass media industries.

In light of the relevant controversies in the WSIS process, special attention must be given to improving the global coordination of the Internet's underlying resources. It must be remembered that the Internet is not a singular communications "platform" akin to a public telephone network; it is instead a highly distributed set of protocols, processes, and voluntarily self-associating networks. Accordingly, the Internet cannot be governed effectively by any one organisation or set of interests. An exclusionary intergovernmental model would be especially ill suited to its unique characteristics; only a truly open, multistakeholder, and flexible approach can ensure the Internet's continued growth and transition into a multilingual medium. In parallel, when the conditions for system stability and sound management can be guaranteed, authority over inherently global resources like the root servers should be transferred to a global, multistakeholder entity.

The international community must have full and easy access to knowledge and information about ICT global governance decision making. This is a baseline prerequisite for implementation of the principles mentioned above, and indeed for the success of the WSIS process itself. We need public-interest oriented monitoring and analysis of the relevant activities of both intergovernmental and "self-governance" bodies including, inter alia, the International Telecommunication Union, the World

Trade Organization, the World Intellectual Property Organization, the United Nations Conference on International Trade Law, the Organization for Economic Cooperation and Development, the Hague Conference on International Private Law, the of Europe, the Asia Pacific Economic Cooperation, the North American Free Trade Agreement, the Internet Corporation for Assigned Names and Numbers, and Wassenaar Arrangement.

As a viable first step in this direction, we recommend the establishment of an independent and truly multistakeholder observatory committee to: (1) map and track the most pressing current developments in ICT global governance decision-making; (2) assess and solicit stakeholder input on the conformity of such decision-making with the stated objectives of the WSIS agenda; and (3) report to all stakeholders in the WSIS process on a periodic basis until 2005, at which time a decision could be made on whether to continue or terminate the activity.

Conclusion

It is people who primarily form and shape societies, and information and communication societies are no exception. Civil society actors have been key innovators and shapers of the technology, culture and content of information and communication societies, and will continue to be in the future.

Human rights stand at the centre of our vision of the information and communication society[14]. From this standpoint, action plans, implementation, financing mechanisms and governance must all be shaped by and evaluated on the basis of their ability to meet life-critical human needs.

Host countries and institutions contributing to and participating in the post-Geneva WSIS process should fully respect the principles enunciated in the Declaration adopted at the Geneva Summit, including those relating to human rights that are fundamental to the information and communications society. These include, but are not limited to the freedoms of expression, association and information.

Toward this end, and in preparation for the second phase of WSIS, an independent commission should be established to review national and international ICT regulations and practices and their compliance with international human rights standards. This commission should also address the potential applications of ICTs to

[14] Nothing in this declaration may be interpreted as implying that civil society wishes to engage in any activity or to perform any act aimed at the destruction of any of the rights and freedoms set forth in the International Bill of Rights and other human rights treaties.

the realization of human rights, such as the right to development, the right to education and the right to a standard of living adequate for the mental and physical health and well-being of the individual and his or her family, including food, housing and medical care.

The full realisation of a just information society requires the full participation of civil society in its conception, implementation, and operation. To this end, we call on all governments involved in the preparatory processes of WSIS to work in good faith with non-governmental and civil society organisations and fully honour the recommendations of Resolution 56/183 of the United Nations General Assembly. In particular, participating governments must honour civil society's right to participate fully in the remaining intergovernmental preparatory processes leading to the second phase of WSIS.

We commit ourselves independent of the modalities of participation granted to us by governments to pursuing by all just and honourable means necessary the realization of the vision of the information society presented herein. To this end, civil society organisations will continue to cooperate with one another to develop a Plan of Action for the second phase of WSIS. We call upon the world's leaders to urgently assume the heavy responsibilities they face, in partnership with civil society, to make this vision a reality.

Civil Society Essential Benchmarks for WSIS[15]

WSIS Civil Society Plenary

Introduction

The approach to the "Information Society" on which the WSIS has been based reflects, to a large extent, a narrow understanding in which ICTs means telecommunications and the Internet. This approach has marginalised key issues relating to the development potential inherent in the combination of knowledge and technology and thus conflicts with the broader development mandate given in UNGA Resolution 56/183.

Civil society is committed to a people-centred, inclusive approach based on respect for human rights principles and development priorities. We believe these principles and priorities should be embedded throughout the WSIS Declaration of Principles and Action Plan. This paper sets out the benchmarks against which civil society will assess the outcomes of the WSIS process and the commitment of all stakeholders to achieving its mandate.

Human rights

The WSIS Declaration of Principles and Plan of Action, should take as their foundations the international human rights framework. This implies the full integration, concrete application and enforcement of civil, political, economic, social and cultural rights, including labour rights, the right to development, as well as the principle of non-discrimination. The universality, indivisibility, interrelatedness and interdependence of all human rights should be clearly recognized, together with their centrality to democracy and the rule of law.

All Principles of the Declaration and all activities in the Action Plan, should be in full compliance with international human rights standards, which should prevail over

---

[15] Document adopted by the Civil Society Plenary during Prepcom 3ª, November 2003. The essential benchmarks listed in this document reflect work in progress by the civil society content and themes group of the WSIS process. While there is consensus on the priorities stated here, this document does not represent absolute consensus, nor does the order of the essential benchmarks constitute a strict ranking in order of importance. For more information on the WSIS CS CT group, contact: Sally Burch, sburch@alainet.org. Final version: 11-Dec-2003. On the web at http://www.prepcom.net/wsis/1069062981246 in html form and at www.worldsummit2003.de/ download_en/CS-Essential-Benchmarks-for-WSIS-14-11-03-final.rtf as an rtf.

national legislative frameworks. The "information society" must not result in any discrimination or deprivation of human rights resulting from the acts or omissions of governments or of non-state actors under their jurisdictions. Any restriction on the use of ICTs must pursue a legitimate aim under international law, be prescribed by law, be strictly proportionate to such an aim, and be necessary in a democratic society.

Article 19 of the Universal Declaration of Human Rights is of fundamental and specific importance to the information society, requiring that everyone has the right to freedom of opinion and expression and the right to seek, receive and impart information and ideas through any media and regardless of frontiers.

Poverty reduction and the Right to Development

Given the unequal distribution of wealth among and within nations, the struggle against poverty should be the top priority on the agenda of the World Summit on the Information Society. It is not possible to achieve sustainable development by embracing new communication technologies without challenging existing inequalities.

Civil society organisations from different parts of the world unite in their call to governments to take this matter very seriously. We want to emphasise that challenging poverty requires more than setting of 'development agendas'. It requires the commitment of significant financial and other resources, linked with social and digital solidarity, channeled through existing and new financing mechanisms that are managed transparently and inclusively of all sectors of society.

Sustainable development

An equitable Information Society must be shaped by the needs of people and communities and based on sustainable economic, social development and democratic principles, including the Millennium Development Goals.

Only development that embraces the principles of social justice and gender equality can be said to centrally address fundamental social, cultural and economic divides. Market-based development solutions often fail to address more deep-rooted and persistent inequalities in and between countries of the North and South.

Democratic and sustainable development ~~of~~ in the information society can therefore not be left solely to market forces and the propagation of technology. In order to balance commercial objectives with legitimate social interests, recognition should be given to the need for responsibility of the public sector, appropriate regulation and development of public services, and the principle of equitable and affordable access to services.

People and communities must be empowered to develop their own solutions within the information society, in particular to fight poverty and to participate in development through fully democratic processes that allow community access to and participation in decision-making.

Social Justice

Gender Equality

An equitable and inclusive Information Society must be based on gender justice and be particularly guided by the interpretation of principles of gender equality, non-discrimination and women's empowerment as contained in the Beijing Declaration and Platform for Action and the CEDAW Convention. The Action Plan must demonstrate a strong commitment to an intersectional approach to redressing discrimination resulting from unequal power relations at all levels of society. To empower girls and women throughout their life cycle, as shapers and leaders of society, gender responsive educational programs and appropriate learning environments need to be promoted. Gender analysis and the development of both quantitative and qualitative indicators in measuring gender equality through an extensive and integrated national system of monitoring and evaluation are "musts".

Disability

Specific needs and requirements of all stakeholders, including those with disabilities, must be considered in ICT development. Accessibility and inclusiveness of ICTs is best done at an early stage of design, development and production, so that the Information Society is to become the society for all, at minimum cost.

Labour rights

Essential human rights, such as privacy, freedom of expression, and the right of trade unions to communicate with employees, should be respected in the workplace. ICTs are progressively changing our way of working and the creation of a secure, safe and healthy working environment , appropriate to the utilisation of ICTs, respecting core labour standards, is fundamental. ICTs should be used to promote awareness of, respect for and enforcement of universal human rights standards and core labor standards.

Indigenous Peoples
The evolution of the Information Society must be founded on the respect and promotion of the recognition of the Rights of Indigenous Peoples and their distinctiveness as outlined in the ILO Convention 169 and the UN Draft Declaration on the Rights of Indigenous Peoples. They have fundamental rights to protect, preserve and strengthen their own identity and cultural diversity. ICT's should be used to support and promote the rights and means of Indigenous Peoples to benefit fully and with priority from their cultural, intellectual and so-called natural resources.

Literacy, Education and Research

Literacy and free universal access to education is a key principle. All initiatives must embrace this principle and respond to needs of all. Knowledge societies require an informed and educated citizenry. Capacity building needs to include skills to use ICTs, media and information literacy, and the skills needed for active citizenship including the ability to find, appraise, use and create information and technology. Approaches that are local, horizontal, gender-responsive and socially-driven and mediated should be prioritised. A combination of traditional and new media as well as open access to knowledge and information should be encouraged.

Cultural and linguistic diversity

Communications media and information technologies have a particularly important role to play in sustaining and developing the world's cultures and languages. The implementation of this principle requires support for a plurality of means of information and communication and respect for cultural and linguistic diversity, as outlined in UNESCO's Declaration on Cultural Diversity.

Access and Infrastructure

Global universal access to communication and information should be a target of the WSIS action plan and the expansion of the global information infrastructure should be based on principles of equality and partnership and guided by rules of fair competition and regulation at both national and international levels. The integration of access, infrastructure and training of the citizenry and the generation of local content, in a framework of social networks and clear public or private policies, is a key basis for the development of egalitarian and inclusive information societies. The evolution of policy should be coordinated internationally but enable a diversity of appropriate solutions based on national and regional input and international sharing of information and resources. This should be people-centered and process-orientated, rather than technologically determined and expert dominated.

Governance and enabling environment

Democratic governance

Good governance in a democratic society implies openness, transparency, accountability, and compliance with the rule of law. Respect for these principles is needed to enforce the right to take part in the conduct of public affairs. Public access to information produced or maintained by governments should be enforced, ensuring that the information is timely, complete and accessible in a format and language the public can understand. This also applies to access to information produced or maintained by corporations where this relates to activities affecting the public interest.

Media

Article 19 of the Universal Declaration of Human Rights is the touchstone for an independent, pluralistic and free media. Media pluralism and diversity should be guaranteed through appropriate laws to avoid excessive media concentration. Security and other considerations should not compromise freedom of expression, media freedom and access to information

Community media

Community media, that is media which are independent, community-driven and civil-society based, have a specific and crucial role to play in enabling access and participation for all to the information society, especially the poorest and most marginalised communities. Community media should be supported and promoted. Governments should assure that legal frameworks for community media are non-discriminatory and provide for equitable allocation of frequencies through transparent and accountable mechanisms.

Internet governance

The global governance of ICT must be based on the values of open participation, inclusiveness, transparency, and democratic accountability. It should establish and support universal participation in addressing new international policy and technical issues raised by the Internet and ICT. No single body and no single stakeholder group is able to manage all of the issues alone. Many stakeholders, cooperating in strict accordance with widely supported rules and procedures, must define the global agenda.

The non-government sector has played a historically critical role in Internet Governance, and this must be recognized. The strength of the Internet as an open non-Government platform should be reinforced, with an explicit and stronger role for Civil Society. The role of Governments should be no greater than that of any other stakeholder group.

Public Domain of Global Knowledge

Limited intellectual monopolies
Human knowledge, including the knowledge of all peoples and communities, also those who are remote and excluded, is the heritage of all humankind and the reservoir from which new knowledge is created. A rich public domain is essential to inclusive information societies. Limited intellectual monopolies, such as copyrights or patents, are granted only for the benefit of society, most notably to encourage creativity and innovation. The benchmark against which they must be reviewed and adjusted regularly is how well they fulfill their purpose.

Free Software
Software is the cultural technique of the digital age and access to it determines who may participate in a digital world. Free Software with its freedoms of use for any purpose, studying, modification and redistribution is an essential building block for an empowering, sustainable and inclusive information society. No software model should be forbidden or negatively regulated, but Free Software should be promoted for its unique social, educational, scientific, political and economic benefits and opportunities.

Access to information in the public domain
Today, more than 80% of mankind has no access to the reservoir of human knowledge that is the public domain and from which our new knowledge is created. Their intellectual power remains uninitialized and consequently unused, lost to all humankind. The reservoir of human knowledge must be made equally available to all in online and offline media by means of Free Documentation, public libraries and other initiatives to disseminate information.

Open access to scientific information
Free scientific information is a requirement for sustainable development. Science is the source of the technological development that empowers the Information Society, including the World Wide Web. In the best tradition of science, scientific authors donate their work to humankind and therefore, it must be equally available to all, on the Web, in online Open Access journals and online Open Archives.

Security and privacy

Integrity and security
Definitions of criminal and terrorist purposes in existing and emerging policies and legislation are ambiguous and prevent the use of information resources for legitimate purposes. The legitimate need for infrastructure integrity must avoid shift to the highly politicized agenda characterized by language referring to the integrity of the military field and the use of information resources for criminal and terrorist purposes.

Right to privacy
The right to privacy should be affirmed in the context of the information society. It must be defended in public spaces, online, offline, at home and in the workplace. Every person must have the right to decide freely whether and in what manner he or she wants to receive information and communicate with others. The possibility of communicating anonymously must be ensured for everyone. The collection, retention, use and disclosure of personal data, no matter by whom, should remain under the control of the individual concerned. The power of the private sector and governments over personal data, including monitoring and surveillance, increases the risk of abuse, and must be kept to a minimum under clearly specified, legal conditions.

Statements of Regional and Thematic Civil Society Caucuses

The Latin American and Caribbean Regional Ministerial Preparatory Conference for the World Summit on the Information Society, from the point of view of the NGOs[16]

Magaly Pazello, translated from Spanish original by APC News[17]

BAVARO, Dominican Republic -- Immediately after the World Social Forum, the Latin America and the Caribbean Regional Conference (one of the Preparatory Conferences for the World Summit on the Information Society) was held in Bávaro, Punta Cana, Dominican Republic, from the 29th to the 31st of January, 2003. Organised by Indotel, ECLAC, the ITU (International Telecommunications Union-the UN agency that is organising the World Summit) and the World Bank, this conference is part of the preparatory process for the World Summit on the Information Society (WSIS) to be held in two parts: the first in Geneva (December, 2003) and the second in Tunisia (2005).

Almost all countries in the region were represented at Bávaro, as well as UNESCO, United Nations Development Programme, the World Health Organisation, the Inter American Development Bank and other representatives of the United Nations, the European Union, the Organisation of American States, various programmes and institutes, development banks, some universities, the private sector (which ranged from mass media to telecommunications companies), and Civil Society (with the presence of a large number of networks, amongst which were the DAWN Network, the APC Women's Networking Programme, ALAI, Funredes, the international community radio association, AMARC, Computer Professionals for Social Responsibility (CPSR) and Chasquinet). There were also delegations from the USA and Canada which, after some discussion, were finally accepted as participants in the negotiations for the Final Declaration, with speaking and voting rights.

---

[16] 03/14/2003 More information: http://www.indotel.org.do/wsis Translation from Spanish original: APC

[17] Magaly Pazello is with the DAWN network for APCNews and also a member of the APC Women's Networking Support Programme

Also present were representatives of the governments of those countries where similar regional conferences have been held prior to this one, such as Mali, Japan and Russia, as well as countries which have hosted previous events, such as Spain and France, and the host countries for the WSIS, Switzerland and Tunisia.

The main objective of the Conference was to "carry out a regional evaluation of the challenges and opportunities presented by the Information Society for Latin America and the Caribbean, and at the same time to work towards the elaboration of a regional position for the World Summit on the Information Society".

Topics dealt with at the Regional Conference:

- the transition towards the Information Society
- the characteristics of the regulatory frameworks necessary for the development of the Information Society in Latin America and the Caribbean
- human capital requirements in the Information Society
- the financing necessary to obtain the benefits of the Information Society

The Conference was organised in plenary sessions and thematic debating sessions, to which non-governmental organisations (NGOs) were invited to contribute as panellists. Parallel to the conference, a one-day workshop was held with the private sector, INDOTEL (the local host agency for this Regional Conference), the ITU and the Economic Commission for Latin America and the Caribbean (ECLAC), where representatives of development banks were also present. This workshop was open to all participants, although it clashed with the main plenary session.

Unfortunately, the Civil Society event, organised by the Global Knowledge Partnership (GKP), was held on February 28, making it impossible for many of the NGOs and networkswho were also at the World Social Forum in Porto Alegre, Brazil to attend. The results of this event, which were quite interesting, were presented to the Plenary on the last day of the Conference. GKP describes itself as a network of networks, made up of three sectors: public, private and Civil Society. This organisation has held workshops in all the other regional conferences and its objectives focus on: the Millennium Challenge as a main guideline; centring the Information Society debate on people rather than on technology; and relating the challenges to productivity with a view to overcoming poverty.

It should be mentioned that there were also parallel or informal meetings among the NGOs and networks present, with the idea of organising a regional NGO meeting. At one of these, the WSIS President, Mr Adama Samassekou and UNESCO were present.

The DAWN (Development Alternatives with Women for a New Era) Network was represented by Magaly Pazello (Brazil) in one of the thematic sessions. Her presentation in the session on human capital (www.indotel.org.do/wsis/bavaro_magaly.doc) focussed on social inequality and the digital divide and was quite general, given that each participant had only 15 minutes to speak. It mentioned that without efficient and effective public policies to overcome poverty, the Information Society could deepen inequalities instead of narrowing or eradicating them, and that this has a much greater impact on poor women, afro-descendents, indigenous peoples and the young poor. She also pointed out that the new information and communication technologies have not contributed to changing unequal gender relations, especially as regards the sexual division of labour. With the exception of DAWN, the Centre of Investigation for Women's Action (CIPAF) and the APC Women's Networking Support Programme (WNSP), there did not appear to be representation from other women's groups, and even less from feminist groups (only DAWN and CIPAF).

We observed that there is a large gap between the perspectives of those movements active in the information society and other social movements, seen in the language used in the declarations, which is often quite backwards and seems to rely on requests for hand-outs, particularly where gender is concerned. Dialogue is needed amongst these movements so that actions around the Information Society do not return to the past, or even worse, allow the language already consecrated in the United Nations to be revised and exclude language already achieved in the so-called UN Social Cycle (the cycle of conferences of the 90's). There was no consensus around contributions which went beyond a welfare-type approach to themes related to women, excluded ethnic groups, the disabled, the young, the old, and "marginalized" groups.. The contributions of the NGOs present went no further than the reductionist viewpoint which transforms so-called excluded groups into a single label, without taking into consideration their specific qualities and above all their political contributions and activities over the last 20 years. So it is extremely important that the various social movements talk to each other so that the debate around the Information Society improves in quality and visibility, and can really have an effect at the decision-making level.

Final Declaration

The negotiations around the Bávaro Final Declaration were slow and suffered from a "small issue" between the USA and Cuba: 40 years of embargo. The Cuban delegation informed NGOs who contact them that they used the access to information and communication theme, to try to gain access to the Internet cables which come out of the US and connect the rest of the continent. The USA will not tolerate this. The discussions over the paragraph related to the transparency of the governing Internet bodies were also difficult, and to manage to include three little words, "democratisation", "transparency" and "representativeness" was very hard. The NGOs present were able to propose contributions to the final text of the Declaration, preparing a short document with their contributions and suggestions for each paragraph which was distributed to some delegations.

The Conference lasted for three days and only in the early hours following the third and final day of the meeting was agreement reached on a provisional (final) text for the Final Declaration, which contained the dissenting views of the US and Canadian delegations. The very two countries which before had been excluded from the Conference and given no chance to contribute to the document because the event had not been conceived as including all of the Americas.

Of note in this process was the ease in getting access to the national delegations, since we all shared the same space, as well as to representatives from the UN, the World Bank and the private sector. On the one hand, it is very interesting, because it suggests that NGOs can start up close and even informal dialogues, yet on the other hand it may allow these very moments of dialogue not to be any more than just that, without creating any possibility for exchange and input into the decisions taken around the negotiated document. In fact, this big opening up was just one side of the story, because the NGOs justly complained of not having any real help for their participation, such as funding for the journey to Bávaro (which is very expensive) or online discussions prior to the Conference. Really very few NGOs or networks were present.

But one has to recognise that although the Regional Conference had been planned for the same dates as the World Social Forum, after various requests there was enough political good faith on the part of the governments and ECLAC for the dates to be moved by one day, allowing the NGOs at the Forum to also attend the Conference. This was a key part of the discussion amongst NGOs in the CRIS-AL mailing list. Those of us who have followed other negotiating processes can compare and affirm that the Bávaro Regional Conference was more open than many other processes carried out by ECLAC in the region. Many of the NGOs present at Bávaro lacked expertise in working in negotiating processes with government delegations. It is not easy to move amongst governments and to take into account the range of negotiations which often occur in other political arenas but which play a key role in the WSIS also. This is a disadvantage faced by NGOs in a regional and global process, and for this reason it is extremely important to create capacity-building opportunities to learn about political lobbying and negotiation.

Statement from Australian Civil Society[18]

Roundtable for Australian Civil Society

Executive Summary

Civil society has enormous power and benefits. Effectively-used information and communications technologies help civil society to develop valuable current knowledge, consolidated networks, beneficial social innovations, global progress, accumulation of past culture, a means for coping with change, personal life-skills, local content, shared community aspirations and values, and productive interactions with government and business. This Statement describes how these can be achieved in Australia.

The key topics it covers are indigenous communities, spatial isolation, democratic pluralism, inclusion and interoperability, access to content and technology, effective use of technologies, volunteers, privacy, knowledge sharing and intellectual property. At each topic, potential for improvement is described.

The Roundtable for Australian Civil Society (RACS) was established by the Centre for Community Networking Research (CCNR), Monash University and Communities on the Internet (COIN), Central Queensland University as a result of seed funding from the National Office of the Information Economy (NOIE) in June 2003 with aim of coordinating a civil society input into the World Summit on the Information Society (WSIS) 2003.

RACS undertook a round of consultations with a number of Australian peak bodies representing civil society families identified by WSIS. This Statement represents the views of this initial engagement and acts as a focal point to seek growing input from the Australian Civil Society, as a base for future inputs to the WSIS processes. The Statement will form a part of the official Australian documentation into WSIS 2003 and is being presented to a number of forums during 2003.

The Statement clearly recognises Australia's ability to contribute to policy development, research, praxis and service delivery, while addressing issues of digital inclusion and effective use of ICT through a prism that validates civil society in key decision-making.

---

[18] On the web at http://www.ccnr.net/wsis/

It recognises the need for Australian governance processes to allocate resource and policy prominence to the intersection between civil society with digital inclusion and effective use of IT products and services. It makes the clear point that this issue (authorized by the UN), is of sufficient import for Australia's future to be considered in the same significance as education, health, security, infrastructure, industry development were to previous generations.

Ongoing dialogue with any interested person or group is encouraged. We believe that this Statement will stimulate widespread debate about the use of ICTs in Australia. Please make your suggestions known.

Civil society in Australia: an adaptation

The concept of "civil society" as a discrete non-government, non-business sector with a particular set of interests and public voice is one that has only emerged in recent times in Australia. Ordinarily, governments at all levels are considered as fully representative of citizens' interests, though there has been a long history of organisations supporting citizens' activities independently of government. It should be also noted that in Australia there is no recognised religious establishment or state church, though many religious groups have a strong role in the delivery of welfare and educational services. The place of institutions of higher education within the civil society has hardly been explored, though most of the members of this roundtable work within academia.

To find organised elements of civil society we have looked to: trade unions, religious groups, foundations, community organizations, social movements, non-government organizations and non-profits, volunteer organisations, charities, cooperatives, professional associations, educational institutions, clubs, public media, and others.

This Statement aspires to support an engaged and informed civil society, which is aware of, and empowered by the multifarious capacities of Information and Communications Technologies (ICTs). It is based on the view that the use of ICTs should not drive the direction of civil society but that, given the right conditions, ICTs can act as enablers, facilitating self-organisation, digital inclusion, participatory decision-making, and a more knowledgeable society.

How this statement was written

The Centre for Community Networking Research, Monash University, and COIN Internet Academy, Central Queensland University, initiated a consultative process in the second half of 2003 to develop this Australian civil society statement for the World Summit on the Information Society (WSIS). This was done through:

- Formation of a key working group of people - the Australian Roundtable on Civil Society (RACS) in non-governmental organisations, particularly universities, non-profits and indigenous organizations, with a known interest in ICTs. Members of this group met in Canberra in May, 2003 and Melbourne in October 2003. The National Office for the Information Economy has provided support for this process.
- Broader consultations and submissions by e-mail and in person, including nurturing contacts at conferences, in Australia and overseas, attendance at PrepComs for the WSIS, board meetings, and other events.

Indigenous Australians

Members of the working party recognise the potential benefits of ICTs to indigenous people's development. The flexible nature of IT applications and the ability to utilise audio-visual media means that IT can play a vital role in the preservation and promotion of traditional culture. It can also provide access to education, training, and employment for the large proportion of indigenous Australians who live in very remote locations.

Australia's indigenous peoples are the original custodians of our land, and their role in preserving heritage, current, and future culture and memory is critical to the process of reconciliation between them and other Australians. For many indigenous Australians, cultural and linguistic differences, geographic distance, and social inequality are major impediments to their participation with ICTs. These differences can only be overcome through targeted initiatives and self-management that are not reliant on market provision solely, but are supported by the state. However, the importance of meaningful consultation, decision-making and implementation of ICTs in the context of many other challenges facing indigenous Australians cannot be underestimated or ignored.

For example: Cape York Digital Network and other regions of the Outback Digital Network are projects are rolling out ICT centres in remote indigenous communities in Northern Australia. CYDN is managed by Balkanu, a non-profit indigenous economic development organisation. These centres typically have 6 computers (3 PCs, 3 thin clients), a videoconference unit, and a Cisco Aironet wireless omni-antenna. A local person is employed to supervise the centre and to teach the public how to use various applications. They are also working with the

Women In Technology project in two communities. For details visit www.cydn.com.au and www.odn.net.au

Digital Inclusion and Spatial Isolation

As with other countries in the Asia-Pacific region, we have been strongly influenced by spatial isolation, and this continues to be the case. Some of the nations which are the world's most disadvantaged, in terms of ICTs and development, are in Australia's regional location. We recognise that ICTs can contribute significantly to bridging geographic, cultural, political, and other gaps, and advocate maximum use of ICTs for all forms of development. ICTs can provide a unique virtual space, if equitably organised, as a medium of communicative transactions.

Australia itself is a large island continent with a small population concentrated in a few cities. Distance has historically affected the cost of all forms of communication and social development within the country and internationally, particularly for people living outside of the cities, and this continues to be the case, despite the heightened capacity and speed of ICTs.

As a consequence, a priority for us is equity in access to communications, including:

- Subsidised or free access to telecommunications, including ICTs for people in regional, and remote areas, apart from pure market considerations. The importance of community service obligations to ensure equity by service providers of telecommunications is paramount.
- The equitable development of broadband and other technologies. Where these are not possible, every effort should be made to develop inclusive interactive options, including more effective use of narrowband, satellite, and wireless technologies.
- Strategies to ensure that there is effective use of ICTs, above and beyond connectivity and access. The particular and local characteristics and capacities of different communities of interest should be taken into account, and supported in the development of the networked society projects and programs, and they must be evaluated for social effectiveness at every point.

Democratic Plurality through ICTs

Members of the working party are strongly of the view that the future of ICTs in this country, and regionally, is bound up with the cultural pluralism that is expressed through a healthy democracy in a country of great cultural diversity. ICTs offer an extraordinary and apparently limitless capacity to foster communication between all people, no matter what their language, location, or disability.

Specifically, as other civil society statements have made clear, and as the Universal Declaration of Human Rights, Article 19, indicated long ago, governments should:

- Ensure that market forces do not interfere with the open communications process, and in fact, should support the development of free or cheap access as widely as possible to the ICTs, particularly the Internet.
- Support the development of freely available open source platforms and software which support a range of network protocols.
- Promote the right for all to be electronically enabled citizens and have the right to free expression online.
- Support the rights of individuals and groups to protect personally sensitive data and records from exploitation, and unwanted intrusion must be carefully considered against the right to free access to as much information as possible by all people.
- Through the use of multiple platforms, serve as many diverse communities as possible, a "democratic commons," to be developed to enhance the democratic political process, including opportunities for e-democracy and e-government as a partnership between government and civil society.
- Ensure political and military security against terror, guided by equal rights of free expression.

National governments should also ensure that the ICT industry itself is a vehicle demonstrating not only good corporate governance, but also good human governance, genuinely recognising basic human rights and the International Labor Organisation (ILO) core conventions. Job security, against the trend to convert permanent jobs to precarious jobs, part-time, casual and contract positions, must be protected. The rights of workers in society to freely join a union and to negotiate collective agreements, particularly important in new growth areas such as the "call centre" industry, where women are the dominant group, must also be protected, to ensure equitable benefits. The ICT industry should be promoted as a model employer industry in every aspect which shares the benefits of development.

Inclusion and interoperability

National governments, including the Australian government, should work to ensure that ICTs promote social inclusion. In the short term, the Internet may well replace other telephony, integrate radio and TV as well, and become mobile, and we should be prepared for creative solutions to emerging and future technologies. Given the tremendous technical innovations and social changes which are almost inevitable consequences of such endemic change, the challenge of full inclusion should be seen as a task to can enhance all forms of development - whether community, business, political or contributing to social capital.

Costs of access, technical skills, language, disability, geographic location, and community capacity are a few of the factors which are interested in community development rarely assisted by means of trickle-down or market-force panaceas.

To this end, national governments should:

- Recognise and support programs which encourage compatibility and promote *effective use* of current, emerging and future ICTs amongst different communities of interest.
- Make freely available technical protocols, standards and platforms, including open source, to support the interoperable communication of information in the world's languages by speech, text and other media.
- Recognise and support the capacity of ICT platforms, standards and protocols to provide interoperable communications tools for vision-impaired and blind people, particularly though World Wide Web Consortium standards and guidelines.
- Recognise and support the capacity of ICT platforms, standards, and protocols to support various interoperable adaptive technologies for people with other physical and psychological impairments, particularly though World Wide Web Consortium standards and guidelines.

Access to content and technology

Australia has, comparatively speaking, one of the highest access rates to Internet services in the world, though there are signs that access to new forms of convergent ICTs will increasingly become a privilege for the affluent. There is a clear link between income and Internet access. Only 10% of households with incomes of less than $25,000 had Internet access in 2000 compared to 69% of those with incomes over $100,000 (according to the Australian Bureau of Statistics, 2002). Linked with inequitable access to education, community organisations, or to business, this gap is reinforced by traditional patterns of inequity (family status, employment patterns, language, and disability, geographic location). There is a danger that "government online" will only benefit those who either have access, or the money to pay for access to information. Government policies must ensure that roll-out does not privilege the wealthy only. Access means access at a reasonable price.

The concept of access also includes a number of other characteristics:

- The ability of people to obtain and then use information, particularly government information, freely and in ways that is suited to their particular circumstances, on line or in person-to-person contexts.
- The ability of people to access the intellectual content of information without being restricted by a lack of information literacy or the inadequate presentation, intellectual or cultural, of information.
- The ability of people to access the technology in a socially appropriate environment, whether that is the home, business or a community setting.
- The ability of people to make effective use of ICTs for capacity building.

Finally, access is not just about access to content created by others. Meaningful access also includes the ability to use ICTs to create new content, to experiment with knowledge and skills and take risks. It includes the capacity to establish more effective channels of communication and to use the available tools to facilitate self-organisation. There are truly transformative possibilities in the use of ICTs by civil society. The use of ICTs must be driven by the seminal needs of civil society.

Globally, access to mainstream technological devices such as the telephone is a privilege in many developing countries, (e.g., only 3 per 1000 people in Uganda), and even more exaggerated patterns are demonstrated for access to ICTs, including the Internet (see www.bridges.org). We therefore believe that global and international programs about the potential of ICTs need to take into account the realities of current technical, wealth and skills structures which serve to exaggerate disparities.

Developed nations achieved their high penetration rates using monopolies and forced cross subsidy of rural access and disadvantaged society access. Policies, such as those of the World Trade Organisation (WTO), which mandate privatisation and deregulation, effectively barring under-developed nations from using these proven strategies to improve their telephone penetration, should be reconsidered.

Effective Use, not just Technology

The picture of an equitable ICT future, whether in Australia or globally, is not just about technical infrastructure but about at least four significant additional components. Experience shows that an over-emphasis on technical imperatives is a recipe for failure. Many reports (see www. bridges.org) make clear that digital inclusion consists of a careful interplay of controllable variables, focusing on effective use, confirmed by the experience of all of the participants to the writing of this document:

- Skills
- Access
- Training
- Support/Sustainability

Skills: Without the provision and transmission of both technical and community development or education skills, to as many people as possible, the literacies that can be enhanced by ICTs will remain in the hands of a minority.

Access: Access should not be determined by market influences alone; a carefully-constructed combination of technical connectivities and relevant socially-based access assists with differences related to wealth, gender, disability.

Training: Training programs are particularly important as a means of "broadcasting" the opportunities which ICTs offer to all people. Expert training should be as widely diffused as possible. There is a clear need for an expanded group of "knowledge workers" who can bridge both technical and social issues, supported through community-service obligations of telecommunications corporates and governments, to support (in turn) all civil society organizations. Volunteers play an increasingly over-burdened role.

Support: ICTs do not come for free - the viability of ICTs, including the Internet for many civil society organizations, is dependent upon ongoing support from government. Volunteers, in particular, can only do a certain amount for free, and their knowledge around technical issues is not necessarily all-encompassing.

Government, in partnership with civil society and the private sector, through corporate social responsibility programs and projects, need to engage effectively in achieving positive social and economic outcomes from the use of new ICTs through exploring the mixes which work best. Opportunities for people to decide for themselves about the right mix of the technical, skills, access and training are critical, and there are many examples of ICT initiatives which have used this approach to invigorate communities.

We emphasise that the use of technology is not the goal of social development engagement with ICTs. In our view, governments and business tend to ignore this, believing that engagement with the technical artefact alone will ameliorate social problems, or act as an instant, valued learning experience. This naivety ignores the well-known lessons of social and community development in many countries over many years.

Civil society needs to be able to have much more input into the transformative process and governments should not fear such engagement.

Volunteers in the Civil Society

Non-profits employed 6.8% of employed people in 2000-2001 and the economic value of volunteers was estimated at $8.9 billion (according to Australian Bureau of Statistics, 2002).

A number of recent studies in Australia have demonstrated that the costs of ICTs, and problems associated with accessing appropriate skills, training, and support are impeding the engagement of volunteers in the management of community-based, non-profits. However, many third sector organisations can see no rationale for getting engaged electronically. This is probably the case in many other countries. However, given the fact that ICTs allow us to interactively communicate in unforseen ways, it is likely that there are many missed opportunities. Encouragement and leadership is needed to increase the pool of creative ideas and opportunities. Governments should regard volunteers as an integral part of the whole "electronic equation," as a means of electronically contributing to the development of a healthy "wired society". Investment in support of volunteers is an investment in social and human capital which will in turn, be passed on to other people and other social connections (via family, work, business).

Rights to Privacy

Civil society rights (personal, and group or community) need to be protected and the government and private sectors should not diminish these rights through inappropriate use or restriction on the use of ICTs for either security or commercial reasons. Real risks around the use of ICTs should be minimised. The problems associated with perceived risks (privacy, spam, pornography, fraud) also need to be addressed more effectively.

There should be international protocols and agreements which provide remedy for invasions of privacy, be they junk mail or other forms of abusive electronic intrusion.

Knowledge Sharing and Intellectual Property

The widening of ICT-based community networking in civil society is a potential means of bringing into play "undiscovered public knowledge" -- knowledge that would otherwise remain unexpressed, or confined to small groups. In Australia public networks which foster, aggregate and organise websites of community groups, have provided a new locus for societal knowledge production and collective memory.

However such public networks are chronically vulnerable, through dependence on multiple and short-term grant funding (e.g., Australia's "Networking the Nation" program). Governments need to recognise that community networking, in all its diversity, is a fundamental, continuous social process of knowledge production and use, comparable to any other in the educational and cultural sectors. Existing educational and cultural institutions are recurrently supported by government funds to foster public production, use and preservation of knowledge, with safeguards as appropriate for intellectual property.

Examples of such institutions are universities, research organisations, public broadcasting, libraries, archives, museums, performing arts organisations, institutes of sport. Comparable ongoing institutional support framework is required urgently for community networks. Community-based knowledge results from the daily experiences of people in all facets of life, and has the potential to enrich mutual understanding and collective memory in society, and thus the building of social capital.

The time has come for the first generation of short-term information society programs such as "Networking the Nation" to be converted to permanent policy, funding and institutional arrangements, to support community networking as a means of knowledge creation and sharing, benefiting citizens both present and future. Such arrangements support recognition of intellectual property wherever appropriate, including respect for limitations imposed by traditional law, or lore. The required institutional framework to foster community networking can be effected through enhancements to the roles of existing public knowledge institutions specifically for these purposes.

A continuing dialogue

Given the complexity and speed of change associated with emerging technologies, there should be ongoing processes to support discussion of diverse viewpoints about how such technologies should be used and governed for social development. Civil society needs ICT champions.

Too often "free market" voices (as the most familiar) prevail, and the notion of ICTs being for common (non-profit) good and capacity building is undervalued and under-represented in various forums, discussions and consultations. If ICTs are to be a force for social good, governments must champion and include the voices of civil society in developing policies, programs, structures and legislation around the governance of ICTs. However, civil society is dispersed and divergent. Government must continue to encourage those voices by providing funding support for an independent, ongoing dissemination of its message, and evaluation of effective use of ICTs for community development.

Leadership by existing groups should be further supported by a programme of action research conducted collaboratively at the local, regional and international levels, leading to an ever-improving body of shared evaluative knowledge, which reflects a fine-grained assessment of community needs. Without such leading research, which focuses on grounded models of social action, there will be no appropriate prime mover to promote the appropriate use of ICTs and all of the social benefits that flow from them.

The participants in the Australian Roundtable on Civil Society (RACS) have welcomed the opportunity to participate in the process to date and would welcome the opportunity to sustain and nurture a continuing dialogue. National and international councils for developing policy on ICT issues and which facilitate that dialogue should be supported by government at every opportunity.

Statement of the International Symposium on the Information Society, Human Dignity and Human Rights[19]

International Symposium on the Information Society, Human Dignity and Human Rights

In the middle of the 20th century, the world community agreed to human rights as the common normative framework at the same time as incredible advances began to be made in digital and genetic information. By the beginning of the 21st century an invaluable regime of human rights norms and mechanisms had been established and, through human rights education and learning broadly understood, a "human rights culture" had begun to take root in many parts of the world; at the same time, important advances in information and communication technologies had created the "information society" and large segments of the population, primarily in developed countries, had altered the way they communicate and live. These two trends of a human rights culture and the information society are intimately related and hold the potential of enhancing each other.

Human rights obligations of states in the WSIS context

The development of the information society, and in particular the vision of it articulated by the World Summit on the Information Society (WSIS), must be built on the reaffirmation of the 1993 Vienna Declaration and Programme of Action adopted by the World Conference on Human Rights that human rights are universal, indivisible, interrelated and interdependent and that their protection is the first responsibility of governments. The human rights obligations states have committed themselves to in the United Nations Charter, the Universal Declaration of Human Rights, the International Covenants on Human Rights and all other U.N. and regional human rights instruments require them to ensure that the information and communications society does not result in any discrimination or deprivation of human rights resulting from the acts or omission of their agents or of non-state actors under their jurisdiction. They also have human rights commitments arising out of other international conferences and summits. WSIS provides a critical opportunity to reaffirm human rights in the context of information and communication policy. There is a growing awareness among WSIS leadership of the importance of human rights in

[19] Palais des Nations, Geneva, 3-4 November 2003
In Preparation for the World Summit on the Information Society, Geneva 2003 - Tunis 2005
On the web at http://www.iris.sgdg.org/actions/smsi/hr-wsis/pdhre-statement-en.html

this context and welcome steps have been taken to include the voice and concerns of civil society in the WSIS process. Greater commitment to human rights and enhanced participation and transparency will be necessary for the Summit to achieve its full potential.

Host countries and institutions contributing to and participating in the post-Geneva WSIS process should be expected to fully respect the principles enunciated in the Declaration adopted at the Geneva Summit including those relating to human rights that are fundamental to the information and communications society, in particular, freedom of expression, association and information for civil society as well as with regard to visiting NGOs.

Consistent with those responsibilities, governments participating in WSIS should not only foster the information and communication society as a means of promoting the Millennium Development Goals and poverty reduction but they should also ensure that it contributes to the promotion of and respect for all human rights, civil, cultural, economic, political and social. Such a human rights framework for the information and communication society can promote the liberation of all human beings from fear and want, contribute to human security, advance human and sustainable development and support gender equality.

The human rights of particular importance to the information and communication society are freedom of expression and information, freedom from discrimination, gender equality, the right to privacy, the right to fair administration of justice, the right to the protection of the moral and material rights over intellectual creations, the right to participate in cultural life, rights of minorities, the right to education, and the right to an adequate standard of living, including the right to health, the right to adequate food, and the right to adequate housing. All of these rights belong to the corpus of internationally recognized human rights and should be furthered through the information and communication society.

Challenges to human rights from the information and communication society

Several trends that characterize information and communication in most of the world today constitute challenges to and in many cases serious dangers for a human rights-based information society. Central to these challenges is the exclusion of most of the people in developing countries from the advantages of advances in digital and genetic information, the commodification of information and knowledge, and the growing concentration of ownership and control of the means of producing and disseminating information and knowledge. Equally important are limitations, surveillance and censorship by the state or private parties, especially in the post September 11, 2001, environment.

The massive disparities in access to information and to the means of communication-known as "the digital divide"-are a result of the unequal distribution of wealth among and within countries. The digital divide is at the same time a cause and a consequence of the unequal distribution of wealth in the world and within countries Like poverty, with which it is closely connected, it severely diminishes the capabilities of people to enjoy their human rights. Information and communication technologies (ICTs) enable and empower individuals and groups, particularly those who are exposed, marginalized and vulnerable. Unless ICTs are made available on a vast scale to those who are at the losing end of the digital divide, the information and communication society will remain a force of relative impoverishment of large swaths of the world's population and consequently a source of instability and deprivation.

The digital divide results in unequal access to information and to the means of communication and information and thus produces massive exclusion. All avenues must be explored to ensure for all equal and affordable access to information, the means of communication and the necessary technology and infrastructure. Public authorities, the private sector and civil society in the developed countries have a special responsibility to share the benefits of the information and communication society with the peoples in developing countries.

The information and communication society offers unprecedented opportunities to advance shared knowledge in areas critical for human development. In particular, ICTs are invaluable to the realization of the rights to health, education and adequate food through a wide range of technologies. Special attention must be paid to using the information and communication society to advance gender equality, consistent with the principle, affirmed in the Vienna Declaration and Programme of Action, that women's rights are human rights. The human rights of traditional cultures in the emerging information society require special measures of conservation and protection of their traditional knowledge and culture. Special measures are also required to improve the situation of and to protect those who are vulnerable, exposed or excluded, in particular, children, the elderly, people with disabilities, minorities, refugees and asylum seekers.

Human rights education and learning

The information and communication society benefits from new technologies which can serve critical functions for human rights education and learning and more generally contribute to social change through the realization of human rights.

ICTs must be put at the service of education and lifelong learning for all. In particular, as privileged instruments of human rights education and learning, they should help to enable and empower humans across the world and across generations and cultures to know, claim and own their human rights and to respect and promote those of others in a spirit of solidarity. ICTs will make a major contribution to societal development on the basis of a commonly shared culture of human rights.

Freedom of expression and information

Full respect for freedom of expression and information by States and non-State actors is an essential precondition for the building of a free and inclusive information and communication society. ICTs must not be used to curtail this fundamental freedom. There must be no censorship and no arbitrary controls or constraints on participants in the information process, on the content of information or its transmission and dissemination. Pluralism of the sources of information and the media must be safeguarded and promoted. Any restrictions of freedom of expression and information must pursue a legitimate aim under international law, must be prescribed by law, be strictly proportionate to such an aim, and be necessary in a democratic society to respect the rights or reputation of others or for the protection of national security or of public order (ordre public), or of public health or morals. National security legislation to combat terrorism must respect freedom of expression and information standards and be subject to judicial review, as well as international scrutiny.

Article 19 of the Universal Declaration of Human Rights and of the International Covenant on Civil and Political Rights is of fundamental importance to a human rights-based information and communication society, not only by requiring that everyone has the right to freedom of opinion and expression and the right to seek, receive and impart information and ideas through any media and regardless of frontiers, but also because it implies free flow of information, free circulation of ideas, press freedom, and availability of the tools to access information and share knowledge.

The trend to provide public access to the information produced or maintained by governments and protected under "freedom of information" legislation should be extended to all countries that do not have such legislation, ensuring that government-controlled information is timely, complete and accessible in a format and language the public can understand.

Freedom of expression should be protected through the Internet in the same way it is protected offline and Internet service providers should be guided by this freedom rather than by codes of conduct that are not based on human rights.

Human right to privacy

Modern technology can and should be used to protect privacy; at the same time, it provides unprecedented possibilities for massive violations of the human right to privacy. The use of increasingly invasive means of surveillance and of interception of communications, of intrusive profiling and identification and of biometric identification technology, the development of communication technologies with built-in surveillance capacities, the collection and misuse of genetic data, genetic testing, the growing invasion of privacy at the workplace and the weakening of data protection regimes give rise to serious concerns from the point of view of respect for human dignity and human rights. New means must be developed to protect the human right to privacy, such as the right to know about one's personal data held by public and private institutions and to have them deleted where not strictly necessary for a legitimate purpose in a democratic society. The development, transfer and use of technology permitting illegitimate invasion of privacy must be controlled and curbed.

It is fundamental to an understanding of the information society to recognize that information is power. Control of personal information and the deprivation of the right of privacy are ways or exercising power over individuals. The protection of personal information and privacy is central to the autonomy of the individual and to respect for human rights. The considerable experience with the elaboration of laws and national and international jurisprudence to protect privacy should be studied and applied in countries where the right to privacy is not adequately protected and the best practices should be emulated.

The development of communications infrastructure and ubiquitous computing threatens privacy in new and intrusive ways; it is, nevertheless, possible to develop and adopt privacy enhancing behaviours, technologies, and infrastructure consistent with privacy law. These choices must be favoured through national law, deontology codes for developers and market incentives. Steps to preserve privacy, at the international, regional, national, community, institutional, and individual level, must start with the establishment of national data protection laws to protect individual rights with respect to the collection, use, and disclosure of personal information, with independent oversight, and access to effective redress. Education across all sectors of society with respect to privacy rights and the risks inherent in the technology is vital so that individuals can take the necessary steps to enforce legal rights.

Certain measures taken in combating terrorism and cybercrime have eroded civil liberties and abrogated privacy rights. Cooperation in the field of criminal investigation must be accompanied by adequate enforcement of civil liberties and independent oversight of data collection.

Cultural and linguistic rights and diversity

The international community has increasingly come to regard plurality of identities, including cultural diversity, as an asset and a fundamental value to be defended and promoted. Fostering diversity is crucial to respecting cultural rights, promoting tolerance and fighting discrimination at all levels of society. The preservation and promotion of cultural and linguistic diversity and interaction must be hallmarks of a thriving information society. ICTs can and must be used to promote diversity and respect for cultural rights and identity, including indigenous knowledge, rather than for their restriction or suppression. This diversity is reflected positively by community radio, indigenous means of communication and local media.

People in the information society are more than consumers; they are also providers of information and of creativity. Steps must, therefore, be taken to give them access to infrastructure under acceptable economic conditions through proactive measures by governments, under cultural and linguistic exceptions to international trade agreements.

The public domain and intellectual property rights

A rich public domain is an essential element for the growth of the information society and provides the reservoir from which new knowledge is derived. Everyone therefore should enjoy the right, reaffirmed in article 27 of the Universal Declaration of Human Rights, freely to participate in the cultural life of the community, to enjoy the arts and to share in scientific advancement and its benefits while at the same time having an equal right to the protection of the moral and material interests resulting from any scientific, literary or artistic production. International agreements and treaties and national policies concerning the creation, sharing and trade of intellectual goods and cultural creations must be aligned according to these competing needs. Facilitating meaningful participation by all, in particular by civil society organizations, in developing the intellectual property framework is a fundamental part of an inclusive information society.

Initiatives for high-quality open-source and public domain software and technologically neutral platforms and the development and use of open, interoperable, non-discriminatory and demand-driven standards that take into account needs of users, consumers, and the underprivileged should be promoted. Furthermore, a fixed percentage of spectrum, satellite and other infrastructural bandwidth capacity should be reserved for educational, humanitarian, community and other non-commercial use.

Concentration of ownership in the hands of a few major corporations limits the opportunities for information and communications technologies to reflect adequately the pluralism of perspectives and diversity of cultures. Legislative and other measures should avoid excessive media concentration and ensure that the media and ICTs respond to the principle of public service and guarantee equal opportunities of access to media ownership for all social sectors. Public service broadcasting is an essential means of counter-balancing the commercial motivation of the media and ensuring the enjoyment of the right of everyone to participate in cultural life and the right of political participation

The regime of knowledge ownership and management includes patents, copyright, trademarks and other legal and technical monopolies on knowledge granted by society, and public domain, fair use and other instruments to enable access. The primary goal of this regime is to strike a balance that will both maximize access and use of this knowledge and at the same time encourage creativity as widely as possible within society. International agreements and treaties, and national policies concerning creation, sharing and trade of intellectual goods and cultural creations must comply with this principle.

Intellectual property regimes and national and international agreements on patents, copyright and trademarks should not prevail over the right to education and knowledge. This right must indeed be exercised through the concept of fair use, that is, use for non-commercial purposes, especially education, and research. Moreover, intellectual work and ideas, including programming methods and algorithms, should not be patentable. The production and use of free and open-source software and content must thus be encouraged and covered by adequate public policy.

Human knowledge is the heritage and property of all humankind and the reservoir from which new knowledge is created. The information and communication society will not contribute to human development and human rights unless and until access to information is considered a public good to be protected and promoted by the state. Information in the public domain should be easily accessible to support the information society. Intellectual property rights should not be protected as an end in itself, but rather as a means to an end that promotes a rich public domain, shared knowledge, scientific and technical advances, cultural and linguistic diversity and the free flow of information. Public institutions such as libraries and archives, museums, cultural collections and other community-based access points should be strengthened so as to promote the preservation of documentary records and free and equitable access to information. Scientists, universities, academic, research and other institutions have a central role in the development of the information society and the sharing of research results, scientific knowledge and technical information.

Democratic governance

Good governance in the information and communication society must be based on the values of participation, transparency, accountability and the rule of law. These principles apply to the democratic management of international bodies dealing with ICTs. Given the borderless characteristics of ICTs, decision-making bodies should ensure the respect of principles of democracy and openness, as well as of legality and sovereignty. In particular, the management of the core resources of the Internet, which are the Internet protocols, standards and identifiers, such as domain names and IP addresses, must serve the public interest at the global, national and local levels. Furthermore, any decision made on protocols, standards and identifiers should be compatible with international human rights standards, and specially the rights to freedom of expression, to privacy, and the principle of non-discrimination. Such decisions should also allow a better-balanced flow of information.

The proper use of ICTs can strengthen democracy by improving the means and access for civil society to participate fully in public affairs. ICTs can improve access to justice and make public services more responsive, transparent and accountable. The rule of law is essential for the information society to become a space of confidence, trust and security where human rights are fully respected.

Both States and non-State actors have a duty to respect and promote human dignity and human rights in the building of the information society. Any regulation and self-regulation regarding communication and information must be based on strict respect for human rights and must contribute to their promotion. The private, public service and community media, as well as journalists, whose independence and access to information must be protected, have major responsibilities in the information and communication society as a means to preserve and advance democracy.

Monitoring mechanisms

In preparation for the WSIS in Tunis in 2005, an Independent Commission on the Information Society and Human Rights, composed of highly qualified experts with a broad geographical representation, should be established to monitor practices and policies and submit recommendations to the Summit. Its mandate could include a review of national and international ICT regulations and practices and their conformity with international human rights standards, the governance of current decision-making bodies in the ICT field, and the potential applications of ICTs to the realization of the right to development and the essential human rights for sustainable human development, including the right to health, the right to adequate food and the right to education.

Furthermore, the importance of the issues of human rights of WSIS justifies the establishment, within the procedures of the Commission on Human Rights or its Sub-Commission, of a position of Special Rapporteur on Human Rights and the Information Society, with a mandate to monitor developments in this area, including threats to privacy, freedom of expression, freedom from surveillance, and applications of ICT to the realization of economic, social and cultural rights and to human rights education and recommend measures conducive to advancing human rights in the information society.

Speaking for Ourselves: Southern Africa and the WSIS[20]

Tracey Naughton[21]

The African Charter on Broadcasting was the initial reason for southern African communication NGO's to become involved in the WSIS.

It was developed at a gathering of media practitioners and freedom of expression advocates from throughout Africa at the UNESCO-supported conference called to celebrate the 10th anniversary of the Windhoek Declaration. This was held during May 2001 in Namibia.

The Windhoek Declaration, penned in 1991 was the basis upon which the UN declared May 3rd World Press Freedom Day. The declaration has served as an advocacy tool for auditing the extent to which governments throughout the African continent honour their commitments towards upholding and promoting media freedom, independence and diversity. Despite this, the region remains an international focal point of media violations.

The right to communicate is almost non-existent for the majority population.

Most African countries do not yet have free and independent broadcast and information environments.

The Windhoek Declaration focussed on promoting independent print media, and was silent on issues such as broadcasting liberalisation and the globalisation of the communications industry which have increasingly come into play in the last decade.

The original Windhoek Declaration was adopted at a time when Africa saw theemergence of multi-party democracy. Namibia had just become independent and apartheid was breaking down in South Africa. The African Charter on Broadcasting has been adopted at a time when the prevailing wind is one of globalisation and the opening of markets to worldwide competition. It argues that Africa needs the space to develop its own cultural industries and local content, a form of market protection.

---

[20] On the web at http://www.wsis-cs.org/africa/documents.shtml

[21] Tracey Naughton is Regional Broadcast Program Manager, Media Institute of Southern Africa – MISA. Paper Presented at For Our Media 111 Barranquilla, Colombia May 2003

The African Charter on Broadcasting is a sequel to the Windhoek Declaration. It has become a key tool in advocating for enabling information environments in Africa. It serves as a policy blueprint rather than a set of rules to be imposed.

The African launch of the Charter took place on May 3rd, 2002 as part of the African Commission Sessions on Human and Peoples' Rights. This is part of the African Union system.

An implementation objective set for the Broadcast Charter was to assert it as an African position in the context of the WSIS. The task of driving this advocacy process was given to five organizations that are based in southern Africa. They are:

- MISA
- ARTICLE 19
- AMARC
- APC
- SACOD

Our focus is in the southern African region - SADC - Southern African Development Community that includes 14 countries.

The campaign to strengthen the Charter coincided with the holding of the World Summit on Sustainable Development, itself a ten years later follow up to the RIO Earth Summit. There were lessons to be learnt that caused us to approach the WSIS with caution and a degree of skepticism.

- Civil society was excluded from the main arena of negotiations
- Parallel events had limited impact on the main agenda
- Only civil society groups with an extremely pertinent point or a high profile got any media coverage

Our focus in the WSIS was gaining enhanced status for the Charter to strengthen it as an advocacy tool. The more status it has, the more cognoscense will be afforded to it by governments that are reluctant to open the airwaves.

Our first port of call was the African Regional WSIS Meeting held in Bamako, Mali in 2002. There the Charter was adopted as an African position and was named in the declaration.

At that meeting which was focused mainly on government input, we realised that:

- Most African countries had little idea of what they should be proposing.
- Most African countries have little agreed policy on the Information Society (other than generally thinking it probably is a good thing).
- Many African delegations were able to identify problems and locate them in development contexts, but due to lack of experiential knowledge, few potential solutions were raised.
- We faced serious capacity issues in the official delegations.
- There was no grass roots involvement.
- The issues had to be grounded in a global framework.
- We had to get involved - the African information society could not be developed by governments alone. We had an opportunity and a responsibility to galvanise a broader input to the process.

As a partnership of the five organizations we developed a project called "Speaking for Ourselves".

The overall intention of the project is to ensure that people who are directly affected by communications issues in the SADC are mobilised, capacitated and have a say in the policy positions that are put by national delegates to the WSIS meetings, be they government, civil society or private sector players.

The principle that informs the project is that people who are directly affected by issues know best what the potential solutions are.

Our objectives are:

- To have an impact on the dominant economic drivers of the information society by exposing the reality of the majority of people who are excluded and linking this to the negative effects of globalisation.
- To have an impact on the policy that frames the information society using the African Charter on Broadcasting as the starting point.
- To have people currently excluded from the information society involved in the process and to build a platform in the WSIS for these voices to be heard.
- To assert and endorse the right to communicate as a human right that exists in conformity with Article 19.
- To assert the legitimacy of civil society in shaping the information society at national, regional and international levels.

Here is what we have achieved to date:

Capacity development
ICT policy curriculum developed and piloted - soon to be available on the APC web site;

ICT Policy workshops conducted in Addis Ababa (Ethiopia), Johannesburg (South Africa) and Kampala (Uganda). 150 people trained and mobilised to:

- run workshops in 38 African countries
- lobby governments to include our people and our input in the official delegations and documents
- to be focal points for national mobilisation

Electronic network established and active in policy development;

Four rural women participated in PrepCom 2 with high profile impact.

Policy, Position, Perspectives
Published a booklet for PrepCom 2

Developed a position paper on the Right to Communicate (ARTICLE 19 publication). This was the basis for input into the Right to Communicate debate held at PrepCom 2.

Developed a response on the Draft Declaration and Plan of Action which is currently being debated and refined through the network of mobilisers on the African continent and the people they are working with.

Developed an Advocacy Tool Kit for civil society campaigns. This includes resources that expand on sections of the African Charter on Broadcasting.

We have also made plans to install and African village and telecentre at the Summit itself. Visiting this installation will be an interactive experience designed to bring home the African reality and perspectives on the information society.

Some of the Issues we will raise are:

- International Bandwidth Costs

The current burden of paying for International Internet Bandwidth Costs is unfairly weighted onto countries in Africa. The existence of these reverse subsidies is the single largest factor that is contributing to high bandwidth costs in Africa. The simple fact that it costs 15 times more to make a phone call from Africa to within Africa than from outside Africa to Africa demonstrates the impact of globalisation on Africans.

Africa has two percent of the world's phone lines and twelve percent of the population. Fifty percent of these phones lines (and in some counties eighty to ninety percent) are in capital cities where only ten percent of the population lives.

- Teledensity (telephone lines per one hundred inhabitants) is 0.5 in southern Africa - excluding South Africa - compared to 4.5 in emerging economies and 52.6 percent in industrialised counties.
- The cost of renting a phone connection in Africa averages twenty percent of income per capita compared to a world average of nine percent and only one percent in high income countries.
- Literacy - people who are highly literate in their home language often cannot read or write any of the languages that dominate the Internet. Radio remains the most important communication tool in Africa but even this source is compromised by the state monopolization of the airwaves.
- Unequal gender relations - It is not uncommon for women in Africa to not be allowed to use the radio ñ where there is one in a home ñ while the man is out. This is considered a waste of batteries. Women in Africa are far more likely to walk on a dirt track than to surf on the electronic super highway.

As Esther Mudlhovo says, Rural Africans are burdened by survival. Top on our minds are the means by which we can maintain our families. Information that is worth the most is that which contributes to fulfilling our daily needs. None is better than that given by us, about us, for us.

These women who work all day to grind enough maize to feed the family each night pointed out that they don't have any spare time to be finding out what is happening in places they canít imagine. It is enough to find out when relatives living in the next village are ill or die.

This young woman asked me why she would think of a computer when she lives in a shack made of tin and plastic. Nurumbu who is 14 is one of many girl children who cannot afford to go to school for want of US$7 a year.

Raphael lives with 19 family members and only one of them has employment, as a security guard in Windhoek, the capital of Namibia. It is a 7-8 hour journey by donkey cart to the nearest telephone. It is generally not worth taking a sick person that far so they either get better, or die.

But I donít want to portray a continent where there is no hope because against all the odds there are very positive communication projects that do get information to communities.

REHO-TV is located in a small town populated by the Baster community which fled from both the English and Afrikaans administrations in the Cape of South Africa over a hundred years ago, to a dry area in Namibia. They defend their right to speak Afrikaans, just as they have defended their right to occupy the land they settled on. They started the station because the national broadcaster is predominantly in English and several indigenous languages.

Two men - one a funeral undertaker the other an auto-electrician started the local TV service, which was broadcasting for three hours each evening until their license was withdrawn for not paying their fees which rose sharply and did not consider the differences between commercial and community operators. The station has been off air for three years. I have recently found a benefactor who has offered them half of the funds required to get back on air if they can raise the rest from within the community. This is a challenge because it is a very poor community, but it is looking like the back shed operation will come back to life.

Moutse Community Radio was started by rural women who defied the Chiefs who refused to grant permission for the station to be run by women. It serves as a source of information where there wasnít one during the long years of Apartheid in South Africa. Particular attention is paid to survival issues and programming includes advice on agriculture, primary health care and budgeting.

In Kanzinzila village in the Caprivi region of Namibia a 24 year old disabled man who has never attended school repairs the broken radios for his and several other villages. Self taught, a few years ago after hearing of the outside world from his schooling brothers, he convinced the village headman to gather enough money from villagers to buy a car battery, a television set and a solar panel. He then established a TV viewing set up for the village. As time has gone by the efficacy of the battery and the panel have declined and it now takes two weeks to recharge the battery using the solar panel. This then works for three to four evenings.

Postrick told me that the village was surprised to see recently that America was bombing the whole of Iraq because they were after one man. They were incredulous that so many people had to die because of one person. He also said that the TV is an important link between the younger generation who attend school and the older one that has not been educated at all. He has seen an advertisement for large screen televisions and is hoping the village will be able to raise enough capital to buy one some day.

Maria Shendembr became the adult literacy teacher for her village after two years of unemployment when she had completed secondary school. She did a three week course to prepare her and now earns a small government income for teaching. She supports the 11 children and her mother who were left when her father died of AIDS.

And so to Geneva - one of the world's most expensive cities - with our depleted Currencies.

In the context of these stories the WSIS has many challenges and with a combination of reality inputs and solution orientated policy positions we in southern Africa - indeed now Africa, for our coalition has grown rapidly ñ hope that the WSIS will be a point of departure for a more concerted global effort to develop affordable, accessible access to information for those who are on a side of the divide that it will be difficult for many delegates to imagine.

We know that it is possible to have information without development but it is not possible to have development without information.

Iranian Workshop Examining the United Nations – Civil Society Relations[22]

Document of the Iran Civil Society Organizations Training and Research Center

Introduction

Today, dialogue is the necessity on which the sustainability of local, national and international society is dependent upon. The ability of the key actors of society to communicate represents the liveliness and productivity of that society while conflict and violence represent the failure of society to reach a mature state. By recognizing this necessity, The Iran Civil Society Organizations Training and Research Center has placed social dialogue as the center of its program such that dialogue is looked at as a strategy. Furthermore, the center promotes the benefits of social dialogue at all levels in order to cultivate the spread of democracy, strengthen civil society and make accessible sustainable development to Iranian society. In order to promote the culture of dialogue to achieve the given goals, design and implement social dialogue in a practical manner and to encourage civil society organizations to engage in dialogue, the center has prepared social dialogue projects at three levels: "civil society organizations", "government, the private sector and civil society organizations", and "Iranian civil society organizations and UN agencies". Thus far, three phases of these dialogues have taken place. Currently, the UN Secretary General's Panel of Eminent Persons has been formed in order to stabilize the relationship between civil society and the UN and Ambassador Bagher Asadi is a member of this panel. It is, therefore, a special opportunity for me and my colleagues to express the thoughts and views of Iranian civil society representatives regarding the relationship between civil society and the United Nations. Additionally, with the assistance of Ambassador Bagher Asadi, honorable member of the Secretary General's panel, the Iran Civil Society Organizations Training and Research Center organized a one day summit on the 6th of October with the presence of over 40 representatives of Iranian civil society. The key topics included "an assessment of the current state of conditions", "opportunities and challenges" and a "presentation of suggestions and solutions". What will follow in this report is a summary of ideas presented by participants of the workshop and the center's past summits.

[22] The work shop on United Nations – civil society relations was held on October 6, 2003 by The Iran Civil Society Organizations Training and Research Center (ICTRC) with participation of representatives of non-governmental organizations. This document contains the solutions and the guidelines for the relation between civil society and the United Nations that were discussed in the work shop. On the web at http://www.irancsos.net/english/

Current Conditions

Civil society organizations have been an active participant in the activities of the United Nations from its onset. This participation has been in the form of cooperation with ECOSOC, DPI, the secretariat, programs, funds, agencies related to the UN, etc. through activities ranging from the transfer of information, development training, assistance with policy to implementation of UN programs. This cooperation has been accomplished both officially and unofficially at the local, national and international level. The Opportunities: Workshop participants emphasized the following points regarding the relationship between the two parties: 1-The Secretary General's call for a 12 person panel This measure represents the United Nations will to improve and adjust the relationship between the United Nations and civil society organizations. Furthermore, the measure indicates that the United Nations officially acknowledges that civil society organizations are a key player in the political power structure and recognizes that the current associations between UN agencies and civil society organizations are not at the desired level and are in need of revisions. 2-In the past decade, by accepting the documents from the Johannesburg Summit and the development goals of the MDG, the United Nations has created new opportunities to play a significant role in the development process. 3- The encouragement of civil society organizations to participate in the development process and carry out capacity building strategies by the United Nations.

The Challenges

Workshop participants emphasized the following challenges facing the relationship between the two parties. 1-The system of "bad governance" dominates the United Nations and its agencies. The most important challenge is the lack of cooperation between benefiting groups in the decision making process and implementation, the lack of clarity in programs, the lack of proper information and the lack of responsiveness. 2-The communication mechanism between the UN and civil society organizations by means of governments is unacceptable. This method of communication between civil society organizations and the UN leads to the establishment and growth of GONGOs and is the reason for their active participation in UN summits. 3-The UN has no clear strategy towards civil society organizations at either the international or national level. The view of UN agencies towards civil society organizations is an imbalanced one where the civil society organization is looked at as merely a tool. 4- The continual changing of the UN agencies goals regarding civil society organizations, the limited cooperation between these two entities and the ambiguity of the mechanism for cooperation between these two entities is another challenge. 5- Because of the rentier state of relations imposed upon

UN agencies, individuals with previous work experience with the UN are able to obtain projects in the framework of civil society organizations. This results in a limited number of civil society organizations having the ability to work in cooperation with the United Nations. 6- The dominance of the North and other external pressures on UN agencies results in the failure to cooperate. As a result, civil society organizations from the South have less influence on international summits. 7- The lack of a dominant policy at the international level to facilitate relations between civil society organizations and the United Nations. 8- The unexplained position of civil society organizations for UN agencies. 9-There exists a lack of confidence and trust between civil society organizations and UN agencies. 10-The unfamiliarity of civil society organizations with the activities of UN agencies 11- A lack of confidence in creating relations with UN agencies by certain civil society organization 12-The inability to identify the capabilities and capacities of civil society organizations by UN agencies

Outline of Successful Associations

Workshop participants have stated the following points as successful examples of cooperation between UN agencies and civil society organizations. 1-Cooperation between the UNDP and the non-governmental organization "Payam Avaran Tose-eh" in the water and earth strategy for the Hableh River 2- Cooperation between the UN working group for NGOs with the "Noavaran Pars" group for the purpose of organizing a 3 day training workshop on the subject of "clear policy and management of non-governmental organizations" and "cooperation between the UN and NGOs" 3- Compensation for publishing the book, "An Analysis of Non-Governmental Organizations in the Islamic Republic of Iran" by the UNDP office. 4-The organization of a workshop on women and violence with cooperation of the Center for Women's Studies 5- The organization of training workshops and summits with the participation of all NGOs active in the field of drug prevention entitled the "Dariush Plan" 6-Cooperation between GEF and environmental NGOs in the field of transfer of information technologies

Outline of Unsuccessful Associations

1- The dissolving of the UN working group on non-governmental organizations. 2- The discontinuation of support for the sustainable development of civil society in the framework of the Center for Resource and Communication for Civil Societies

Suggestions and Solutions

1-The United Nations was established after World War II. During that time period, the only players in the international arena were governments. Today, however, with attention to global transformations and the appearance of new groups of actors, the United Nations must modify and re-define itself in order to play an effective role. 2-The United Nations, governments and civil society organizations must define a new mechanism for their relationships based on respect. 3-Next to the office of the secretary general, an office should be established in the United Nations for facilitating cooperation between the UN and civil society organizations. 4-A democratic set of regulations must be put into place for governing the relationships between UN agencies and civil society organizations. 5-UN experts must receive the necessary training on a continual basis as facilitators between these two entities. 6-A group of civil society organization members must be selected to follow national and international regulations and report to the secretary general of the UN upon the conclusion of each year. 7-Attempts should be made at the national level in order to re-establish the dissolved UN Working Group on NGOs 8-The design of a transparent system of communication 9- In addition to communication, UN agencies must provide the appropriate information regarding their programs to civil society organizations and civil society organizations should have access to this information.

Asia Pacific Statement: Civil Society Observations and Response to the Tokyo Declaration[23]

Asia Pacific Regional WSIS Conference

January 15, 2003

Preamble

Civil society entities have been fully committed to promoting and defining the information society, particularly since the Prep Com I of the United Nations World Summit on the Information Society (WSIS) on July 1, 2002 in Geneva.

Despite the efforts to integrate different perspectives and views from every level of the region by most stakeholders throughout the preparation for WSIS, which is to be held in December 2003, some government representatives opposed to the participation of non governmental organizations (NGOs) in the drafting committee of the Asia Pacific Regional Conference on the WSIS, which was formed to facilitate the accomplishment of official output of the conference (Tokyo Declaration). This is in contradiction of the avowed principle of WSIS to be inclusive of all stakeholders in shaping the future information society.

The regional conference was originally designed as a forum for discussion for all stakeholders rather than exclusively governments and inter-governmental agencies so as to fully incorporate opinions from various communities, including the grassroots voices in the region to guarantee full-scale evolution of the information society.

The event was convened by the Government of Japan (Ministry of Public Management, Home Affairs, Posts and Telecommunications and Ministry of Foreign Affairs) on 13-15, January 2003 to prepare for the year-end Summit. Participants invited include representatives of the government of 37 countries and territories, 26 international organizations, 58 private sector entities and 199 NGOs.

Civil society firmly believes that, efficiency, economic growth and productivity should not be the only priority of the information society. Information communication technologies (ICTs), therefore, should be regarded as merely modern

[23] On the web at http://www.wsisasia.org/wsis-tokyo/tokyo-statement.html

instruments for the pursuit of ultimate goals, which includes the promotion of gender equality, equitable and sustainable human development, empowerment of the people and all fundamental human rights.

We, the undersigned organizations, are convinced that these voices of civil society, or the people, must be adequately presented despite being deminished by negotiations in the regional conference's drafting committee, and therefore propose this paper to reflect the grassroots perspectives so as to promote comprehensive and balanced evolution of the information society. These voices of civil society are inspired and built upon the Asian NGOs' previous outputs, which are respectively The Declaration of the Asian Civil Society Caucus at Prep Com I in Geneva, The World Summit on the Information Society: an Asian Response and the Joint Statement from Asia Civil Society Forum Participants on World Summit on the Information Society.

1. Communication rights should be fully recognized as a fundamental and universal human right to be protected and promoted in the information society.

2. The participation of civil society in the information society at all levels should be ensured and sustained, from policy planning to implementation, monitoring and evaluation. The information society should be promoted with collaborative efforts of civil society, governments and private sector entities altogether.

3. Fundamental issues, such as poverty, democracy, gender justice/gender equity, environment and the impact of globalization should be taken into account apart from technological and economic evolution in the development of the information society.

4. Special attention shall be given in the information society to marginalized groups, such as indigenous peoples, women, people with disabilities, older people, refugees, migrants and those who lack access to formal education and higher technical training.

5. In all forums to discuss ICT policies, the participation of women and consideration of gender issues should be supported and promoted so as to realize women's full potential as contributors and beneficiaries of the information society.

6. Young people, the first Asia-Pacific generation growing up with the internet, need support in adapting to changes in education, employment and participation within society, especially when youth are at the forefront of technological development and adoption of our region - their expertise and energy can assist in bridging the digital divide.

7. Transparency and accountability of the government as well as civil society participation in policy, programme and service development, should be enhanced in the formation of the information society.

8. Governments must ensure that market competition is fair and that monopolies are not perpetuated.

9. While governments should promote and facilitate infrastructure building, provide training, and create an enabling environment for ICT to be accessible for all, they should not play the role of regulators of information flow and content.

10. Privacy and government surveillance issues should be the priority concern in the assessment of whether national compulsory projects utilizing ICTs, such as electronic national ID card and electronic health care card initiatives and national fingerprint database building, should be implemented.

11. Availability of both traditional and newer technologies should be guaranteed to promote equitable access to information at all levels of the information society.

12. Technological progress based on community needs with emphasis on local content to preserve cultural and linguistic diversity should be promoted.

13. Surveillance on people by governments, consumers by entrepreneurs, employees by employers, by utilising new information and communication technologies are a severe threat to human rights. We call on all parties to take appropriate measures to protect the right to privacy including freedom from surveillance at all levels of information society. We are opposed to any kind of censorship imposed by anyone that restricts freedom of expression.
Privacy and personal security should be ensured in the information society when promoting ICTs. Values of human rights, democracy, and freedom of expression should never be threatened/compromised by any kind of surveillance and censorship.

14. Community based media should be supported and promoted. The equitable and affordable access to information for all should be assured in the information society.

15. Civil society acknowledges its role as a major content provider in the information society and should, therefore, be active in the promotion of public awareness on the quality of content of information circulated in the society.

16. In the protection of intellectual property rights (IPR), priority should be given to cultural and human development instead of mere economic development and

commercial profits. The protection of IPR should not deter the free and balanced flow of ideas and innovations. Public information commons, including open source technologies, should be promoted by all stakeholders in the information society.

17. We recognize that safeguarding the environmental resources is central to achieving a healthy networked community for all. Life cycle management in the production flow of ICT related goods must be promoted and implemented by the global ICT sector. Also, special attention should be given to people who are living in small islands under the endangered environment by hazards or global warming/ small islands in an environment endangered by hazards or global warming.

Youth Forum Declaration: Res, Non Verba[24]

Youth Caucus

The world we live in is not fair at this moment. Some of us benefit daily from the empowering force of ICTs while others, to whom simple communication could mean the difference between life and death, hope and downheartedness, a sparkling future and stagnation, do not have access to any form of ICTs.

This is not our destiny. Young people have united and urge you to join them in building the fundamentals for the digital bridge.

Yesterday we faced many problems but today we face many challenges. We, the youth, present to you the issues that we consider pertinent:

Education

Education should play a crucial role in the life of all people. ICTs should be an integral part of today's education; and we advocate the improvement of education worldwide.

Governments and companies should be encouraged to support ICT centers in order to teach those who have not yet had the opportunity to immerse themselves in ICTs. ICT learning centers, which should contain useful equipment donated by private companies, should be opened to the public. This equipment must also be used to entertain children, thus introducing them to the concept of the computer and ICTs. Efforts should also be made in the training of ICT trainers.

In addition, those who have been educated through scholarships or other funds shall then be obliged to help overcome the digital divide in their country, by sharing the knowledge acquired to public schools, universities or acting as a community or social worker. This would also help fight illiteracy, which still adversely affects many countries.

---

[24] On the web at www.itu.int/wsis/docs/geneva/misc/**youth_forum**.doc

Access and infrastructure

All governments should ensure that basic, affordable, ICT infrastructure, such as the connection through radio transmitting stations, be placed in the rural areas.

The critical challenge is about distribution of technology and deployment of infrastructure to all areas within the countries themselves. ITU is requested to assist developing countries that have a solid plan for distribution of these technologies.

Local action

The local population of developing countries should be made aware that they are the ones to provide solutions to overcome the technological challenges they face. They should be made confident in this knowledge through inspiration from their leaders. Promotional campaigns should also be undertaken in the countries to gain full support of the population.

In order to bridge the Digital Divide within a country, there should be community service initiatives spearheaded by the youth in collaboration with the private and public sectors. These actions will educate the communities on the use of ICTs, erase illiteracy and ensure that local, applicable and affordable ways of providing ICTs to rural areas are obtained.

The population should be made aware of the desirability and value of ICTs in their daily lives and that it is not simply a luxury. Therefore, ICT content should be derived from its users to reflect their needs and services, should be user-friendly, simple, and overcome the language barrier.

Regulation

The youth realize that effective regulation of ICTs is key to development and that it should be focused on users' needs. We recommend that nations create a healthy regulatory environment through the actions of an independent and effective regulatory body that makes ICTs accessible and affordable to consumers. We believe that the future of ICTs depends on market liberalization, coupled with universal access policies, that encourage investment in developed and developing nations.

Investment and finance

ITU should act as a facilitator: for bringing together investors, viable projects, especially micro projects and private initiatives; and, promote the financing of those that are feasible and sustainable.

To permit the success of Small to Medium Scale Enterprises (SME), governments should offer incentives, such as, micro-credit at low interest rates with repayment extended over long periods of time. In addition, governments should be transparent so as to encourage foreign investors.

Aid and funding given to support ICT technologies should be provided with no 'strings attached' so that the funding is channeled to the relevant context. The only conditions made should be those that ensure that projects meet their aims.

Youth Action Plan

Actions speak louder than words!

Education is not only about educating young people. We recognize that the elderly in the community could benefit from ICTs. We as the youth commit ourselves to introducing our grandparents to the Internet by letting them send an e-mail to all youth forum participants.

Considering the success of previous Regional Youth Fora such as Africa 2001 and Asia 2002, we believe it is necessary to continue those initiatives already established by the ITU, including a similar event of a Youth Forum orientated to Europe as well as the Americas. We also urge that ITU continue to organize World Youth Fora.

We the youth, shall furthermore strengthen the Digital Bridge by promoting the re-use of ICT equipment. Youth fellows promise to contact at least one company or organization within their local network for collecting abandoned ICT equipment that can be valuable to developing countries. The Youth Fellows from the developing countries will also contact their governments, to draw their attention to this project. In so doing, youth will be giving a strong positive signal to their communities. The global network of World Youth Fellows will together help in distributing the equipment.

With the passage of time an opportunity lost is lost forever. We, as youth, should refresh our minds, seize our ideas and make a difference. We recognize the extreme importance of the World Summit on the Information Society (WSIS) for achieving the goals that have been identified by all people, and most particularly the Youth. We hope our voices will be heard and our Declaration will be accepted as a sign of youth commitment. Moreover we ask all players at WSIS to implement the WSIS Action Plan.

Actions, not words, how wonderful our lives will be if we all play our part.

The Declaration of the Global Forum of Indigenous Peoples and the Information Society[25]

Global Forum of Indigenous Peoples

Introduction

We, representatives of Indigenous peoples, nations and tribes of the World, assembled in Geneva from 8-11 December 2003 for the Global Forum of Indigenous peoples, nations and tribes and the Information Society. The Global Forum is an official meeting for the first phase of the World Summit on the Information Society and is facilitated by the United Nations Permanent Forum on Indigenous Issues.

As the representatives of Indigenous peoples, nations and tribes, Nations, and Tribes and recognizing the full diversity of Indigenous peoples, nations and tribes, who live in both, urban, rural and remote settings, we declare the following fundamental principals for building the information society that is inclusive of our cultural diversity and indigenous information communications styles and respects our rights in forming partnerships in action. All the following statements apply to Indigenous peoples, nations and tribes, our Elders, women, men, youth and children, in order that States abide by and respect them.

The Information Society is the result of a global revolution in the fields of economics, technology and social development. Its primary aspects are knowledge, information, communication and access to services and products. These elements of the Information Society, by their very nature are reflective of the political and economic status of the dominant society. This global revolution has had and continues to have a profound and deep impact on the cultures and communities of the world's Indigenous peoples, nations and tribes, most of whom continue to live in extreme poverty without basic provision for food, water, shelter, electricity and other basic infrastructure.

At the heart of our vision of the Information Society is respect for the dignity and human rights of Indigenous peoples, nations and tribes, which must be affirmed, if the economic, information and digital divide which separates technology rich nations

[25] On the web at www.worldsummit2003.de/download_en/ **indigenous**-Declaration.rtf

and the private sector from the most marginalized peoples of society including Indigenous peoples, nations and tribes, is to be bridged.

In this context, Information and Communication Technology (ICT) should be used to support and encourage cultural diversity and to preserve and promote the language, distinct identities and traditional knowledge of Indigenous peoples, nations and tribes in a manner which they determine best advances these goals. The evolution of the information and communication societies must be founded on the respect and promotion of the rights of Indigenous peoples, nations and tribes and our distinctive and diverse cultures, as outlined in international conventions. We have fundamental and collective rights to protect, preserve and strengthen our own languages, cultures and identities.

The prerequisite for the inclusion of Indigenous peoples, nations and tribes in the Information Society is the provision of adequate infrastructure in States for tele-communications, radio, television, the internet and ICT providers, with the free, prior and informed consent of Indigenous peoples, nations and tribes concerned. This requires access to basic community infrastructure such as electricity and energy sources. It is the desire of Indigenous peoples, nations and tribes that the provision of infrastructure and energy by achieved in sustainable ways and the use of alternative technologies should be investigated to ensure the environment is protected. States should take immediate action to address the needs of all Indigenous peoples, nations and tribes in their countries and should support developing nations and countries in transition, in their effort to provide ICT infrastructure.

Some Indigenous peoples, nations and tribes have made strides in bridging the information divide with the assistance of state and private sector support and financial subsidies. Our achievements demonstrate that equitable partnerships between Indigenous peoples, nations and tribes and others can be attained. These indigenous approaches and programs are resources, which can be transmitted to others through indigenous to indigenous training projects in order to meet the need of the vast majority of Indigenous peoples, nations and tribes, who have a critical need for culturally appropriate capacity building programmes. Capacity building programmes should begin at the grassroots level and should ensure gender equity.

Human Rights

We declare that our participation in building and implementing the information society must be based on our right to self-determination, and honour and respect of the spirit and intent of Treaties. Towards this end, we ask that States consider the rapid adoption of the Draft Declaration on the Rights of Indigenous peoples, nations and tribes, which we regard as minimal standards for the achievement of equity and social justice.

We declare that the protection and preservation of our indigenous languages and development of our traditional knowledge cannot be separated from our right to maintain and strengthen our distinctive spiritual and material relationship with our lands, territories, resources, air, inland waters and coastal seas. Access to ICT should not replace indigenous/traditional ways of knowing. Indigenous peoples, nations and tribes have a right and cultural obligation to preserve and transmit our ways of life, which includes our ways of knowing, to younger generations.

We declare that our cultural protocols, traditions, customary law and natures law, especially concerning sacred information and knowledge, must be respected. Arrangements for equitable benefit sharing must be based on our free, prior and informed consent.

We declare our desire to work collectively with others in the Information Society to create an ethical code and standards for best practices, which will be inclusive of our cultural values.

Education and Culture

We have the right to fully access and participate in decision-making processes (at all levels) concerning State Education (and the use of modern technologies). We also have the right to establish and control our own education systems based on our cultural methods, in our own languages and to plan and control our ICT application, as we see fit. We have the right to establish and control ICT training and application in indigenous educational systems, based on our own cultural methods of teaching and learning (of wisdom and cultural knowledge), in our own languages. We need to be key members and an integral part of the ICT capacity building for our communities.

We call on States, civil society and the private sector to partner with Indigenous peoples, nations and tribes, nations and tribes, to provide the needed resources for the development and implementation of "indigenous-to-indigenous" training projects, including "elders-and-youth" initiatives. This process will allow for the building of local capacity and expertise, and for programs that will be self sustaining.

We are entitled to culturally appropriate forms of distance learning as a complement to our methods of oral, personal, and intergenerational learning that are an integral part of indigenous learning and the transmission of language and culture.

To ensure equitable access to the Global Information Society, we need to develop our own approaches in the utilization of ICT that can be adapted to our own patterns and protocols of communication.

We are entitled to education and capacity building methods that are rooted in our languages, cultures and traditional knowledge that are fundamental in validating and affirming indigenous self-esteem and identity.

To promote mechanisms that enable Indigenous peoples, nations and tribes to realize culturally adaptive applications to the ICT best practices and technology need to be shared among various Indigenous peoples, nations and tribes. In order to do so, regional, national and international meetings and workshops have to be held to exchange information about educational projects between indigenous individuals, groups and peoples.

Social and Economic Development

We have the right to determine and develop priorities and strategies for exercising our right to development. All development measures including those relating to the implementation of the Information Society, must be controlled by the Indigenous peoples, nations and tribes concerned and carried out in equal partnership with them. Participation, negotiation, and free, prior and informed consent of Indigenous peoples, nations and tribes must be recognized as key elements of any development process.

We have the right to establish and control our own Information Communication and Technology (ICT), further developing our fundamental right to social and economic progress.

We have the right to participate in all manner of media and Information Communication Technology in mainstream ICT systems, nationally and internationally, in order to further strengthen our social and economic development strategies.

We have the right to appropriate capacity-building and support in developing a sounder financial base, in order to keep up with technological developments and to build partnerships and networks.

Health

Technology can assist in meeting our dire need for primary health care. It is a vehicle to success in achieving the Millennium Development Goals relating to infant mortality and maternal health care. Technology can also support preventative health education and through Tel-med applications, provide services over vast geographic distances. Information technology should be used to promote and protect our traditional healing practices as well as to improve our access to mainstream health services. This potential can only be realized through collective efforts and equitable partnerships between Indigenous peoples, nations and tribes, States, civil society and the private sector. This is considered a high priority.

Indigenous Cultural Property (includes Traditional Knowledge and Indigenous Intellectual Property and the Media)

We are the owners and guardians of the Traditional Ancestral Knowledge of our cultures that have been transmitted through aeons by our oral traditions and ceremonial cultural practices. Existing intellectual property regimes that favour individual property rights within the public domain are insufficient for the protection of indigenous intellectual property, which is the collective inheritance of Indigenous peoples, nations and tribes and the legacy of future generations.

Indigenous peoples, nations and tribes have the right to both fully explore existing legal regimes and to develop *sui generis* legal systems, in order to safeguard traditional knowledge and to ensure protection of sacred and/or secret content. This right encompasses the wealth of traditional knowledge, including but not limited to ethno-botanical and genetic applications of traditional knowledge and traditional knowledge systems relating to medicinal and agricultural practices.

An indigenous media agency should be established, in cooperation with relevant United Nations organizations, to advise on legal protection and dissemination of information on indigenous political, cultural and economic situations; and stories, articles, videos, images, and products of indigenous peoples, nations and tribes, utilized for commercial purposes, through all forms of media, including print. Furthermore, relevant United Nations agencies, coordinated by the Permanent Forum of Indigenous Issues, should in cooperation with Indigenous peoples, nations and tribes, elaborate a code of ethics regarding mainstream media researching or reporting on indigenous communities.

An internationally recognized indigenous products symbol should be encouraged and supported by States, in order to protect Indigenous peoples, nations and tribes intellectual property, for all ICT innovations belonging to Indigenous peoples, nations and tribes either individually or collectively.

The United Nations and Member States should promote mechanisms to ensure the effective protection of the collective knowledge, innovations, and practice of the Indigenous peoples, nations and tribes, linked to cultural and biological diversity.

Environment

The environment is a concern for us all. ICTs, including radio and video, provide excellent opportunities to showcase and educate about the natural beauty and diversity in which we live and can further our efforts to protect our lands and territories. Indigenous peoples are interested in producing multi-media education materials to assist in environmental education.

Indigenous and non-Indigenous peoples, nations and tribes share the responsibility of protecting the environment and to live in sustainable ways. ICTs should be used to promote sustainable forms of living for the benefit of our whole planet.

There should be no construction of ICT equipment on Indigenous territories without the free, prior and informed consent of the indigenous peoples.

Environmental and cultural impact assessments on indigenous territories (lands, waterways, airspace, seas and oceans) must be carried out with the effective participation of the indigenous people/s before any ITC construction takes place.

ICT construction, whether on lands, waterways, airspace or in the oceans, should not proceed if there are concerns of negative environmental or cultural impacts.

Our Road to Tunis

To assure the meaningful participation of Indigenous peoples, nations and tribes in Tunis in 2005 and in all preparatory conferences leading up to Tunis, the following recommendations need to be implemented:

The Tunis Global Forum of Indigenous peoples and the Information Society (GFIPIS) should be convened at the same site of the Tunis WSIS and should precede the WSIS by four (4) days. Registrations for the GFIPIS should include access to WSIS.

Indigenous members of the Permanent Forum on Indigenous Issues, in coordination with regional indigenous organizations, should be included in 2004 during the planning of the Tunis WSIS.

Travel and per diem grants for lodging and support for Indigenous peoples, nations and tribes should be funded by States and private sector and provided within sufficient time to allow proper planning and participation. Contributions should be sent to the Permanent Forum, which should ensure equal allocation among the indigenous regions taking into account gender, age and geographic equity.

A broad based effort should be made to inform Indigenous peoples, nations and tribes about the dates, location and all relevant matters of the Tunis regional preparatory conferences in early 2004. Email announcements should also be distributed to all participants of the annual sessions of the United Nations Permanent Forum on indigenous Issues.

Plan of Action of the Global Forum of Indigenous Peoples and the Information Society[26]

Global Forum of Indigenous Peoples

Following are suggested courses of action to improve indigenous connectivity and equitable access to the new information society, on the Road to Tunis in 2005.

Economical and Social Development:

Indigenous peoples are interested in building partnerships with other indigenous peoples, States, the international system (including financial bodies), and the private sector to:

- Ensure regular and sustained support for isolated indigenous communities, so they can maintain connectivity;
- Build partnerships that are crucial for the establishment and sustainability of community connectivity, especially through funding/resourcing and training;
- Promote cooperation among those who have access to new technologies and those who do not;
- Ensure that Indigenous peoples who have access to new technologies can share their skills in such areas as advertising (for trade of indigenous communities) with those who do not.
- Ensure ICTs are made available to communities on the basis of equity and are accessibility to all.
- Recognize the potential of the Internet for indigenous peoples to promote their own culture and history beyond economic profit.
- Explore possibility for an indigenous satellite.
- Assist Indigenous communities to explore and develop technologies themselves.

---

[26] Geneva, 11 December 2003. On the web at www.worldsummit2003.de/download_en/ indigenous-Declaration.rtf

- Explore e-commerce applications which are very important for indigenous enterprises in assisting them to develop a needs analysis, a business plan, and develop partnerships and plan how to sustain their e-commerce projects.

- Establish a worldwide indigenous association of indigenous organizations and businesses that have made the leap to connectivity, so that they can assist and make this technology available to indigenous communities who are not yet connected.

- Raise awareness about the necessity of satellites to accomplish any form of communication in remote areas;

- Promote radio/wireless as cheaper and better strategies for small communities.

- Raise awareness of appropriate technologies for the local situation and such issues as the use of landlines, which are very expensive but work better in large communities.

- Fund capacity building in communication projects for indigenous communities, prioritizing access by youth, women and Elders.

- Access to information for indigenous women and indigenous youth and projects for capacity building.

- Assist indigenous peoples to decide what ICTs they need and assess what education is needed to have access to the knowledge of this new technology.

- Develop computer software in indigenous languages that allow indigenous peoples to write in their own languages and to expand the use of computers in communities where indigenous languages are still in common use.

- Properly resource indigenous peoples to allow their full participation in the information society.

Culture and Education

Indigenous peoples are interested in building partnerships with other Indigenous peoples, States, the international system (including financial bodies), and the private sector to:

- Assist indigenous media in transmitting information (through print, audio and video) without excessive cost.

- Adapt information technologies to the needs of indigenous communities.

- Assist indigenous peoples to publicize their realities, recognizing that indigenous peoples should decide what should be published and what should not.

- Develop and promote ICT projects that motivate all young learners (including indigenous youth) to understand other cultures and also to take part in the preservation of their own cultures.

- Promote education and capacity building about information technology to ensure that indigenous peoples can utilize it effectively and appropriately.

- Ensure that relevant UN bodies including the UNPFII, WIPO, and UNESCO should work together on these issues to ensure that these issues (that are cross-cutting) are adequately addressed, recognizing that no single UN body has a mandate that allows for the comprehensive addressing of these issues. Such a partnership should encourage complimentary in addressing these issues.

- Produce a secure database portal of Indigenous languages written and oral.

- Create educational programs, where indigenous students can be trained to improve their technical skills.

- Assist indigenous peoples to develop our own strategies of communications.

Environment

Indigenous peoples are interested in building partnerships with other indigenous peoples, States, the international system (including financial bodies), and the private sector to:

- Ensure that ICTs, including satellite dishes, should not be placed on indigenous lands or territories unless the free, prior and informed consent of the Indigenous Peoples of those territories have been secured.

- Establish procedures concerning the placement of ICT equipment on Indigenous peoples lands that require widespread advertisement and notification, to ensure that the Indigenous Peoples belonging to those territories are fully informed and that their free and prior informed consent is obtained prior to any work commencing.

- Ensure that indigenous peoples fully participate in environmental and cultural impact assessments on their indigenous territories (lands, waterways, airspace, seas and oceans) before any ITC construction takes place and that construction relating to ICTs whether on land or in the seas should not be undertaken where there is a negative environmental or cultural impact.

Health

Indigenous peoples are interested in building partnerships with other indigenous peoples, States, the international system (including financial bodies), and the private sector to:

- Develop and implement indigenous specific health strategies at both community-level, regional, national and international levels.

- Ensure that High tech health care enhances and build on traditional ways of healing.

- Allow indigenous peoples, through their indigenous evolutionary processes to find their own uses for modern technologies, through capacity building and learning about its potential.

- Work with indigenous communities, to assist them in identifying what improvements are needed firstly in their health care, before they can identify how technology can help in other areas.

- Ensure that (recognizing the under-resourcing of indigenous health in many countries) moneys saved through high tech health delivery are redirected back into other indigenous health areas.

Human Rights

Indigenous peoples are interested in building partnerships with other indigenous peoples, States, the international system (including financial bodies), and the private sector to:

- Acknowledge that this Global Forum of Indigenous Peoples and the Information Society - Programme of Action is built on the previous precedents of World Conferences, noting the unqualified use of the term indigenous peoples in the Johannesburg Declaration and the relevant recommendations made at the World Conference against Racism, Racial Discrimination, Xenophobia and Related Intolerance.

- Recognized that Indigenous peoples were identified as vulnerable groups by the World Conference against Racism, Racial Discrimination Xenophobia and Related Intolerance, and as peoples, suffer multiple forms of discrimination. In particular, indigenous women were at the intersectionality of race and gender discrimination. Therefore, particular attention should be given to the negative uses of modern technologies to promote and proliferate racial hatred, discrimination, gender bias and stereotyping. As the World Conference recommended, special measures should be adopted to address discrimination against indigenous peoples.

- Develop special measures to include marginalized segments of society including Indigenous peoples, and to ensure that they are not further marginalized by the information society.

- Ensure that the right to freedom of speech is exercised without any discrimination.

- Develop a code of conduct for the use of the information society, encouraging respect and promotion of cultural diversity.

Traditional Knowledge

Indigenous peoples are interested in building partnerships with other indigenous peoples, States, the international system (including financial bodies), and the private sector to:

- Ensure that international organizations, including WIPO and other bodies, dealing with issues of relevance to Indigenous peoples and the information society, develop effective participation mechanisms to allow full and effective participation of indigenous peoples, including travel grants for regional representatives to participate in relevant meetings.

- Assist Indigenous Peoples in exploring *sui generis* legislation to protect their collective intellectual property rights.

- Raise awareness with UNESCO that it needs to consider more effective protection mechanisms for cultural heritage.

- Promote to the theme of Traditional Knowledge protection with the United Nations Permanent Forum on Indigenous Issues as their special theme for their 2005 session.

Charter of Civil Rights for a Sustainable Knowledge Society: Version 3.0

Document of the Heinrich Böll Foundation

The "Charter of Civil Rights for a Sustainable Knowledge Society" was instigated by the Heinrich Böll Foundation (www.boell.de) as a contribution to the preparatory process of the "World Summit on the Information Society" (WSIS) on behalf of German civil society entities and individuals[27].

The first draft was submitted to the second Preparatory Committee (PrepCom2) of the "World Summit on the Information Society" in January 2003. The present revised version incorporates suggestions and criticisms voiced in intensive offline and online discussions in spring and early summer of 2003.

The "Charter" aims to enrich as well as influence the preparatory consultations among all stakeholders in Germany as well as at the international level. The principles and viewpoints expressed are intended to be guidelines for policy-making at all levels. The final version of the "Charter" will be submitted to the World Summit in December 2003.

The "Charter of Civil Rights for a Sustainable Knowledge Society" calls for the unhampered and non-discriminatory use of knowledge and information based on the principles of sustainability. The challenge for the knowledge society consists in securing the availability of knowledge and keeping access to information resources open. Knowledge and information are the primary means of providing citizens with a reliable basis for action.

---

[27] The following individuals have contributed to the drafting of the Charter:
Markus Beckedahl, Network New Media; Gabriele Beger, German Association for Information Science and Practice; Ralf Bendrath, FOGIS; Dr. Johann Bizer, Data Protection and Data Security; Dr. Christoph Bruch, Humanistic Union; Jutta Croll, Digital Chances Foundation; Olga Drossou, Heinrich Böll Foundation; Wolf Goehring, Fraunhofer Institute for Autonomous Intelligence Systems; Dr. Ralf Grötker, free-lance journalist; Arne Hintz, Indymedia; Dr. Jeanette Hofmann, Social Science Research Center Berlin; Prof. Hans J. Kleinsteuber, University of Hamburg; Prof. Rainer Kuhlen, University of Konstanz and German UNESCO Commission; Alvar Freude, odem.org; Nils Leopold, Humanistic Union; Prof. Bernd Lutterbeck, Technical University of Berlin; Annette Mühlberg, General Union of Service Industries Ver.di; Oliver Passek, Network New Media; Dr. Andreas Poltermann, Heinrich Böll Foundation; Jan Schallaböck, Network New Media; Petra Schaper-Rinkel, Free University of Berlin; Dr. Thomas Schauer, Research Institute for Applied Knowledge Processing (FAW); Rena Tangens and padeluun, Art d'Ameublement; FoeBuD Big Brother Awards Germany; Till Wetermayer, Network New Media.
Information about the consultation process of the "Charter" and those involved can be found at:
www.worldsummit2003.de (German) or www.worldsummit2003.org (English)

The Charter questions the increasing privatisation and commercialisation of knowledge and information. A society in which the intellectual property regime transforms knowledge into a scarce resource is not a sustainable society.

A knowledge society is sustainable when it preserves and promotes historically achieved human and civil rights for future electronically determined environments.

A knowledge society is sustainable when access to knowledge is unhampered and inclusive. It is sustainable when it promotes cooperative forms of knowledge production as the basis for innovation and creativity.

A knowledge society is sustainable when its knowledge forms the basis for effective means of preserving our natural environment. The increasing consumption of natural resources currently threatening our environment is in part a result of the mass propagation of information technologies.

A knowledge society is sustainable when access to knowledge and information provides all peoples of the world with the opportunity for self-determined development in their private, professional and public lives. It is sustainable when it preserves for future generations access to diverse media and information resources.

A knowledge society is sustainable when development in the North is no longer carried out at the expense of the South and when the potential of men is no longer realised at the expense of women.

The "Charter of Civil Rights for a Sustainable Knowledge Society" is based on the following rights and values. These must be preserved and promoted for all citizens of the global knowledge society:

1. Knowledge is the heritage and the property of humanity and is thus free.

Knowledge represents the reservoir from which new knowledge is created. Knowledge must therefore remain permanently accessible to the public. Limitations on public access such as copyrights and patents must be the exception. Commercial exploitation of knowledge conflicts with the interest of society in knowledge as a public good. Knowledge as a common good must have a higher status in the hierarchy of social values than the protection of private claims.

2. Access to knowledge must be free.

The central objective of a knowledge society organised according to the principle of sustainability is that access to all medial forms of knowledge must be possible for present as well as for future generations, for all peoples, at all times, in all places and under fair conditions. This applies to all domains of society, not only to science. Only free access to knowledge and information makes democratic participation in public affairs possible and stimulates creativity and innovation in science, business and culture. Only democratic control mechanisms can be allowed to limit the principle of free access.

3. Reducing the digital divide must be recognised as a political objective of high priority.

The digital divide - that is, the division of the population into groups that have access to the new media and groups that are excluded - has developed along traditional, for the most part social, ethnic and gender divisions. The existing unjust distribution of opportunities for all is increased by unequal access to information and communication technologies. This is a global problem which affects the relations between countries and within societies.

It is essential to enable all citizens access to old and new media. Overcoming unequal access opportunities must take into account local conditions and specific needs and must proceed according to sustainable principles. The establishment of public-access points and the furtherance of information and media competence will enable people both in developed and developing countries to find their bearings in the world of media information, to evaluate the content on offer, to produce their own content and to profit from information for their own personal pursuit of well-being.

4. Everyone has an unlimited right of access to the documents of public and publicly controlled bodies.

Access to information and knowledge as well as free communication are necessary prerequisites for personal development, for political participation and for the development of humanity as a whole. Freedom of information makes political decisions transparent, helps reduce corruption and improves the management of information in public administrations. Classifying administrative activities as secret must always require legitimisation by law and should be kept within a tight legal framework.

All citizens have the right to inform themselves through publicly available resources and to have unhampered, unfiltered access to documents of public and publicly controlled organisations - without manipulation or control. Information and knowledge in private hands should also be accessible in case of a special public interest. Governmental and public administration institutions must commit themselves to the comprehensive electronic publication of all information of public interest.

5. Employee rights must be upheld and furthered in electronically networked environments as well.

The protection of human dignity, the right to personal development, and to equality are individual rights of great importance in the work environment as well. A necessary prerequisite for realising these rights for employees is the right to form coalitions, including the right to promote one's own interests and to gather in freely elected organs of representation.

Employees must have free and uncensored Internet access at their workplace. Employees and their representative organs must have access to the communication system (Intranet) of their company. The right to privacy must be protected in the work environment. Electronic surveillance and user-profiling must be prevented.

6. Cultural diversity is a prerequisite for individual and social development.

Culture is realised in languages, customs, social behavior patterns, norms and ways of life, but also in human artifacts (such as arts, crafts and technology). The emergence of the global knowledge society must not be allowed to lead to cultural homogenisation. Instead, the creative potential of current information and communication technologies must be used to preserve and promote the heterogeneity of cultures and languages as a precondition for the individual and social development of present and future generations. A dialogue of cultures can only be realised in a climate of diversity and equal rights.

7. Media diversity and the availability of information from independent sources are essential for the maintenance of an enlightened public.

Media and their content are increasingly controlled by only a few global media conglomerates. It is a public responsibility to support existing and new forms of media participation. Non-profit media and those public service media that are controlled by democratic structures must be extended. The rights to freedom of opinion and to a free press must be supplemented by general rights to freedom of communication. The right to communication must include the right to participate in all kinds of communication processes and to contribute actively to the media.

8. Open technical standards and open forms of technical and software production guarantee the free development of infrastructures and thus self-determined and free communication forms.

Proprietary solutions in regard to protocols and standards in network technology, computer architecture and software application lead to the formation of monopolies and are detrimental to innovation. When governments hold monopolies on infrastructures and when private-sector players have proprietary monopolies on technologies, there is the additional danger that the power to set standards will affect content and lead to restrictions in the freedom of information and communication.

Only open technical standards will promote free and open software development and self-determined communication.

9. The right to privacy is a human right and is essential for free and self-determined human development in the knowledge society.

Respect for privacy allows for both participation and detachment in regard to social activities and opportunities. Every person must have the right to decide freely whether and in what manner he/she wants to receive information and communicate with others. The possibility of receiving information anonymously, irrespective of the source, must be ensured for everyone.

The power of the private sector and of governments over information increases the risk of manipulative access and surveillance and must be kept to a legally legitimized minimum. The collection, analysis and release of personal data – no matter by whom - should remain under the control of the individual concerned.

Civil Society Statements Through Phase One of the Summit

A Latin American Civil Perspective on the Information Summit[28]

Olinca Marino[29]

Information Society

The concept of Information Society belongs to the current colloquial language used. Nowadays, the term "Information Society" is lightly used as a synonym with media, technology and Internet. It's in fashion. However, when we use this concept, do we ask what information society we are building? Is information society civil organizations are building the same society other social sectors are interested in? Is it about building only one information society? The debate is still open, more interesting and important than ever. The next World Summit on Information Society organized by the UNO follows this fashion.

What civil society proposes

Groups that have made fundamental contributions to the field of communication including radio stations and other community media, news agencies, telecenter projects, and Internet community providers, and other initiatives encouraging communities to use new information technologies, have many years of work experience. Therefore, they can considerably contribute to the preparation process of the World Summit on Information Society, WSIS.

Civil society organizations have key principles to build their concept of information society and have emphasized this process to stress the importance of protecting this concept. In the first place, for organizations, equality seems to be the cornerstone for its construction. In several congresses held in the region and in national chapters about the World Summit, one posture seems to join the regional civil society: to

---

[28] On the web at www.ourmedianet.org/papers/om2003/Marino_OM3.eng.pdf
[29] Olinca Marino is the Information Coordinator, LaNeta Program, Mexico. Paper delivered at the third meeting of OurMedia/Nuestros Medios in Barranquilla, Colombia, May 2003.

leverage an equal construction of the information society based on economic and social sustainable developments, and on gender justice. In the opinion of most civil society organizations, it is evident that the information society can not only be supported by the market force. They had initial fears with respect to the responsibility for the organization of the WSIS, which was entrusted to the International Telecommunications Union, ITU, the consultative organ for large corporations like Siemens, Motorola, Bell, Nec, Alcatel, Ericsson and AT&T. According to the Summit organization body, the Summit should have a common vision and better understanding of the transformation towards an Information Society.[30]

Also these groups with wide community experience look for an Information Society based on right to communication as a human right. They think Internet and Communications access and use are fundamental rights as a guarantee to hear community voices. Therefore, the purpose of civil society organizations is to implement information and communication technologies as instruments to encourage democratic governability and citizen participation. Civil groups also have proposals on literacy and education, defend cultural and linguistic diversity, public domain of global knowledge, and information Security as part of the socalled information society.

Participation and mobilization

For many civil society organizations, the Information Summit is considered as a means, not an end. They expect to take this occasion as an opportunity to have a national and regional debate on priority topics related to information and communication. They want to generate a movement in the organizations an citizens about communication themes of their interest. Many civil groups have participated from the beginning on the WSIS official process. Some of these groups want to open dialog spaces in several countries with their government, oriented towards building civil mechanisms for the design and implementation of communications, information and telecommunications public policies. For other organizations – that have had unnoticeable Latin American participation – the Summit is important to generate another kind of movement oriented towards a protest on the unequal development of the digitalized society. They are organizing in another way to highlight the inequalities and actually demand the same basicprinciples that motivated the chosen organizations to participate in the official process. An example of civil diversity is

[30] Civil organizations are also concerned about the fact that the United Nations intervenes in the Summit, which will help develop a solid base for the economic development through new stable job opportunities and highly qualified jobs, as well as create local goods, equipment, software, content and service manufacturers, especially if there is no big debate.

the range of alternative meetings to beheld in Geneva in December 2003 to shape and strengthen the wide global scope of civil society.

Civil participation, the starting point to defend in the WSIS process For civil society organizations, information society is a diverse society under construction whose development should imply transparent participation. Thus, diverse organizations that are involved in the WSIS process, fiercely defend what has been too difficult to accomplish within the Summit: to take into account not only the voices from the government and corporations in the discussion process, but also communities' needs, contributions, and proposals at the working table. From the beginning of the official process – that publicly began with the first Preparatory Conference in July 2002 – it was clearly stated to take respect and the guarantee of civil society inclusion as the initial action. Diverse and transparent participation was then the first action and defense of civil society organizations before the WSIS.

Therefore, the following aspects are very important:

- Civil organizations should keep exerting pressure in the WSIS official process to guarantee the effective inclusion of proposals from different sectors that constitute the civil society.
- Any efforts made by the organizations, groups and other initiatives to generate proposals including peoples and communities in their ruling center.
- Any initiative that encourages debate, analysis, and diffusion of civil society's postures in and out of the Summit's official process.

Civil Organization Initiatives in Latin America

The CRIS Campaign

CRIS [Communication Rights in the Information Society] was created as a global campaign in 2001 to influence the process, and the World Summit agenda. This campaign is oriented towards promoting democratically citizen mobilization for the right to communication, even beyond the WSIS framework. CRIS' mission is to "help build an Information Society based on transparency, diversity, participation, and social and economic justice principles, and is inspired by equality between genders and between different cultural and regional perspectives". To fulfill this mission, the CRIS campaign is oriented towards influencing on the definition of procedures, as well as on guaranteeing transparency in participation processes. CRIS has tried to widen the participation margin within the Summit official process, and it is basically looking for promoting the inclusion of social, economic topics and relevant policies that do not limit to simply use new information technologies.

Six are CRIS co-founding organizations in Latin America: The Latin American Association of Radio Broadcasting Education (ALER), The World Association of Community Radio Broadcasters (WACRB), the Third World Institute (ITM), la Rede de Informações para o Terceiro Setor (RITS), the World Association for Christian Communication (WACC) and the Latin American Information Agency (ALAI). The campaign is currently composed of a large number of organizations and individuals that work on communication for the social change at the local, regional, and global levels. It is difficult to exactly say the number of participants in the campaign since there is no registration form or any other instrument alike. The CRIS' modus operandi and raison d'être is to support scenarios that have been spontaneously generated or consolidated within the Summit framework to reflect, build networks, and take actions based on the analysis and proposals on the information society. That is to say that the creation of local entities is fostered to diversely analyze, discuss, and/or make proposals for the creation of one or more Information Societies. These agencies such as radio stations, discussion groups, assemblies, e-mail listing, school groups, telecenters, human rights organizations, women groups, and technical or academic groups, are convinced of the protection of communication rights.

E-mail lists as participation power

Electronic lists have had a major role in the organization of the civil process in the region with respect to the WSIS. In the last months, several organizations have been involved in the analysis and debate based on their participation on mail lists dealing with topics related to the information society. The origin of the Latin American Caucus is in these lists – which we will talk about later. Among the lists we can mention:

The Crisal list

In February 2002, CRISAL – CRIS electronic space for Latin America – was created. Using this e-mail list, activists, researchers and other people interested in ICTs and the rights to communication have participated from Argentina, Bolivia, Brazil, Colombia, Costa Rica, Chile, Ecuador, Guatemala, Haiti, Honduras, Mexico, Nicaragua, Panama, Paraguay, Peru, Puerto Rico, the Dominican Republic, Uruguay and Venezuela. There are currently on average 300 people participating in CRISAL[31]. This list is aimed at offering information and inviting several civil society players in the region to collectively cooperate in the definition of WSIS procedures, and to promote the adoption of relevant themes about a sustainable human development perspective. Initially, the civil coordination in the region was discussed.

[31] http://comunica.org/mailman/listinfo/crisal_comunica.org

Based on this discussion, the first collective Latin American documents appeared and were submitted to the Summit official process.

The Mistica List

The Mistica List[32] exists since 1998. About 350 people, among activists and academic members discuss and make collective documents – some of them very linked to the WSIS – focusing on the "ICTs social impact" in the region. The list facilitates the players' distance participation with some presential probability and keeps a synthesis of what happens in this and other communication processes associated to regional public policies.

The Socinfo list

Based on the great amount of data in English regarding the coordination of civil society in the Summit, socinfo[33] was founded to spread information in Spanish and coordinate actions from the First Preparatory Conference. Currently, it is an information scenario for several organizations providing data mostly from other lists.

Participation in these lists is open and the organizations that exchange data are not necessarily working in the Summit's lobbying process. That is to say that these organizations do not belong to the different entities created to directly work with the UNO, the governments, etc. There are many lists that do not work in Spanish, apart form the LAC caucus list and that one for Latin American education.

Latin American participation takes shape in the LAC Caucus

The Latin American and Caribbean Caucus - LAC Caucus - is the meeting point of Latin American civil information, communication and human rights organizations, some academic actors and other people interested in participating in the WSIS. This is a space for debate, topics, and incidence strategies with the governments. It is open to any organization or person who wants to work driven by the proposals from the regional civil society in the WSIS official process. Caucus is recognized as a civil space for Latin America and the Caribbean by its organizing body.

Caucus makes part of the necessity to build information societies based on human rights and their integral respect, especially the rights to education, to expression, and to regional citizen communication. Caucus consider communication as a public asset and a fundamental process to achieve sustainable economic, political, social and cultural development through ICT tools and other ways of communication and

[32] http://funredes.org/mistica y http://funredes.org/olistica
[33] http://lists.cpsr.org/socinfo

information. LAC Caucus' commitment is to search equal opportunities for genders, races, ethnics, nationalities and social classes in all information society policies and initiatives.

Caucus intends to create strategies to strengthen Latin American and Caribbean civil society presence in the WSIS process. Therefore, Caucus' purpose is to encourage topics of special regional interest including the development of regulatory frameworks to facilitate legalization mechanisms for the community media; the promotion of free software and democratization of country code top level domain names ccTLD; effective participation of our countries in the Internet and all international regulation agents; mechanisms for the legal protection of local knowledge; and community needs to directly participate in the discussion, formulation, follow up and assessment of ICTs public policies in the region.

The purpose of the LAC Caucus can be summarized in one sentence: "to strengthen the presence of the Latin American civil society in the WSIS process and to influence in it effectively". Therefore, best efforts are made to coordinate LAC's civil society organizations participation – on line and personal participation. Documents are being translated, contents are being designed and strategies for the governments and other actors' participation are being encouraged. Another task undertaken by the LAC Caucus is to promote the participation in and support to other initiatives on information societies and the right to communication in the region. The LAC Caucus has its mailing list which gathers about 40 subscribers. It also has its own temporary web site[34].

Other civil society agencies in the WSIS process

Division of the Civil Society

The Summit organization created an official working team called Division of the Civil Society that is currently participating by supporting the civil groups in the entire process. In practical terms, the Division is a team of the WSIS organization that operates as a speaker between the Summit organization and the coordinated civil organizations. It presents proposals before the different civil agencies and recommends procedures. It has its web site[35] to post data from and to nongovernment groups.

Caucus

[34] LAC caucus list: http://mailman.greennet.org.uk/mailman/listinfo/lac
site http://lac.derechos.apc.org/wsis/
[35] Web site http://www.geneva2003.org/wsis/indexa03.htm

Apart from the LAC Caucus, the gender caucus[36], Asia's and Africa's [37] caucus are active. All of them were created before the Latin American one. Apart from the existing Caucus, there are other bodies that have been created within the preparatory meetings.

Bureau of Civil Society and its "families"

This Bureau was formally incorporated during the PrepCom 2 in Geneva in February 2003. Its mission is to facilitate and improve communication and exchange between the organizations and the civil society members and the government and organizing body of the Summit. It does not have a decision vote. To reach the Bureau incorporation, "families" which are working teams that work on a common topic, region or any other work aspect, were first created. In the Latin American case, the LAC Caucus has "family"' duties. Currently there are 22 families and each one has 2 contacts. All contacts constitute the Bureau.

Plenary of the Civil Society

This is the maximum legitimacy space that makes decisions of the civil society. In each prepcom and during the Summit there are presential plenaries of the WSIS civil society. In these plenaries, participation is open to all the participants from the organizations. Between each presential meeting, the plenary works on line on the list plenary@wsis-cs.org.

Obstacles and mistakes

In an attempt to make an overview of the most important obstacles that Latin American civil organizations have encountered in the WSIS process, we can mention the following aspects with respect to their relationship with the governments:

In spite of the statements in an opposite sense, weak political will to stimulate and guarantee participation of civil society is remarkable. This can be seen in the absence of official participation spaces, the little financial support received and the reiterate insistence of some governments to limit the presence of civil organizations as mere observers.

The governments still have a marked tendency to favor a technology and marketoriented scope (competence, deregulation, economic development).

[36] Gender caucus' web site: www.wougnet.org/wsis/wsisgc.html

[37] African caucus' list: Africa@wsis-cs.org

Some governments' lack of political will regarding the possible contributions that can be taken again from civil society is remarkable. Some of them fear to incorporate contributions from the civil sector even in working documents making it impossible to have later contributions in official declarations and action plans. Regarding the governments in the region under the GRULAC[38], their posture is puzzling. Their proposals not always match the political openness they have directly reiterated to the organizations at the moment of signing official agreements.

Official documents are in English and their translation in Spanish appear much later. This situation together with on line discussions in English do not favor timely participation from many civil society sectors.

Regarding the coordination of civil organizations here are the following mistakes:

- The economic situation of the organizations to cover expenses clearly limits the civil participation in the Latin America region. However, in on-line civil participation there are more observers than committed people to work on different activities.
- Civil participation structures so far constituted – such as the families, Caucus and the Bureau of Civil Society – are complex.
- The Latin American civil organizations coordination that has worked so far have to make more contacts with organizations from the Caribbean countries.
- Also regional youth and human rights groups have to participate more.

Achievements in the WSIS' process

Generally speaking, there are more documents counteracting the mercantilist approach of the Summit. Proposals with the support of different regions and specific action areas (gender, education...) have been integrated.

There has been a fruitful analysis process in the Latin American region. If the topics are not alien to the work of many organizations, they have not been analyzed in other aspects with so many players and for such a long time.

There have been successful initiatives that integrate academic sectors to organizations.

[38] Group from Latin America and the Caribbean

The relationships with GRULAC governments

There have been very successful national processes including the national chapters of the CRIS campaign: Bolivia, Colombia, and Costa Rica.

Challenges

Undoubtedly, the major challenge is to include Latin American civil society's proposals and needs in the declaration and action plans.

Another important challenge is to strengthen the civil coordination in the region. In this regard, the following aspects should be consolidated: the LAC Caucus; CRIS' national chapters in other countries; Latin American participation in other Caucus and thematic working groups; as well as greater regional participation in meetings alternative to the Summit.

It is important to have more relationships between the initiatives within the Summit official process and alternative initiatives to it.

It is mostly important that Latin American organizations increase the number of proposals with respect to contents and actions to be taken.

Another challenge is to have economic support to leverage civil participation in the Summit.

To quickly translate data to Spanish and include this language in the debate lists. This will facilitate the integration of more civil society sectors and voices.

A very difficult challenge is to participate in the Summit with real incidence since the risk is that at the end of the process, civil society participation has not had an impact, but has only served as an excuse for organizers to say that all sectors participated in the Summit.

Strengthening Latin American civil Society's relationships

Beyond the specific results in the information policy field, the WSIS process has left interesting and warm experiences from the constitution of coordination bodies at the local, national, regional and global levels. Apart from contributing to building the information society with innovative ways of participation and transparency, civil society is also strengthened with this experience of coordination and membership. Membership initiatives of different civil, academic groups and other players are very constructive for the consolidation of organization structures that not only defend and demand, but that also substantially provide contents. The global exchange has been very enriching and particularly in the Latin American case, the experience has been very rich leaving new networks established in the region in the search of diverse, equal and sustainable information societies.

WSIS, the Neoliberal Agenda, and Counterproposals from Civil Society[39]

Sasha Costanza-Chock

Background on WSIS

The World Summit on the Information Society (WSIS) is a UN Summit that is being organized by the International Telecommunications Union (ITU). The Summit has been constructed according to a so-called 'flower petal' model, with a series of regional meetings feeding into preparatory conferences, followed by a two-phase World Summit: in December 2003, Geneva, a Declaration and Action Plan will be agreed upon, and then in 2005, in Tunis, there is supposed to be a review of accomplishments since 2003 and a renewal of commitments by all the participants [see www.wsis.org]. According to the rhetoric, each 'petal' (regional meeting, preparatory conference, and Summit) is open to 'tripartite participation,' meaning that the governments, private sector, and civil society are all supposed to have a voice. In theory, then, the Summit is a much more open model for a global forum than most UN meetings or bodies. In what sense, then, is it appropriate or realistic to see the WSIS as another instrument consistent with the neoliberal agenda?

To begin with, it is important to understand that the ITU has always served governments and the powerful telecom conglomerates. Originally set up in 1865 to regulate telegraph standards, later radio, and then satellite orbit allocation, the ITU took on the Summit because it has recently been losing power to the telecoms that increasingly set their own rules and to the Internet Corporation for Assigned Names and Numbers (ICANN), which was created by the US government to regulate the Internet domain name system. The ITU is now facing heavy budget cuts and is desperate to remain a player in the global regulation of Information and Communication Technologies (ICTs). Given the background of the ITU, it's no surprise to find the clearest vision of the Summit as a plank in neoliberalism coming straight from the horse's mouth. Yoshio Utsumi, Secretary General of the ITU, has stated at repeated regional conferences, and I quote:

"Developing policy frameworks for cyberspace to deal with issues of cybercrime, security, taxation, IP protection, or privacy – is something like establishing a new

[39] Presentation for OURmedia III, Barranquilla, May 20, 2003 www.ourmedianet.org/papers/om2003/ Costanza-Chock_OM3.pdf

government in the New World. I recall the early history of the colonial states in the USA or the story of El Dorado in Spanish [sic] America. But cyberspace is an invisible world and much more complex. Its inhabitants are not only individuals but include corporations, governments, and even sovereign states. They require new mechanisms for cooperation. We need a much more stronger [sic] political will to solve the issues than our ancestors [sic] did in establishing a state in their newly conquered territories" [Bucharest, 7 November 2002: available at http://www.itu.int/wsis/docs/rc/bucharest/speech_utsumi.doc].

We can see from this statement the imperialist mindset with which the leadership of the ITU are approaching the so-called 'information society.' They are not, of course, the only ones with such a vision. The US position is also clear:

1. Crack down on 'digital piracy' in the developing world, in order to maximize profits for the US based multinational software and media content conglomerates;

2. Fight so-called 'cyberterrorism,' in other words normalize electronic surveillance across the globe and extend the electronic eavesdropping provisions of the USA Patriot Act to the rest of the world. (Of course this already exists in the form of ECHELON, but ECHELON is illegal. The global adoption of an instrument on 'cyberterror' would be a terrible step).

The agenda of the private sector mostly overlaps with and informs the position of the US government: ensure the enclosure of the knowledge commons in the form of Intellectual Property Rights (IPRs) held by corporations, rather than creators, and ensure the liberalization of information and communication systems everywhere [see the contribution to WSIS Content and Themes by the Coordinating Committee of Business Interlocutors at http://www.itu.int/wsis/docs/im/content_themes/contributions/ccbi.doc].

To the most powerful actors on this stage, then, cyberspace is a lawless frontier to be tamed and fenced in under the property rights and surveillance regimes. The Summit will envision a rollout of infrastructure across the globe, of course with lip service to universal access, but only under conditions that ensure the maximization of profit for the multinationals and the normalization of the paranoid panoptic pretensions of the USA/UK ECHELON surveillance system. In place of a global knowledge commons, we will have a crackdown on so-called 'digital piracy' in the developing world. In place of the emergence of a strong coordinated global civil society, we have the chilling effect of state surveillance apparatus, with the US Empire's war dogs leading the pack towards Total Information Awareness [now renamed 'Terrorist Information Awareness:' see http://www.darpa.mil/body/tia/TIA%20DI.pdf].

On the 'inclusion' of civil society

Does all this mean that the WSIS agenda is entirely set by the wealthy nations and the private sector? Can it be dismissed as yet another tool of neoliberalism? It's not so simple. For one thing, the most powerful nations and the multinationals have been fairly uninterested in the entire Summit process, sending low-level representatives, if anyone, to preparatory meetings. They seem to be mostly ignoring the WSIS, focusing on other forums like the World Trade Organization (WTO) and World Intellectual Property Organization (WIPO) to push the privatization of information and communication systems.

At the same time, there have certainly been positive developments within the Summit process. There have been head nods to civil society participation, formal accreditation for NGOs, and small openings for crafting official UN language. The supposed goal of 'bridging the digital divide,' while at best a naïve formulation that obscures the underlying economic divide that increases as a result of neoliberal policies, is still a positive ideal, and we should welcome a stated commitment by governments to achieve universal access. There is language encouraging governments to adopt Open Source software (although this will be blocked for the most part by the US and the private sector.) There is language that emphasizes attention to power inequalities, gender, youth, indigenous, migrants, and other marginalized peoples. We also might expect some funds to be made available for development communication projects as a result of the WSIS action plan; at least a few of these projects will likely be well conceived and implemented and will bring access, tools, and skills to underserved populations.

However, the negative experience so far is also clear: civil society has been shut out of the process, civil society and the private sector have been formally lumped together, and there are few funds for participation by people from the 2/3 world (global South, plus poor and marginalized peoples from the North). The WSIS is shaping up to be an ineffective talk shop with no teeth. That may turn out to be a blessing, since human rights are not at the core - crucially, the Draft Declaration section on infrastructure is informed instead by the trickle-down neoliberal vision cloaked in the language of 'enabling market environment' and 'public-private partnership,' code words for the privatization of information and communication systems [see the Draft Declaration, section 6, at http://www.itu.int/dms_pub/itu-s/md/03/wsispcip/td/030721/S03-WSISPCIP-030721-TD-GEN-0001!!PDF-E.pdf].

To be fair, the whole question of 'civil society' participation has been complicated by the decision to allow individual private firms to register as civil society participants, in addition to their representation by delegates from trade associations (and often, by the government delegates as well.) While Canada, Australia, some African countries, and the EU have all pushed for 'civil society and private sector' contributions in the form of working papers, China and Pakistan blocked this proposal during both PrepComs. While some countries may be trying to shut out civil society in order to avoid discussion of internal human rights violations, the conflation of the private sector with civil society also resulted in some more progressive national delegates opposing the meaningful inclusion of 'civil society' on the valid grounds that this would open a back door to greater corporate influence. It is sometimes difficult to sort out which instances of exclusion are due to careful planning by the ITU Secretariat or by national delegates, and which are due to bumbling Secretariat inexperience in dealing with civil society. The upshot, though, is clear: civil society has been marginalized and excluded at every step of the way.

Alternatives

In response, a variety of groups have already begun planning alternative, parallel, countersummit, and protest activities around the WSIS:

- European Independent Media Centers, NoBorder Network: These groups met in April (along with delegates from the CRIS campaign) to discuss an alternative conference the weekend before WSIS, to bring together political and media activists, artists, and cultural workers. They envision a space where "the antiglobalization movements meets the tactical media movement," and will facilitate skillshares and tactical media laboratories before and during the Summit, with radio, TV channels, and web coverage. They have issued a call to 'refuse and resist war and infowar, border management and digital rights management, restrictions on freedom of movement and freedom of communication' [http://www.geneva03.org/moin.cgi/GenevaCall].

- US Media Activists: In the USA, the Summit has not really been on the agenda. The press has completely ignored it, the private sector is only sending low-level representatives so far, it's unclear how involved the Bush administration will be, and the social movements and media activists who do work on communications have all been focused on the June 2nd Federal Communications Commission decision to allow further consolidation of US media systems in the hands of corporate conglomerates [see http://www.reclaimthemedia.org]. Still, some activists and organizations are trying to build on the momentum of the campaign against media monopoly to educate US activists, advocacy groups, and policymakers on the global implications of US communications policy, and to link the domestic issues to the international movement for communication rights.

For example, Free Press Media Reform Network, an umbrella organization that hopes to link policymakers with grassroots media activists, will hold their formative conference in Madison, Wisconsin, in November 2003. While the focus will be on US media policy reform, the organizers are interested in making links to the global communication rights movement. They will include an international strand within their conference that may include discussion of the WSIS and alternatives, possibly generating input to events in December [see www.media-reform.net].

There has also been discussion of a 3rd Break the Media Blackout event. Organizers from the media arm of the Poor People's Economic Human Rights Campaign are interested in a US conference to take place the weekend before the Summit, parallel to the alternative activities in Geneva that are being organized by the IndyMedia Centers and NoBorders Network and hopefully linked to them. They envision poor people's organizations meeting with media activists for skillshares and hands-on tactical media labs as well as education on the global communication rights/media justice movement. They hope to create some kind of statement or message to be delivered in Geneva [see http://www.kwru.org/conference for information about the 2002 Break the Media Blackout Conference].

Some discussions have also begun around parallel activities in San Francisco and in Austin, Texas.

- World Forum on Communication Rights: Perhaps most exciting, the Communication Rights in the Information Society [CRIS: http://www.crisinfo.org] campaign has proposed the launch of a World Forum on Communication Rights. To be held the second day of the WSIS, December 11th, this Forum is conceived not as a one-time event but as the expression of an ongoing process. The first World Forum on Communication Rights will aim to 1. create a Declaration on Communication Rights, with reference to and synthesis of past declarations; 2. provide examples of violations and successful implementations of Communication Rights; 3. create a Set of Actions. The World Forum on Communication Rights will deal with the public domain and alternatives to IPRs, the public sphere and media, the closure of the internet, the promotion of Free/Libre Open Source Software, governance innovation and grassroots communications technology [see http://www.crisinfo.org/live/index.php?section=2&subsection=2&id=32].

- World Social Forum: In Porto Alegre, participants in the 'media, culture, and counter-hegemony' strand agreed that a countersummit would be important, alongside continued 'inside' participation [see http://www.worldsummit2003.de/en/web/190.htm]. In addition, a discussion has been growing around the possibility of a Thematic Social Forum on Communication Rights, perhaps to take place in 2005 as an alternative to the Phase II WSIS meeting in Tunis.

This last proposal takes us to the most important point: if WSIS is best thought of as an organizing opportunity, rather than a forum we can really participate in or a body that will have real power, what are we organizing towards in the long run?

Beyond wsis: building a global movement for communication rights

For those of us trying to build a global movement for communication rights, WSIS is most useful as an agenda-setting event, organizing impetus, and news hook, not as a democratic forum where our concerns will be addressed. It is an opportunity to strengthen the links between the anticorporate globalization (global justice) movement and the fight against wholesale privatization of information and communication systems, or the fight for communication rights. The global justice movement can't proceed without tackling this area; and of course, communication rights can't be won if the movement stays within a relatively small circle of NGOs, media activists, and academics.

To that end, WSIS can be thought of as a potential catalyst for us to develop our own global organizing process and structure around communication rights. As MJ Kim has pointed out, the corporate sector has their own agenda: they are focused on IPRs and privatization of ICT infrastructure, and they lobby hard in every venue.[40] The US has its own agenda, focused on surveillance and cyberterrorism, and they will also lobby hard everywhere. These powerful actors constantly venue-shift, taking the battle from national legislatures to multilateral agreements, from the WTO[41] to

[40] The Coordinating Committee of Business Interlocutors (CCBI) has recently released a statement with a 6-point program: "1. Focus on Information Society Building Blocks; 2. Recognize the Importance of Pro-Competitive Policies and Private Sector Investment; 3. Link ICT investment to economic development, social growth and poverty reduction; 4. Incorporate Measuring and Accounting tools in Summit pronouncements; 5. Prescribe National ICT Strategies; 6. Acknowledge the critical role of Business in the Future of the Information Society" [http://www.itu.int/wsis/docs/im/content_themes/contributions/ccbi.doc].

[41] For example, at the WTO ministerial meeting in Cancun in September, the US will try once again to overturn what is now known as the 'cultural exception' and bring the audiovisual sector into the WTO [see the US proposal at http://docsonline.wto.org/DDFDocuments/t/S/CSS/W21.doc]. If successful, this will mean the elimination of national funding for content production and of quotas on foreign content. Activists are already planning a day of tactical media skillshares combined with policy education, to take place just before the ministerial and train the assembled movements in how to report on their own days of action during the meeting.

WIPO, from the FTAA to ICANN. The global justice movement needs its own space to develop a communications agenda, in order to take the fight to each institution, body, and process, and to the streets in front of each as well. In a way, we need our own version of the ITU – an international forum where the network of networks can develop a progressive agenda on communication rights, with concrete measures and plans of action. WSIS is an opportunity to launch such a forum; to bring together different generations of media activists, strengthen our networks, and voice clear opposition to both state and corporate control of media and communication systems.

To that end, social movements and media activists who are trying to decide whether to engage with WSIS at this point should consider how to best use the event to their advantage, but not get bogged down in spending most of their resources trying to influence the official Declaration and Plan of Action. At the same time, we need to be very clear: It would be shameful to sign on to the Declaration and Action Plan as they are unfolding at this point. By the end of PrepCom 3 we should have a clear counterproposal that denounces the privatization of communication systems, the airwaves and satellite orbits, and the fruits of human creativity and knowledge, demands the removal of the neoliberal language from the Declaration and Action Plan, and threatens a walkout of the Summit itself if these conditions are not met. [They will not, of course, be met.]

If a walkout does become necessary, it should not take place at PrepCom3 but should be delayed until the Summit, since it is a card that can only be played once and will make a much greater impression in December– the PrepComs are not newsworthy, the WSIS December meeting may be to some degree. There, as many civil society organizations as possible (and if possible, national delegates as well) should stage a walkout on the second day – from WSIS to the World Forum on Communication Rights. In one possible scenario, this would be a highly visible, physical movement of people from one venue to another. Others argue for a less 'confrontational' style; a kind of open invitation to the parallel forum.

A brief point about the possibility of more confrontational tactics: at the moment, it doesn't seem necessary to try and shut WSIS down, in part because the Declaration and Plan of Action is still very unclear, and also because it probably won't have much impact. It seems more important to articulate our own vision and strengthen the foundation for our own movement. On the other hand, the symbolic significance could change: especially if Bush attends, it would be worth amplifying confrontation to take a stand against US imperialism in all its manifestations – military, economic, informational - and for communication rights and media justice.[42]

Regardless of the actual form of the walkout, the first day of the Summit should be used to make the intention clear to the full assembly – if possible, one of the Civil Society speaking slots on the first day should be used to announce the demands, the parallel process, and a post-World Forum on Communication Rights press conference. That press conference should provide statements not only from representatives of those in attendance, but also videotaped or live remote statements from key civil society groups, social movements, and figures from around the globe.

Finally, all of the opportunities provided by the Summit notwithstanding, we need to remember that the key decisions about privatization of audiovisual content in the near future will be taken elsewhere, for example at the WTO in Cancun in September, where proposals have already been introduced by the USA, Switzerland, and Brazil[43] to liberalize the AV content industries. Interventions at the WTO and WSIS could be keys to galvanizing a strong communication rights movement.[44] This movement can then intervene in other processes.

Conclusion

To sum up: the Summit has thus far excluded civil society. We can't let the ITU, powerful nations, and the private sector use civil society to give a stamp of legitimacy to a thinly veiled neoliberal agenda of privatization of information and communication systems, privatization of common resources like the electromagnetic spectrum and satellite orbits, erosion of the knowledge commons, and the elimination of communication rights. Rather than boycott the Summit, though, we should participate, using WSIS as an organizing opportunity to develop our own alternatives, strengthen our own vision and plan of action for demanding communication rights, and linking this movement to the global justice movement.

I think it's a waste of time to spend our efforts at WSIS, or at the World Forum on Communication Rights, hammering out carefully crafted statements line by line. We

---

[42] A note here about the term 'media justice,' and the question of racism in the media: media racism should be central to media justice movement, just as environmental racism was central to the emergence of the environmental justice movement (Art McGee has pointed this out). Use WSIS to launch an international media justice movement, led by people of color. (Conference on Racism and Communications, as part of WFCR?).

[43] By the way, I believe the proposal from Brazil came from the old administration, and someone should lobby the Lula administration to retract it. The Brazilian proposal is available here: http://docsonline.wto.org/DDFDocuments/t/S/CSS/W99.doc.

[44] I don't know whether audiovisual content or other aspects of media and communications systems will fall under the FTAA; if so, that's
another important space to intervene.

should approach it as a moment for political theater and an organizing opportunity, which means thinking about ongoing initiatives that can be launched there. We should think about emerging from WSIS with the basis of an organizing structure for a more democratic Forum of our own. The World Forum on Communication Rights is a step in this direction. A Thematic Social Forum on Communication Rights / Media Justice, possibly to be held in 2005 in counterpoint to the second phase of WSIS Tunis, could be another step on the long road to communication rights for all. Thank you.

The WSIS: whose freedom, whose information?[45]

Solana Larsen[46]

The UN's World Summit on the Information Society (WSIS) in Geneva is intended to create ways of bridging the global 'digital divide'. But will its political tensions and complex agenda make it less of an "internet-Kyoto" and more of an arid talk shop?

You can't eat a computer. But having access to information and communication technologies can mean life or death, when it comes to delivering to people around the world necessities like clean water, medical help, education and employment.

Around a third of the world's population has still never made a phone call. Less than one tenth have experienced the internet. This disparity is often referred to as the 'digital divide'. It is not only one of the most important indicators of development today, it has a dynamic link to the persistence of inequalities.

This week in Geneva the first phase of the UN World Summit of the Information Society (WSIS) will gather more than 130 of the world's governments – plus interested representatives of business and what are called 'civil society groups' – to discuss how the world should administer the spread of technology and the internet. The second phase will take place in Tunisia in November 2005.

Thorny issues like internet governance, security, intellectual property, open source software, and not least, who should pay for new infrastructure and technology in the developing world, are on the programme.

It is a gargantuan agenda which WSIS will funnel into a declaration of principles and an action plan for all participants to undersign at the summit's conclusion. Sadly, it is already clear that both will contain gaping holes. The summit is in real danger of becoming nothing but a talk shop.

Nonetheless, it is already clear that its divisions are crystallising some of the significant new issues of start of the century, as divisions between rich and poor

---

[45] On the web at http://www.opendemocracy.net/debates/article-8-10-1630.jsp 9 - 12 - 2003

[46] Solana Larsen is Media & the Net Editor and moderator of the discussion forums at openDemocracy. A Danish-Puerto Rican, she holds an MA in international journalism from London, and has headed dozens of cultural and social projects in the Copenhagen NGO sector. Today, she works for openDemocracy out of New York City and occasionally contributes stories to Danish talk radio

governments, between the global north and south, and between NGOs and state power, criss-cross traditional left-right differences.

Not so civil

The preparatory meetings have gone less than smoothly. A complete breakdown of negotiations has been close more than once. Countries disagree radically on so many things that it is hard to come up with language that can be agreed on by consensus. Nonetheless, for all the hot air, the evasions, the clichés and the diplomatic subsidies, important issues are in play and innovation is occurring.

For the first time at a UN summit, non-governmental participants have been invited to take part in drafting the documents. But some governments – among them China, Egypt, Mexico, and Pakistan – refused to negotiate in their presence.

Civil society participants, who represent over 940 interest organisations, universities, think-tanks, and religious groups, were locked out of meetings on some of the most contentious issues. In frustration over the failure of government to come to terms, they have formed a body and created an alternative declaration.

The only thing everyone can agree on is that there should be more telephones and computers for everyone. In 2000, the UN's member states promised to uphold a list of "Millennium Development Goals". One goal demands there should be a computer with internet access for every 100 people around the world by 2015.

With little more than ten years to get online computers within walking distance of even the poorest of the world's citizens, a meeting of nations is not happening too soon.

The issues that divide

A clear plan is nowhere in sight. China won't hear any mention of human rights and wants governments to have full control over the internet. The United States and Europe have helped weaken proposals on open source software in favour of proprietary software (like Microsoft's). And many of the wealthiest countries would like all mention of financial support for the developing world erased from the declaration of principles.

The reality is that WSIS is not just about bringing computers to the poor. It is also about making money from selling them equipment and software; privatisation of national communications industries; investment and infrastructure. And it is about seizing power over the internet as it spreads. Many governments want to rein it in and have more direct control.

There are five major issues that stand out at the summit and remain irresolvable for the near future.

Bridging the digital divide

Who will pay for the development of infrastructure in Africa and the rest of the developing world? The poorest nations are hoping the summit might lead to commitments from the rich to cover some of the costs. The president of Senegal, Abdoulaye Wade, is behind a proposal to create a "digital solidarity fund" for the poorest countries. He suggests it would be "painless" for $1 from the purchase of every computer, software package, or network equipment to go to the fund. Other suggestions include taxing international telephone calls or commercial use of the radio frequency spectrum.

The United States, European Union, Canada and Japan have all declared themselves against the idea, and suggest Africa would be better served by establishing an environment in which the private sector would develop the needed infrastructure – for instance through deregulation. The World Bank has also been dismissive of a fund, saying it would cost too much money to manage it on a daily basis compared with the benefits.

Open Source versus Microsoft

One of the most inhibiting barriers to the spread of computers in the developing world is the cost of software like Microsoft Windows, which is not only expensive but needs to be updated regularly at a steep price. Governments can save billions simply by switching to free and open source software like Linux, which can be updated or modified gratis by anyone, helped by a global community of programmers. India, Peru, Brazil and South Africa are among nations who have already started switching over to viable alternatives to Microsoft.

In what many suspect is a response to the mounting business threat from open source software, Bill Gates and Microsoft have been donating billions of dollars worth of software and aid to the developing countries where open source is most popular. Accusations abound that United States and European Union delegates at WSIS are in the pockets of Microsoft lobbyists. Certainly, in the centre of the negotiations, the draft for the WSIS declaration of principles has gone from outright "support" of open source software for the developing world to "promoting awareness" about "different software models, and the means of their creation, including proprietary, open source and free software".

Intellectual property

The issue of intellectual property has become explosive with the advent of digital technology, which enables anyone to make a quick and perfect copy of anything that can be stored on a computer. Since the original Napster, free file-sharing software has accelerated, hurting the profits of the music and film industry (and by extension the American economy). The legal battle between rich copyright holders and regular computer users in Europe and America has been fierce. But the loaded guns of the entertainment business are also aimed at developing nations like China where piracy is both rampant and a significant gain for the economy.

Hollywood lobbyists are given a lot of credit for new, stringent international legislation for the protection of copyright. The extension of copyright periods, and closure of old loopholes like "fair use", impact on what is allowed to enter the public domain. Developing nations may have less free access to content from literature and science, to policy statements, basic statistical data and social and political analysis – all in different ways important tools of development.

Freedom and security

Fear of terrorism fuels the emphasis on "security" at WSIS. Reliability and integrity of the internet is also required for growth of the United States's priorities. "Network security" is at the top of their list.

China and Russia are attempting to switch the emphasis onto "information security" and "military security", causing alarm among critics that the declaration of principles could be used by nations to legitimise censorship and invasions of privacy through surveillance.

Their alarm may be justified. In the draft declaration, a free and independent media are currently only promised "in accordance with the legal system of each country". This is a significant step back from Article 19 of the Universal Declaration of Human Rights that guarantees "freedom to hold opinions without interference and to seek, receive and impart information and ideas through any media regardless of frontiers".

Once again, China is stubbornly opposed to such basic rights. But there are many others with dirty track records, such as Tunisia, the 2005 host of the WSIS. After nearly a year and a half, this country still holds the editor of satirical website Tunezine, Zouhair Yahyaoui, in jail for being critical of the country's president, Zine El Abidine Ben Ali.

Internet governance

Nobody owns the internet. But one of the most important organisations involved in its management is the Internet Corporation for Assigned Names and Numbers (ICANN). It decides who assigns names to the number addresses on the net. It's a non-profit organisation with board members around the world, but it is based in California and answers to the US department of commerce. The European Union, the United States, and the Mexican and Canadian governments are all happy with this arrangement.

Developing countries like Brazil, South Africa, India and Bangladesh feel that ICANN is too American and corporate-controlled, and would prefer to see internet governance follow the guidance of the International Telecommunications Union (ITU), which happens to be the organiser of WSIS on behalf of the UN. China agrees, and is furthermore furious with ICANN for allowing Taiwanese representation on their government advisory board. Which form of internet management will be more democratic: a complex government bureaucracy that could inhibit the growth of a medium fuelled by speedy innovation – or a body that answers to US rules?

If the negotiations at WSIS can be used as a gauge for what government management of the internet might look like, we should be very concerned.

Old and new divides

The fact that these five major issues are being discussed on a global scale at the WSIS is great. Yet even as it starts, many observers disdain the summit and dismiss its chances of success. The challenge of creating an "internet-Kyoto" which could secure a more democratic, global information society is in the balance.

The quarrels between governments move along the axis of rich and poor, north and south. These divisions predate digital technology. "Anyone who has been paying attention to issues of the so-called digital divide will tell you that it is simply a symptom of the injustices that already exist between rich and poor countries," says

Sasha Costanza-Chock from Communication Rights in the Information Society (CRIS), a campaign to ensure communication rights are central to WSIS.

Negotiations between civil society groups have not been marred by the same problems as those of governments. Instead, most of the groups share a vision for development. But is this because they are genuinely representative, or mainly self-selected?

Who is right and who wrong?

One of the interesting developments that seems to be emerging from WSIS is the shared identity between its civil society participants. The evolving reality called 'information society' is so encompassing that groups as different as Rotary International and the Global Alliance for Women's Health have found themselves on the same side of the picket line.

In plenary sessions at preparatory meetings, the non-government group organised a communications network, whose email lists and numerous working groups have finished an alternative declaration of principles. This seeks to promote freedom, justice and equality. "I'll bet you if you put the two declarations next to each other, the civil society declaration will give you a much better, more coherent and progressive picture of what governments should be doing," says William Drake, a board director at Computer Professionals for Social Responsibility.

But will it be so clear-cut? No doubt governments need to set their differences aside, get their priorities straight, and listen to the unofficial groups from an emerging global civil society that is working to bring information and communications technologies to the *whole* world, developing as well as developed.

But on the eve of the WSIS summit, the divisions are more apparent than the unities and what is fascinating and acutely necessary to understand, is that these divisions are cross-cutting and not simply polarising.

The two familiar oppositions in the discussion of information society issues – that between governments and non-governmental, or 'civil society', groups on the one hand, and that between the rich north and the poor south on the other – intersect, but do not neatly overlap.

It is often the governments of the global south, ostensibly representing millions of the world's poor (like China) which most vigorously seek to deny a proper voice to

NGOs in discussion and decision-making, whereas it is often the governments of rich countries (like the European Union member states) which are ready to accommodate them. If campaigning NGOs truly represent a broader, democratic constituency of interest and are accountable for their views (propositions that need to be argued for and not assumed as fact) then it cannot be said that their natural 'allies' in their progressive project are the governments of predominantly poor countries.

The lack of overlap between different sorts of division is also reflected in the arguments over which body – ICANN or the ITU – should take the lead in the future governance of the internet. The defence of ICANN may appear to symbolise conformity to a US-defined authority over the internet. But it could also preserve its space from governance from state diktat. The apparently 'multilateral' and variegated system implied by granting authority to the ITU (as advocated by many governments from the global south) might prove to be an attempt by states to carve up power among themselves in a way that limits the space of freedom granted to their own citizens.

In this mosaic of arguments at the WSIS summit, who is the champion of freedom in the information society? The responsibility of those who seek to expand open, democratic space and discussion about new technologies is to argue the case in terms of practicality as well as principle, utility as well as ideology, and citizens' rights as well as ownership or control of institutions.

Unzipping the World Summit on the Information Society[47]

Alan Toner[48]

The World Summit on the Information Society (WSIS) has already attracted the attention of the critical media community. Here, Alan Toner of Autonomedia and New York's Information Law Institute examines what's at stake at the Summit and how its agenda reflects changes in the post-industrial location of power, describing some working strategies for intervention in the WSIS process from 'independent' and contestatory communications groups formed outside last year's European Social Forum.

A tale of two terms

We begin with a tale of two terms: the well aired and well known 'Information Society', and its rather furtive and less well known relation, 'intellectual property' (IP). One of the decade's great shibboleths, 'Information Society' was a phrase recycled throughout the '90s by policy hacks, academics and gurus alike. Employed variously to herald the expansion of digital networks, the permeation of labour by information processes, and the shift from tangible to intangible goods, 'Information Society' seemed to imply something inexorable, a consequence of the massive mediatisation of the preceding years, outside any one set of strategic interests – something, we were constantly reminded, 'we would all have to adapt to.'

What this rhetoric largely occluded was the wave of expansionist intellectual property laws which accompanied the 'informaticisation' of society. These legal constraints, at whose epicentre sits the Trade Related Aspects of Intellectual Property Rights (TRIPS), annex to the General Agreement on Trades and Tariffs (GATTs), have served a very strategic set of interests within the post-industrial scene. They have effectively reversed the notional role of IP laws from the protection of cultural production and scientific/technological innovation to the limitation of these creative forces, and served to fix relations between advanced post-industrial states and the former 'third world'. They have done this by creating copyright monopolies which drive concentration of ownership, push up costs of entry into markets, and exclude effective activity for many independent actors.

---

[47] On the web at www.hubproject.org/news/2003/09/78.php

[48] Alan Toner <alan@kein.org> is an activist and researcher working from Rome, Italy. He is part of the Autonomedia collective

Advanced 'post-industrial' states now compel others to observe legal norms that effectively disallow certain forms of innovation, production and organisation. The states thus impacted are effectively limited, through control over invention and information, to a role as factors in the system of global production that has the major powers of the North at its centre. The agreements ensure that even where production is transferred to these areas due to lower labour and production costs, the profits continue to flow to New York, London and Zurich.

Copyright laws protect commerce from competition and from its own customers, allowing it to charge a rent on the past which finances domination of markets in the present – and which, in turn, is taken to guarantee the future. This putative guarantee comes at a certain price: software licenses checked at gunpoint in Brazil; 40 people arrested in Madrid in a swoop on pirate CD/DVD network (industry lobbyists insist such operations bankroll terrorism); a Russian software engineer arrested and jailed in the United States after a conference presentation of his work before thousands; indigenous Indians in Chiapas rioting after a police raid on a market of infringing goods; an 18-year-old Norwegian prosecuted for enabling a Linux based DVD player; American citizens sharing music prosecuted as felons; university researchers charged with criminal trade secrets offences for publishing knowledge derived from their own research works; China summarily executing trademark pirates as disciplinary examples. In AIDS-ravaged sub-Saharan Africa and Asia, pharmaceutical companies have instigated actions through the WTO and in national courts to prevent the cheap manufacture of the anti-retrovirals necessary for people to survive. Where once corpses accumulated to the advance of colonialism or the indifference of commodity capital, now they hang in the profit and loss scales of Big Pharma, actuarially accounted for and calculated against licensing and royalty revenue. With the aid of stringent IP law, companies are able exercise a biopolitical control that takes to new extremes the tendency to liberate capital by restricting individual and collective freedoms and rights – even the right to life itself.

Introducing wsis

You might be forgiven for imagining that one of the first imperatives of an occasion such as the World Summit on Information Society, due to take place in Geneva in December 2003, would be to address the social terrors being carried out in the defence of intellectual property. Unfortunately such topics are firmly off the agenda. The stated 'objective' of the WSIS is defined as the building of 'a common vision and understanding of the information society' in full regalia.[49] WSIS is presented in the literature promoting the event as

> [a] dynamic process [which] promises a fundamental change in all aspects of our lives, including knowledge dissemination, social interaction, economic and business practices, political engagement, media, education, health, leisure and entertainment. We are indeed in the midst of a revolution, perhaps the greatest that humanity has ever experienced [...] The roles of the various partners (Member States, UN specialised agencies, private sector and civil society) in ensuring smooth coordination of the practical establishment of the information society around the globe will also be at the heart of the Summit and its preparation [...] the anticipated outcome of the Summit is to develop and foster a clear statement of political will and a concrete plan of action for achieving the goals of the Information Society, while fully reflecting all the different interests at stake.[50]

Such nebulous policy extravaganzas have been a regular staple of the international scene since the Stockholm Conference on the Environment in 1972, and have ranged thematically from women (Beijing 1995) to sustainable development (Johannesburg 2002). These events have been a key theatre for the emergence of so-called 'civil society', a panoply of NGOs seeking recognition as representatives of minority constituencies, 'universal' values or specialist knowledge. Such constituencies, it is argued, are easily neglected during the legislative process, but necessary in enabling 'deliberative democracy'. An increasingly obvious trait of such affairs has been their inconsequentiality, especially when juxtaposed with the unforgiving machinations of the World Trade Organisation or the potentially lethal repercussions of being the subject of 'assistance' from the World Bank/IMF. Promissory rhetoric and problem-solving enthusiasm may provide a compelling tenor for the media function such events serve, but are misleading as a guide to actual efficacy. WSIS, first mooted at the decision making plenary of the International Telecommunications Union (ITU) in Minneapolis, 1998, seems little different. The summit co-host, Tunisia, has already flagged its engagement with the issues by arresting and imprisoning web activist Zouhair Yahyaoui, editor of online journal TUNeZINE and ardent critic of Tunisia's human rights record. In April, Yahyaoui began a second hunger strike in jail.

---

[49] Resolution adopted by the General Assembly 56/183, World Summit on the Information Society
[50] From Wsis.org

Futures past

Information and communications have been the subject of two previous international initiatives since the Second World War. The first, the UN's 1948 Conference on the Freedom of Information, also in Geneva, was overshadowed by Cold War tensions.

But ensuing attempts at the World Intellectual Property Organisation (WIPO) to revise the Paris Convention governing industrial property (patents and trademarks) and to expand the role of compulsory licensing at the UN Conference on Trade and Development (UNCTAD) were more successful. At UNESCO, demands for a 'New World Information and Communication Order' (NWICO), premised on a critique of media concentration and cultural domination of third world countries by foreign states and commercial interests, postulated the centrality of informational flows to economic development and argued that systemic inequalities in such flows obstructed countries from developing local media industries that could allow them to represent themselves.

Out of the Declaration on Mass Media at UNESCO's 1978 conference came the establishment of a commission to study communications issues, which two years later published 'Many Voices, One World', better known as the MacBride Report, setting out a program promoting diversity of ownership, plurality of opinion and guarantees of cultural identity.[51] Despite the moderation of its claims, the MacBride report incensed media and broadcast associations, especially in the US, culminating in the 1981 'Declaration of Taillores' demanding that UNESCO 'abandon attempts to regulate news content and formulate rules for the press.' Right-wing analysts such as the Heritage Foundation characterised UNESCO as having an 'anti- Western bias',

> rampant budgetary mismanagement, and advocacy of policies that undermine freedom of the press and free markets [....] advocacy of a 'new world information order' (NWIO) to counter an alleged pro-Western bias in global news agencies; specifically, the organisation sought the licensing of journalists, the creation of an international code of press ethics, and increasing government control over the media [...] [52]

Ultimately the United States left UNESCO in 1984 (depriving it of 30 percent of its budget) followed shortly thereafter by Britain and Singapore. All of these negotiations had taken place in multilateral fora, a terrain for which the Reagan

---

[51] Useful background to this period is to be found in Susan Sell's *Power and Ideas: North-South Politics of Intellectual Property and Antitrust* (Albany: State University of New York Press, 1997)

[52] Brett D. Schaefer, *Look Before Leaping to Rejoin UNESCO*, Executive Memorandum #746 [http://www.heritage.org/Research/InternationalOrganizations/EM745.cfm]

administration had little taste, preferring the conditions of bilateral negotiation where US economic and military clout could be wielded with less modesty. Companies such as Pfizer and IBM, as well as trade associations like the Motion Picture Association of America (MPAA) decided that the genteel style of WIPO, the numerical supremacy of the developing countries, and the lack of an enforcement mechanism for international copyright and patent treaties, made it unsuitable for their purposes. That same year, amidst a sharpening debt crisis that undermined the solidarity of the Group of 77, negotiations to revise the Paris convention collapsed, followed twelve months later by the termination of the negotiations for a code on technology transfer. But despite its jettisoning, the spectre of the NWICO continues to haunt old cold warriors such as the World Press Freedom Campaign, who periodically circulate scare stories of its return.

Information (real) politik

The US Administration's new bilateral trade-based strategy debuted in 1983 in the form of the Caribbean Basin Economic Recovery Act, which offered duty-free access to US markets for certain goods, contingent on compliance with US intellectual property norms – a template later employed in numerous other bilateral deals. The following year, US copyright industries united to establish the International Intellectual Property Alliance (IIPA) which was to pursue a trade route towards copyright enforcement. The IIPA's first achievements were the amendment of the US Trade Act to allow the initiation of formal trade retaliations against non-compliant states under Section 301, and conditioning access to US Markets via the Generalised System of Preferences to those satisfying the stipulated level of intellectual property protection. In some cases staff were actually dispatched to countries such as the Dominican Republic to rewrite copyright law.[53]

Subsequently India and Brazil, two countries formerly at the forefront of the enforcement drive in the UN, were singled out for action under 301. In 1986, with the Uruguay Round of the GATT negotiations on the horizon, the IIPA was supplemented by a new industry group, the Intellectual Property Committee (IPC), determined to ensure that corporate IP concerns be inserted into the negotiation agenda and fully integrated into any ultimate agreement. It was the IPC's efforts to orchestrate business lobbying efforts on a global basis which culminated in TRIPS, now administered by the WTO. TRIPS will transfer an estimated 40 billion dollars

[53] For more on the shift to a trade based paradigm of intellectual property see *Information Feudalism: Who Owns the Knowledge Economy?* Peter Drahos and John Braithwaite, New Press, 2003

from the poorest states over the next ten years, according to the World Bank, via patented medicines and seeds, and net rent transfers through royalties and licenses.[54]

Military humanism

The aftermath of the Trade Towers conflagration has been marked by an undisguised turn towards unilateralism by the United States. Clinton had proposed rejoining UNESCO, ending reliance on bilateralism, but recoiled in the face of fierce Republican opposition. Now such bellicose commentators see a missed opportunity: UN institutions, it is believed, hold great potential as a precinct for the continuation of military operations. Here, ideological dissemination and the promotion of 'cultural understanding' can take place, a project Perry Anderson styles 'military humanism'.[55]

Accordingly, after September 11, the US paid some of the dues it owed to the UN. George Bush announced his intention to rejoin UNESCO last September, just before presenting the 'evidence' that would be used to justify the war on Iraq. While old foes of UNESCO like the Heritage foundation may have understood the logic of rejoining, they continued to support 'bilateral aid' (better known as bribery), 'public diplomacy programs' and 'voluntary contributions' to the organisation. But increased accusations of unilateralism following the unendorsed assault on Iraq are encouraging the strategy of exploitation of organisations such as the UN. The fact that they exercise very little power only means that they cannot pose any real threat of constraint, either on business practice or military might. What they do offer, in the words of Ronald Koven are

> real opportunities [...] to advance the ideological interests of the international coalition against terrorism [...] September 11 demonstrated that US security can no longer be defined in purely military terms and that the extremist offensive against American cultural values must be answered through school curriculums, working for tolerance and rationalism and the correcting of cultural misperceptions in foreign publics. [My emphasis.] [56]

Koven's advocacy in favour of UNESCO is doubly significant in that he works for the World Press Freedom Committee, an outpost of cold war thinking and permanent sentinel against any attempt to reinvigorate the NWICO. Assumption of such a pro-

---

[54] 'Intellectual Property Rights and Economic Development', Keith J. Maskus, *Case Western Reserve Journal of International Law*, vol. 32 (2000), p. 471

[55] See, for example, Perry Anderson, 'Casuastries of Peace and War', in *London Review of Books*, Vol. 25, No. 5 dated 6 March 2003

[56] James H. Ottaway Jr. and Ronald Koven, The New UNESCO, *The Washington Post*, Wednesday, July 17, 2002; Page A23

UNESCO position by Koven signals that the organisation is now seen as favourable to the 'free flow' of information.

A conference without content

This evacuation of power from UN organisations poses a dilemma : what can be meaningfully discussed at WSIS? The draft declaration indicates the questionable content of the 'information society' concept itself, comprising 71 different points and resuscitating a ruse reminiscent of the heights of the 'dot com' folly: addition of prefix 'E-' to any given area of human activity to cast it as an 'ICT issue' (E-administration, E-Learning and so on). Meanwhile substantial media-themes have been marginalised to such an extent that the European Broadcasters Union recently threatened to pull out of the WSIS altogether unless its concerns were addressed. Such an embarrassing scene would be the ultimate disaster for the Swiss, who are hosting their first UN event since they joined the organisation in September 2002, desperate for a diplomatic and publicity triumph.

It is in this light that the pious discourse on the digital divide must be considered. This great divide is a matter which thoroughly exercises policy lovers within the G8, who established the suggestively titled 'DOTForce' to suggest how the chasm might be bridged – by free market means, of course. Rhetoric and reality starkly diverge: development agencies set a target of connecting every family and village by 2005 in a context of constantly dwindling budgets and the emasculation of sources of self-financing such as the Accounting Rate Mechanism. [9] Likewise the sole surviving product of the NWICO debate within UNESCO, the International Program for the Development of Communication (IPDC) has been so denied resources as to cripple it entirely: in 2001, contributions to the IPDC program at UNESCO hit an all-time low of US$1.25 million. Given that major 'donors' slashed aid through the '90s – US development funding is smaller as a proportion of the total economy than at any time since the advent of official statistics – the likelihood of any tangible effects arising from the programme is negligible.

Fear on the table

Whilst eschewing controls upon capital, the modern state's appetite for the restriction of individual and collective freedom continues unabated. Thus the exception to the taboo on regulatory initiatives at WSIS: the Cybercrime Treaty, presented at the second preparatory meeting for the Summit under the legend 'Taming the World Wide Web.'

Negotiations on the treaty began in secrecy between the Council of Europe, the US Department of Justice and assorted intelligence interests in 1997. Its text, finalised in November 2001, bolstered police powers of search and seizure and expanded existing international cooperation programs for the collection of evidence and the interception of communications. The treaty, a policeman's wish-list, pays no heed to individual rights and privacy in its articulation of an authoritarian programme of data accumulation. Particularly startling, however, is Article 10, requiring the institution of criminal punishments for copyright infringements where 'such acts are committed wilfully, on a commercial scale and by means of a computer system.' Criminal sanctions in copyright law have historically been circumscribed to commercial counterfeiting operations, but as this provision does not require any pecuniary motivation, it would enable, for example, the criminal prosecution of users of file sharing systems who share their music with others. In a similar vein Article 6 criminalises possession, manufacture or distribution of devices that can be used to gain illegal access.

As must now be clear, behind the WSIS' 'broad and general view' of 'knowledge dissemination, social interaction, economic and business practices, political engagement, media, education, health, leisure and entertainment' lies a very specific and ongoing set of strategies designed to use control of information, and information property, to advance Northern interests on the global scene. Meanwhile the US intends to make sure that these same strategies cannot be simultaneously used against its interests. Its intentions in this respect were signalled clearly by the Intergovernmental Statement which concluded the European Regional Preparation Meeting for WSIS in Bucharest, whose principle 6 is worth quoting at length:

> A global culture of cyber-security needs to be developed – security must be addressed through prevention and supported throughout society, and be consistent with the need to preserve free flow of information [...] Information Communications Technologies can potentially be used for purposes that are inconsistent with the objectives of maintaining international stability and security and may adversely affect the integrity of the infrastructure within States, to the detriment of their security in both civil and military fields, as well as in relation to the functioning of their economies. It is also necessary to prevent the use of information resources or technologies for criminal or terrorist purposes [...] In order to build confidence and security in the use of ICTs, Governments should promote awareness in their societies of cyber-security risks and seek to strengthen international co-operation, including with the private sector.[57]

---

[57] Elsewhere the revenue-sharing 'Accounting Rate Mechanism' instituted by the ITU has been discarded. This term refers to the calculation by which telephone companies divide income from calls between the country of origin and that in which it is received. Until recently this figure was 50% of a fictitious fixed rate, distinct from both cost of

Subsequent briefings in Washington, hosted by the International Telecommunications Advisory Committee, reiterated the administration's commitment to advancing the security agenda in Geneva, insisting that it is one of only three areas (the others being training and infrastructural expansion) where any agreement is 'foreseeable.' So far the US has manifested relative indifference to the WSIS, and the impact of the security agenda will hinge upon the degree to which they apply their muscular approach to the Summit. In the meantime the usual triggers for moral panics on the net – drugs, terrorists, money launderers and paedophilia – can be expected (recent reports of the use of p2p tools for sharing child porn are an example) as well as the continued blurring of the category of 'cyberterrorism' to potentially include any radical use of new media technologies.

The problem with ngos

In April 2002, 15 months after the closure of applications of the job and just four months before the first preparatory conference, an executive director of the WSIS secretariat was appointed: Pierre Gagne, a Canadian bureaucrat with the ITU. The lateness of this appointment means that no significant decisions can be taken at the Summit, even by the usual low standards of such spectacles. Unfortunately, the ITU's insistence that the WSIS would be a 'new' type of summit, built on a 'multi-stakeholder model' involving states, intergovernmental organisations, business and civil society, has not come to very much. There has been little opportunity to make a mark on the Summit's direction. Contact with the organisers is mediated through a WSIS secretariat comprising three divisions, the civil society element being managed by the Swiss Fondation de Devenir, which has assumed the role of 'mediating the mediators'. NGO participants discovered that while decisions on procedural form were to be discussed in the ITU building (where Pakistan and China were doing their utmost to have participation limited strictly to state-actors), they themselves were to be quarantined across the road where a programme of discussions had been scheduled for them by the Civil Society Directorate.

The very participation of the NGOs, restricted though it is, raises questions. To what extent is their involvement solicited merely to give the Summit legitimacy? Without

---

provision or charge to the user. This system once constituted an important source of income for developing countries – in 1996 the United States, for example, had a deficit of 5.6 billion dollars, much of which flowed to poor neighbouring countries. From 1997 the FCC announced a reduced accounting rate, practically capping the amounts transferred. Although the ITU responded with an alternative proposal in 1999, it was by this time too late and many countries had adopted the FCC system. Interestingly, legal restraints on the domestic market for sex-lines in the US catalysed the use of innovative routing mechanisms via peripheral nations such as Guyana, who receives up to 40% of its Gross Domestic Product from such calls. See Frederick E. Allen, 'When Sex Drives Technological Innovation and Why It Has To.' [http://www.plannedparenthood.org/education/updatearch.html]

the NGOs the emptiness of the windy sermonising might be all the more apparent. On the other hand, the absence of any real decision making intent at WSIS means that there is scarcely a process to 'launder'. And social movements as a whole have not agitated effectively around intellectual property and technology, despite the centrality of such themes for those involved in movement communications. As a result efforts at cooption by state and intergovernmental actors would bc premature. Some hope for NGO activity comes in the form of Communication Rights in the Information Society (CRIS), a campaign formed at the World Social Forum in Porto Alegre in November 2001 from a pre-existing alliance of NGOs known as the 'Platform for Communication Rights' including such organisations such as the Association for Progressive Communications and Computer Professionals for Social Responsibility. CRIS is highly critical of the official WSIS agenda for its fixation on technical issues, neglect of the social context, and fetishisation of the digital at the expense of what may be more accessible and useful technologies such as radio. CRIS formulates an explicitly dialogic conception of 'communication rights' predicated on the potential to produce and disseminate messages, as well as the 'freedom' to receive them. Its aspiration is towards a democratisation of the media, rather than the restraint of private actors by the state (although some of its constituent groups continue to advocate ownership controls on a national level).

CRIS have pressured the ITU for more transparency, financing for non-Western participation and adoption of content relevant to its communication rights agenda. Unlike other NGO participants they see the WSIS as a context to be instrumentalised in a broader struggle rather than an end in itself. This attitude turns out to dovetail well with the strategies of the radical media contingent which will be present in Geneva during the WSIS. Indeed, the two groups met in April this year to discuss the potentials for interaction both in- and outside the Summit.

Communications insurgency

Protagonists in an ad hoc network born at The Hub, an autonomous space parallel to the official European Social Forum (see *Mute* 25) had already begun organising their own campaign around the WSIS prior to this meeting. Their Geneva meeting brought together these 'hubbers', largely focused on autonomous media infrastructures and the possibility of social economies existing in defiance of intellectual property, members of the Make World organisation, representatives of CRIS and Italian elements of the Indymedia collective. Together, these groups initiated the organisation of an event immediately prior to the Summit, offering the opportunity to discuss the substantive issues denied delegates at the WSIS in the context of a critique of liberalisation, privatisation and 'free' competition. Against this discursive background, the event will also offer the opportunity for emancipatory communications and participation in a 'polymedia' lab dedicated to broadcasting by any means necessary – via television, radio, streaming media and wireless networks. The event will foreground skills and knowledge sharing. Providing an interface for remote participation through multidirectional streaming and other tools will both open the event to greater participation and also addresses another theme confronted at the ESF Hub in Florence: namely, the means to go beyond summit-hopping and focus on embedded local processes. This environment of experimentation will be accompanied by continuous workshops in practice, advocacy and theory.

Alongside these actions, CRIS have proposed a one day seminar to take place inside the vast Palexpo complex in which the plenary sessions will take place, and where some of their members have to be present as part of national delegations. CRIS has three main aims: to bring together governments and NGOs disaffected by the neoliberal paradigm, initiate concrete projects that could have a more enduring impact in areas such as spectrum allocations policy, and to develop a more radical declaration on the 'information society' that will counter the asinine production of the 'official' summit .

The vagueries of the WSIS agenda offer the chance for an agitation that is broader still, going well beyond questions immediately related to digital regulation and media to embrace the fight against patents for access to essential medicines, restrictions in movement of knowledge under trade secret laws and technology transfer. The hope is that extramural opposition to the WSIS, in collaboration with informed participants on the inside, can monitor any dangers, and exploit what benefits there are to be had from discussing the issues shadowed at the Summit with delegates 'extracted' from its hallowed precincts.

Rather than surrendering to what passes for substantive discussion in those climes, social radicals are mustering the critical tools assembled in recent years to effect an *in situ* demonstration of communications insurgency. Geneva 2003 does offer a rare chance for substantial exchanges with media workers from outside the post-Fordist core, extending existing global networks, and building bridges to material and immaterial workforces affected by and effecting informational regimes.

Practically, an orientation-blueprint for this counter-event may be provided by Yochai Benkler's dissection of the communications structure into three layers: physical, logical and content.[58] The physical layer comprises not only the machines

[58] Jochai Benkler, From Consumers to Users, Shifting the Deeper Structures of Regulation Towards Sustainable Commons and User Access, 52 Fed. Comm. L.K. 561 (2000)

but the copper wire, cables, satellites and spectrum. Logical tasks are performed by (for example) webservers, mail servers and operating systems. The content layer entails entertainment and other forms of informational inputs. According to this model, really existing communications freedom is predicated upon the existence of non-proprietary options at each level. The ad hoc event outside WSIS addresses these three layers in its focus on the capacity of unlicensed wireless networks to liberate carriage from the physical infrastructure, the free and open source software development of network and productivity tools, and the protection of a non-proprietary space of creative and informational work.

Unpacking the layers of struggle

At the infrastructural layer, hitherto comprising cable network, satellite and traditional telecommunications systems, advances in radio technology have rendered former spectrum policy schema redundant, premised as they were on broadcast and reception devices that required tight control over frequency usage to prevent interference. Spread spectrum, software-defined radio and ultra-wide band (UWB) radio technologies have transformed usage potential by allowing coordination by devices themselves. Conservative critics, perceiving a danger to establishment control of media infrastructures, are demanding the institution of full property rights in this spectrum, arguing that this will allow the formation of an effective secondary market and guarantee that the resource will find its useful and valuable application, consistent with free market doctrine. This conflict between open spectrum advocates and property-rights militants is only now coming into public view, as consciousness of spectrum issues has risen with the proliferation of community wireless networks on the unlicensed band around 2.4Ghz and the standard 802.11.

The International Telecommunications Union has responsibility for the international coordination of spectrum allocation and holds a World Radiocommunications Conference every two years, the next of which takes place in June. One of the items on the agenda there will be plans for the use of the frequencies above 5GHz where there are also some trenches of unlicensed spectrum, over which 802.11a devices are functioning. Ultra Wide Bandwidth advocates have argued for a full GHz of spectrum to be allocated to unlicensed use. The US military opposes this proposition with claims that it would interfere with radar operation. Campaigning on this issue towards the construction of alternative media infrastructures is forming an important part of provisions against the WSIS.

At the logical layer, language endorsing preferential use of free and open source software was excised from the Asian Regional Meeting for the WSIS in Tokyo, again at the behest of the United States. But there is a powerful movement to adopt and encourage non-proprietary software models, both on a national level in the former third world and regionally within Europe and some US States. Freedom from proprietary restrictions, it is hoped, might allow 'third world' countries to circumvent obstacles to their autonomous development presented by IP-protected media tools, developing applications tailored to their social and cultural needs, and bringing important forces to the worldwide developer and software engineering community.

The content layer has seen celebrated conflicts in peer-to-peer information exchange using software such as Napster, Audiogalaxy and many others. Whilst every recombinant wanderer on the network may be denounced as copyright infringer or even felon, this *de facto* expansion of the 'public domain' seems set to continue. Exploitation of the GATT/TRIPS provisions in legislatures from the US to the EU and continuous acquisition by the infotainment cartels have utterly failed to prevent the sharing of immaterial 'property' in *ad hoc* autonomous distributed networks. To the establishment's shivers of fear over revenues lost through 'piracy', the file-sharing subject responds with shivers of pleasure at the joy of collective access and continuous cooperative transformation. From Ogg to DivX, setting up file-sharing systems to disabling firewalls, technologies of sharing are being deployed, expressing our identity as commoners, confronting cartels with mass illegality. The task now is to valorise this process of giving and receiving within the network as a constitutive social relationship beyond the mere acquisition of media products. 'Information freedom' no longer constitutes a radical demand in these terms. Instead, the potential of peer relations and resource sharing lies in the capacity for a true autonomous infrastructure and autonomy of action. Stripping the behemoths of their *warez* has been easy; cracking the iron curtain of market domination over individual preference may not prove so simple. This constitutes a real territory of conflict to be addressed during the Geneva '03 event. Our informational freedom, as James Boyle has said, is at best potential:

No theory can grant it to us. It must be taken through collective action and imagination, through the postulation of a fictive 'we' that becomes real only in the context of a practice which presupposes the very community it calls into being. The intellectual land-grab ... can be halted, and even pushed into reverse.[59]

[59] Boyle, op. cit

Seizing... You can't beat the feeling![60]

Document of Geneva03

The WSIS positions itself as an opportunity to develop a common vision of an 'information society' and bundles with it a series of promises; a just world; more transparent government; bridging of digital divides. An examination of the material propositions, trade agreement (WTO, FTAA) realpolitik, and the positions of market dominance and social misery left untouched, and unmentioned, tell a different story.

As communications networks spread information becomes central to both production and the organization of social institutions. But rather than making life easier, informationalization supplements and intensifies production and labor. Spiraling demand for productivity imposes close-quarters labor surveillance; dockers' movements' tracked as they move palettes around a warehouse; the waitress whose orders are memorized and who must balance her float exactly at the end of the shift; the temporary worker assigned to a new data entry office or call center every couple of days. Benefits of digitalization accrue principally to those who have the capital resources and power to capture them, and the fight over the laws regulating the digital sphere is a struggle over the destination of this wealth between global regions and social classes.

The purpose of new legal instruments has not been to 'reform' but to extend and entrench preexisting commercial interests. A clear example are the laws on digital television (DTV) introduced in the US and Italy which intensify monopolistic and oligopolistic control over the media, closing the potential for other voices created by DTV's efficient use of radio spectrum for broadcast. In DTV there has been subterfuge, but copyrights, patents and trademarks have simply been extended and enforced by means of coercion based on trade sanctions under TRIPS and bilateral treaties. When the essential raw materials of production are knowledge and data - both of which can be shared and reproduced infinitely - these laws limit the productive potential of social cooperation, by maintaining an artificial scarcity of that which is in fact plentiful.

The preparation process for this summit has been long and tedious. Initially enthusiastic NGOs have seen their hopes evaporate. The basic reformist agenda has received no significant concessions even within the merely discursive framework the

---

[60] On the web at www.geneva03.org, posted *Wednesday December 10, 2003 at 01:34 AM*

summit offers. Attempts to establish a new fund to finance Southern development have been stymied; language extolling the benefits of free software and public interests in 'intellectual property' (IP) has been expunged; the drive to elaborate a substantial legal concept of communication rights has been blocked. To add ignominy to business as usual, groups such as Reporters Sans Frontiers and Human Rights in China have been barred from participation for having raised rights abuses by participating states.

The failure of the WSIS is no surprise and occurs in a continuum of defeat for reformist movements in the ICT field stretching 25 years. The neo-liberal logic is unrelenting: privatization of telecommunications services over community-oriented development, removal of ownership restrictions in media and more intense concentration of ownership, maintenance of artificial scarcity in radio spectrum so as to benefit broadcast and telcoms incumbents, expansion of IP laws prioritizing private profit over health and education and the maintenance of neo-colonial international ordering.

Against this background, "WSIS? WeSeize!" poses another point of view, another strategy – from below. Ordinary people build every society, including any would be information society, and their unsatisfied needs express themselves in cooperative and often illegal ways vexatious to the rulers. Our task is to help these communities recognize one another, hybridize, and realize their strength. File-sharers resisting copyright laws, free software programmers who challenge proprietary software monopolies, grassroots communications guerillas who breach the wall of the media-advertising complex, casualized call-center workers in search of means of struggle after the departure of the unions, migrants hacking border management in pursuit of a better life.

Blinded by the fantasies of the officially powerful, we underestimate the power of resistance. And widescale resistance brings reform even when it is not requested. Concessions come not because we ask for them but because we impose them- the law formalizes that change post-factum. There comes a moment when the costs of continuing with the old arrangements exceeds that of changing them, domination then integrates what it can and seeks to pacify the rest. Our ability to control the consequences of that passage pivots on our cooperative capacity to ensure that it maximizes our potential to subordinate time and resources to life rather than the accumulation of dead labor for others.

Civil Society Assessments of Phase One

Human Rights Caucus Assessment of WSIS Outcome[61]

Human Rights Caucus

The civil society Human Rights Caucus of the World Summit on the Information Society is relieved that a major setback in the international consensus on human rights has been avoided in the final declaration of Principles. The Caucus, which includes more than 45 organizations, has been working since the first preparatory meetings 18 months ago to ensure that human rights are not left off the WSIS agenda.

The Caucus contributions have somewhat been taken into account. We are pleased that the document begins with human rights. The first four paragraphs include many principles that are supported by the human rights caucus. The essential principles of universality and indivisibility are reiterated and there are references to the Universal Declaration of Human Rights as well as to the Vienna Declaration and the UN Charter. We are also pleased that Article 19 of the UDHR is quoted in full rather than in an abridged version as some delegations were proposing. We feel that the human rights section of the document would be much weaker had we not been active throughout the process. We deplore however the absences of any reference to the fundamental principle of nondiscrimination as well as to international labor standards.

But beyond principles, there is the question of enforcement. The Plan of Action is devoid of any mechanism to advance the human rights agenda. The human rights caucus, supported by the civil society plenary, and the International Symposium on the Information Society, Human Dignity and Human Rights (convened by the People's Movement for Human Rights Education in November 2003) proposed an Independent Commission on the Information Society and Human Rights, composed of highly qualified experts with a broad geographical representation, to be established to monitor practices and policies on human rights and the information society. This is particularly urgent, given the tendency in many countries - both North and South - to sacrifice human rights in the name of "security".

---

[61] Communique of human rights caucus, Geneva, December 12, 2003
For more information: Diana Bronson: +41 (0) 79 296 4782 or dbronson@ichrdd.ca
Antoine Madelin: +41 (0) 79 331 2450 or amadelin@fidh.org

The discussion around security would have been enhanced by a clear understanding that true security can only be achieved by measures that are fully compatible with international human rights and particularly the right to privacy. We deplore the emphasis that continues to be placed on creating a "global culture of cyber-security" which aims at "enhancing trade" instead of implementing human rights (paragraph 35).

Likewise, the caucus remains concerned that the rule of law and the regulatory framework are expected to "reflect national realities" instead of being consistent with the legally binding obligations of States according to the international human rights treaties they have ratified (paragraph 39).

At this Summit, the Human Rights Caucus has sought to provide a forum so that voices that have been silenced by authoritarian governments can be heard. In this light, we have brought some of the top international human rights advocates to speak about the situation in China and Tunisia. They are not the only countries with serious human rights problems. They stand however as proof that infrastructure alone is not enough.

How was the Summit?: A helpful list in case your friends (or any reporters) ask you[62]

Rik Panganiban and Ralf Bendrath

The Good

ICT4D Exhibitions

It was quite inspiring seeing the hundreds and hundreds of great exhibitions and stands in the ICT4D. Comparing this fair to the Geneva Telecom 2003 last month, one can see how colorful and vibrant are the many activities being engaged in by civil society, governments, international institutions and businesses. It makes you think that we need more frequent gatherings where people and groups developing ICT applications to meet real human needs can assemble and celebrate each others work.

Civil Society Declaration

Great work all around assembling such an ambitious document, representing a diverse assemblage of views and vision of hundreds of groups of civil society. Kudos to Sally Burch and Bill McIver for guiding the process, all the drafting committee folks, and caucus and working groups for their input and refinements.

Parallel Civil Society Events

It was incredibly frustrating knowing that there were at any time several interesting meetings going on that you wanted to attend. We hope that groups will make reports, powerpoints, videos and other materials available, so we can see a flavor of what we missed. We went to lots of great events, including the CPSR meeting on ICT governance, the AMARC community media forum, the TRP meeting on "democracy, freedom and digital divide", the World Forum on Communication Rights, and the UBUNTU meeting on global governance and WSIS. Congrats to all the organizers for their great work.

Helping Hands

An whole number of people – especially from but not limited to civil society – were extremely helpful during the whole week. Be it the geeks who set up the free wireless hotspot around the civil society offices, the people who coordinated the press

[62] On the web at www.worldsummit2005.org, posted December 16, 2003. Document of the Heinrich Boll Foundation.

conferences and plenary sessions, the ones who spent nights in smoke-filled hotel rooms finalizing joint press releases and other documents, or the volunteer translators - thanks to all of you!

The Bad

Overpasses

Turns out there was plenty of room in the plenary hall, hundreds of available seats. So making us come up with these complex distribution systems, fight with each other, and put poor Robert Guerra (who helped getting it structured) through the wringer, was all for nothing.

WiFi / Internet Access

This was abyssmal how substandard our internet access was. We confess to being guilty of assuming that at the information society summit that we would have in place adequate information technology. WiFi barely worked, even after having to pay exhorbitant amounts for it. SMTP never worked, so sending email was impossible for most of us. The biggest scandal, though, was the fact that we had no free wireless access, as this had been the case at all the PrepComs.

Noise

The noise factor was a significant and constant nuisance the entire week, with no soundproofing of any meeting spaces and frequent loud music, booming noises, and the overall buzz of a thousand conversations. Many people commented that they had never been at a meeting of this stature where the noise level was so bad.

Official Roundtables

We understand that the roundtable speakers only got 3 minutes to make their interventions. What exactly was the point of bringing all this expertise together if no actual dialogue was going to happen? A number of speakers who had taken the effort of coming to Geneva from distant continents for these roundtables told us they had never felt so useless at any other conference.

The Ugly

Civil Society Speaker Selection

We had selected our speakers in a fairly transparent and democratic manner before the summit. Then somebody in the ITU just took the list and arbitrarily picked and dropped people. We neither know who took this decision, nor why. But it denied civil society its right to choose who speaks on its behalf and brings its points across. This was especially clear in the opening ceremony. The selected speaker from the World Blind Union was nice, but had not participated actively in overall civil society discussions and therefore did not make our points. She even had been under pressure from the ITU secretariat to include specific sentences in her speech. Oh, and by the way: This was even against the rules of procedure.

Tunisian Influence Efforts

According to several reports, the Tunisian government had sent a whole number of people to the summit and accredited them as "civil society" members. Many of them tried to mess up civil society discussions related to the second phase of the summit and especially to the bad human rights record of Tunisia. Some of them were even caught red handed in attempts to steal hundreds to thousands of copies of the critical summit newspaper Terra Viva. This is not only a violation of human rights such as free speech, but it is also very stupid and backfires if you get caught.

Police Repression

The Geneva Police closed down the Polimedia Lab of the Counter Summit "WSIS? We Seize!" downtown Geneva on the day before the summit started. They also surrounded and stopped a demonstration held against the summit on its last day. Protestors using their right to free speech and assembly were questioned and their personal data taken. Those who refused or did not have their passports on them were taken into custody.

Censorship Efforts

The security guards at the entrances of the summit venue also censored radical material activists wanted to distribute. Sometimes this was even the case with material produced by organizations with consultative status at the United Nations like the alternative news agency IPS. The Summit Special Advisor to the UN Secretary General, Nitin Desai, even tried to picture a joint civil society protest note against these measures as lies. "I think these people were attending a different conference," he said. Probably he was at another summit himself.

Privacy Violations

The name badges produced for every summit participant at registration included a radio frequency identification (RFID) chip. The personal data of the participants, including the photograph, was stored on a central database, and the times when and where they left or entered the summit venue were also recorded. There was no privacy policy available, and nobody could or would tell us what happens to the data after the summit.

Brave New Digital World? Reflections on the World Summit on the Information Society

Dr. Peter Leuprecht[63]

The first part of the World Summit on the Information Society (WSIS) took place in Geneva from December 10 to 12, 2003. Its second part is to be held in November 2005, in Tunis. The purpose of this article is to give a brief account of the preparation and organization of the Summit (I.), to present the main results of its first phase (II.), to deliver a critical analysis of these results (III.) and to show that the WSIS gives rise to some critical reflections on the present state of the international community (IV.).

Preparation And Organization Of The Summit

An initiative of the International Telecommunication Union (ITU)

The WSIS stems from an ITU initiative. In its Resolution 56/183, the UN General Assembly endorsed the framework for the Summit adopted by the ITU Council. The Resolution also endorsed the leading role of ITU in the Summit and its preparation, in cooperation with other interested organizations and partners.

According to its website[64], the ITU is "an international organization within the UN system where governments and the private sector coordinate global telecom networks and services". It is composed of 189 member States and 650 "ITU Sector members", i.e. mainly corporations active in the field of telecommunications, such as Alcatel, Microsoft, Nokia, Canon, Hitachi...In accordance with Article 3 of the ITU Constitution[65], "Sector Members shall be entitled to participate in the activities of the Sector of which they are members". There are three of such Sectors, i.e. telecommunication standardization, radiocommunication and telecommunication development. ITU's Plenipotentiary Conference, held in Minneapolis in 1998, "focused on strengthening the participation of the private sector in the work of the

---

[63] Dr. Peter Leuprecht is Associate Professor at the Faculty of Law of McGill University. He attended the first phase of the World Summit and a Round Table with Heads of State in the course of the Summit, as a civil society representative. He prepared and chaired the International Symposium on the Information Society, Human Dignity and Human Rights held before the Summit and referred to in this article.

[64] www.itu.int

[65] Adopted at the Additional Plenipotentiary Conference in Geneva in 1992. The text is available on the ITU website under "Basic Texts".

Union, and adopted a number of resolutions which enhance the rights of Sector Members"[66].

The preparation of the WSIS was thus mainly entrusted to a technical organization in which corporate interests carry considerable weight. This fact inevitably had an effect on the fundamental orientation of the Summit.

Although it was clear from the outset that the questions to be discussed at the Summit would have far-reaching human rights implications, there was considerable resistance against taking human rights concerns on board. Some, not least in the ITU leadership and the Executive Secretariat of the Summit, regarded the introduction of human rights issues into the negotiating process as a nuisance that would detract from what in their view should be a "technical" discussion.

The PrepCom

UN General Assembly Resolution 56/183 recommended that preparations for the Summit take place through an open-ended intergovernmental Preparatory Committee (PrepCom) that would define the agenda of the Summit, decide on the modalities of the participation of other stakeholders in the Summit, and finalize a draft declaration and draft plan of action. It invited the ITU to assume the leading managerial role in the Executive Secretariat of the Summit.

It was mainly in the PrepCom, which was very ably chaired by Mr. Adama Samassekou (Mali), that the political discussion and indeed confrontation took place. It was not until the eve of the Geneva Summit that agreement was reached on the draft declaration and draft plan of action. It was largely thanks to Mr. Samassekou that civil society was associated with the Summit process and it was mainly due to civil society representatives that human rights language was introduced into the negotiating process.

Switzerland and Tunisia as host countries

As host of the first part of the WSIS, the Swiss Government did a remarkable job in creating an open and free environment for the Summit and in fostering active participation by civil society. The Swiss Agency for Development and Cooperation (SDC) headed by Ambassador Walter Fust actively supported, including financially, numerous contributive and side events before and during the WSIS, such as the International Symposium on the Information Society, Human Dignity and

[66] ITU website, under "ITU Overview – History".

Human Rights referred to below. SDC also initiated the ICT for Development Platform, a large exhibition with some 250 participants of great diversity from 75 countries.

Independent experts and NGOs have expressed doubts as to whether the Tunisian authorities will live up to the high standards set by the Swiss authorities. In paragraph 3 of the statement adopted by the International Symposium it is stated:

"Host countries and institutions contributing to and participating in the post-Geneva WSIS process should be expected to fully respect the principles enunciated in the Declaration adopted by the Geneva Summit including those relating to human rights that are fundamental to the information and communications society, in particular, freedom of expression, association and information for civil society as well as with regard to visiting NGOs."

The strong presence of secret police in the Tunisian delegation to the PrepCom and the first part of the Summit as well as some of its actions do not augur well for the atmosphere surrounding the second part of the WSIS.

The International Symposium on the Information Society, Human Dignity and Human Rights[67]

The Symposium held in Geneva on 3 and 4 November 2003 was convened by an NGO, PDHRE (People's Movement for Human Rights Education), with the support of SDC, the European Commission, the Office of the High Commissioner for Human Rights, and the Government of Mali, Chair of the Human Security Network. It brought together independent experts from all regions of the world representing a variety of backgrounds, expertise and perspectives. The Symposium elaborated and adopted by consensus a statement which had considerable impact on the final negotiations in the PrepCom with regard to the inclusion of human rights language in the final documents of the first part of the Summit.

Main Results Of The First Phase Of The Summit

Level of participation

Over sixty Heads of State or Government were present in Geneva, mostly from developing countries. With a few exceptions - Finland was represented by its

[67] Hereinafter referred to as International Symposium. The statement adopted by the Symposium is available at www.pdhre.org/wsis.statement.doc

President, France by its Prime Minister - the rich Western countries were represented at a lower level, a fact that seems to indicate that the subject of the Summit was not taken sufficiently seriously by their top political leadership. This is regrettable. After all, overcoming the digital divide, one of the main objectives of the Summit, requires a strong commitment of the wealthy countries at the highest political level.

The final documents

The first phase of the Summit adopted by consensus a Declaration of Principles and a Plan of Action[68] which, as mentioned above, were cleared by the PrepCom on the eve of the conference. Both are rather lengthy and wordy documents.

The Declaration of Principles, entitled "Building the Information Society: a global challenge in the new Millennium", first attempts to define the participants' "Common vision of the Information society". In paragraph 1, it is stated:

"We, the representatives of the peoples of the world, assembled in Geneva from 10-12 December 2003 for the first phase of the World Summit on the Information Society, declare our common desire and commitment to build a people-centred, inclusive and development-oriented Information Society, where everyone can create, access, utilize and share information and knowledge, enabling individuals, communities and peoples to achieve their full potential in promoting their sustainable development and improving their quality of life, premised on the purposes and principles of the Charter of the United Nations and respecting fully and upholding the Universal Declaration of Human Rights."

According to paragraph 2, "our challenge is to harness the potential of information and communication technology to promote the development goals of the Millennium Declaration, namely the eradication of extreme poverty and hunger..."

Paragraph 3 contains important language concerning human rights, democracy and rule of law:

"We reaffirm the universality, indivisibility, interdependence and interrelation of all human rights and fundamental freedoms, including the right to development, as enshrined in the Vienna Declaration. We also reaffirm that democracy, sustainable development, and respect for human rights and fundamental freedoms as well as good governance at all levels are interdependent and mutually reinforcing. We

---

[68] Available on the ITU website, under www.itu.int/wsis/documents

further resolve to strengthen respect for the rule of law in international as in national affairs."

Paragraph 4 recalls the fundamental importance of freedom of opinion and expression:

"We reaffirm, as an essential foundation of the Information Society, and as outlined in Article 19 of the Universal Declaration of Human Rights, that everyone has the right to freedom of opinion and expression; that this right includes freedom to hold opinions without interference and to seek, receive and impart information and ideas through any media and regardless of frontiers."

It goes on to define communication as "a fundamental social process, a basic human need and the foundation of all social organization. It is central to the Information Society. Everyone, everywhere should have the opportunity to participate and no one should be excluded from the benefits the Information Society offers."

In paragraph 5 the Summit participants further reaffirm their commitment to the provisions of Article 29 of the Universal Declaration of Human Rights. In paragraph 8 they "recognize that education, knowledge, information and communication are at the core or human progress, endeavour and well-being. Further, Information and Communication Technologies (ICTs) have an immense impact on virtually all aspects of our lives. The rapid progress of these technologies opens completely new opportunities to attain higher levels of development. The capacity of these technologies to reduce many traditional obstacles, especially those of time and distance, for the first time in history makes it possible to use the potential of these technologies for the benefit of millions of people in all corners of the world."

According to paragraph 9, "ICTs should be regarded as tools and not as an end in themselves. Under favourable conditions, these technologies can be a powerful instrument, increasing productivity, generating economic growth, job creation and employability and improving the quality of life of all. They can also promote dialogue among people, nations and civilizations."

After these highly optimistic assertions that present ICTs as a kind of panacea, the Summit participants note in paragraph 10 that "the benefits of the information technology revolution are today unevenly distributed between the developed and developing countries and within societies. We are fully committed to turning this digital divide into a digital opportunity for all, particularly for those who risk being left behind and being further marginalized." Neither the Declaration of Principles nor the Plan of Action indicates convincing solutions to overcome this digital divide.

The Declaration of Principles then addresses the particular needs of specific groups or sectors of society, e. g. young people (paragraph 11), women (paragraph 12), marginalized and vulnerable groups of society (paragraph 13), the poor (paragraph 14), indigenous peoples (paragraph 15), etc…

In paragraph 17 it is stated:

"We recognize that building an inclusive Information Society requires new forms of solidarity, partnership and cooperation among governments and other stakeholders, i.e. the private sector, civil society, and international organizations. Realizing that the ambitious goal of this Declaration – bridging the digital divide and ensuring harmonious, fair and equitable development for all – will require strong commitment by all stakeholders, we call for digital solidarity, both at national and international levels."

Under the heading "An information society for all: key principles", the Declaration goes on to deal with "the role of governments and all stakeholders in the promotion of ICTs for development" (paragraph 20), "information and communication infrastructure (paragraphs 21-23), "access to information and knowledge" (paragraphs 24-28), "capacity building" (paragraphs 29-34), "building confidence and security in the use of ICTs" (paragraphs 35-37), "enabling environment" (paragraphs 38-50), "ICT applications: benefits in all aspects of life" (paragraph 51), "cultural diversity and identity, linguistic diversity and local content" (paragraphs 52-54), "media" (paragraph 55), "ethical dimensions of the Information Society" (paragraphs 56-59) and "international and regional cooperation" (paragraphs 60-64).

The Declaration refers to accessibility and affordability of information and communication network infrastructure (paragraph 22) and of software (paragraph 27). In paragraph 27 it is stated that "access to information and knowledge can be promoted by increasing awareness among all stakeholders of the possibilities offered by different software models, including proprietary, open-source and free software…"

According to paragraph 26, "a rich public domain is an essential element for the growth of the Information Society…" However, the public service principle is not affirmed in the Declaration.

The issue of privacy is mentioned in the context of cyber-security (paragraph 35). However, nothing is said about the fact that modern technology provides unprecedented possibilities for massive violations of the human right to privacy.

The formulation of paragraph 42 dealing with intellectual property protection is particularly vague:

"Intellectual Property protection is important to encourage innovation and creativity in the information society; similarly, the wide dissemination, diffusion, and sharing of knowledge is important to encourage innovation and creativity."

Paragraphs 48-50 deal specifically with the Internet. Internet governance was one of the most controversial issues of the Summit. In paragraph 50 it is stated:

"International Internet governance issues should be addressed in a coordinated manner. We ask the Secretary-General of the United Nations to set up a working group on Internet governance, in an open and inclusive process that ensures a mechanism for the full and active participation of governments, the private sector and civil society from both developing and developed countries, involving relevant intergovernmental and international organizations and forums, to investigate and make proposals for action, as appropriate, on the governance of Internet by 2005."

In paragraph 55 dealing with the media, Summit participants reaffirm their "commitment to the principles of freedom of the press and freedom of information, as well as those of the independence, pluralism and diversity of media...Diversity of media ownership should be encouraged, in conformity with national law, and taking into account relevant international conventions..."

There was a strong North/South divergence with regard to the practical steps that should be taken to move from the digital divide to "digital solidarity" to which everybody paid lip service. Countries from the South, particularly Africa, proposed the creation of an international "Digital Solidarity Fund"; countries from the North were far from enthusiastic about the idea. The compromise formulation in the Declaration (paragraph 61) reads as follows:

"We recognize the will expressed on the one hand by some to create an international voluntary 'Digital Solidarity Fund', and by others to undertake studies concerning existing mechanisms and the efficiency and feasibility of such a Fund."

The Declaration of Principles concludes with the following, rather sweeping and euphoric statement (paragraph 67):

"We are firmly convinced that we are collectively entering a new era of enormous potential, that of the Information Society and expanded human communication. In this emerging society, information and knowledge can be produced, exchanged, shared and communicated through all the networks of the world. All individuals can soon, if we take the necessary actions, together build a new Information Society based on shared knowledge and founded on global solidarity and a better mutual understanding between peoples and nations. We trust that these measures will open the way to the future development of a true knowledge society."

The Plan of Action is supposed to translate "the common vision and guiding principles of the Declaration" into "concrete action lines to advance the achievement of the internationally-agreed development goals...by promoting the use of ICT-based products, networks, services and applications, and to help countries overcome the digital divide" (paragraph 1). Paragraph 3 emphasizes the importance of "partnerships" between governments, the private sector, civil society and international and regional institutions, including international financial institutions. According to paragraph 4, "opportunity shall be taken in phase two of the WSIS to evaluate and assess progress made towards bridging the digital divide".

Paragraph 6 refers, in an extremely prudent formulation, to "indicative targets" that "may serve as global references for improving connectivity and access in the use of ICTs in promoting the objectives of the Plan of Action, to be achieved by 2015. These targets may be taken into account in the establishment of the national targets, considering the different national circumstances." They include: "to connect villages with ICTs and establish community access points" (paragraph 6 a), "to ensure that all of the world's population have access to television and radio services" (paragraph 6 h), "to encourage the development of content and to put in place technical conditions in order to facilitate the presence and use of all world languages on the Internet" (paragraph 6 i) and "to ensure that more than half of the world's inhabitants have access to ICTs within their reach" (paragraph 6 j).

Paragraph 12 asserts that "confidence and security are among the main pillars of the Information Society" and refers to "existing and potential threats to ICTs" (paragraph 12 a). There is no reference to the threats stemming from the improper use of ICTs, e.g. as far as invasion of privacy is concerned.

According to paragraph 13 a, "governments should foster a supportive, transparent, pro-competitive and predictable policy, legal and regulatory framework, which provides the appropriate incentives to investment and community development in the Information Society". In a similar vein, paragraph 27 d i advocates "developing countries to increase their efforts to attract major private national and foreign investments for ICTs through the creation of a transparent, stable and predictable enabling investment environment".

There are numerous references in the text to “public/private partnerships”.

Paragraph 27 f of the Plan of Action deals with possible financial mechanisms, including a Digital Solidarity Fund, which are also addressed in paragraph 61 of the Declaration of Principles, in the following terms:

“While all existing financial mechanisms should be fully exploited, a thorough review of their adequacy in meeting the challenges of ICT for development should be completed by the end of December 2004. This review shall be conducted by a Task Force under the auspices of the UN Secretary-General and submitted for consideration to the second phase of this summit. Based on the conclusion of the review, improvements and innovations of financing mechanisms will be considered including the effectiveness, the feasibility and the creation of a voluntary Digital Solidarity Fund…”

Finally, paragraph 29 looks forward to the second phase of the WSIS which “should consider *inter alia*:

“a) Elaboration of final appropriate documents based on the outcome of the Geneva phase of the WSIS with a view to consolidating the process of building a global Information Society, and reducing the Digital Divide and transforming it into digital opportunities.

b) Follow-up and implementation of the Geneva Plan of Action at national, regional and international levels, including the UN system, as part of an integrated and coordinated approach, calling upon the participation of all relevant stakeholders. This should take place, *inter alia*, through partnerships among stakeholders.”

The NGOs produced a challenging Civil Society Declaration to the WSIS entitled “Shaping Information Societies for Human Needs”, which was handed over to the President of the Swiss Confederation on December 12, 2003[69].

It will have to be seen whether substantial progress can be made between the two phases of WSIS and whether the Tunis phase will produce more concrete results, particularly on the contentious issues referred to below.

[69] Available at www.itu.int/wsis/documents/doc_single-en-1179.asp

Critical Analysis Of The Results Of The First Phase Of Wsis

The texts adopted by the Geneva Summit might well have been entitled: "Welcome to the digital wonderland!" They are wordy, full of sweeping statements, commonplaces, clichés, stereotypes and pious wishes. They project an idyllic banality, a naïve belief in technology and in a brave new digital world in which ICTs will solve all problems. However, one should not be deceived by the triumphalist language of the texts adopted. They cover up fundamental disagreements and gloss over diametrically opposed world visions that were expressed at the Summit and, probably even more so, in its margins. Some of these will be referred to below.

A highly political Summit

For some, particularly ITU, the Summit was supposed to be technical. Corporate interests which were strongly involved in the preparation of, and represented at, the Summit saw it as a great opportunity to promote their products. It is mainly due to them that the texts adopted contain a number of articles of faith from the credo of pan-economic ideology. On the other hand, NGOs presented powerful alternative visions and managed to have some of their thinking included, e.g. with regard to human rights. If one looks behind the consensual language patched together *in extremis* on a number of fundamental points, one realizes that this was in Geneva, and will be in Tunis, a highly political and societal Summit.

A blurred frontier

There was some, probably deliberate, confusion between business and NGOs. Some of the corporate interests also tried to use an NGO hat. On many issues of substance, e.g. free software or intellectual property rights, there were obviously profound differences of opinion between the two. Some of the catchwords used in the Declaration of Principles and the Plan of Action are "public/private partnerships" and "partnerships between governments, the private sector, civil society and international and regional institutions".

The "Information Society"

The concept of information society promoted by the Summit is itself questionable. One could argue whether information creates a society. Communication and dialogue are more likely to do so. How should information be treated? As a commodity or as a public good? Should the human being endowed with dignity and human rights or commercial interests be at the centre of the networked information society? Should the human being be seen as a passive consumer or buyer of information or rather as an actor and producer of communication? The Geneva texts fail to address these fundamental questions.

The inclusion of human rights language

The hard fought inclusion of human rights language into the Geneva texts is to be welcomed. It is not really surprising that, being the result of a political compromise, they deal with the human rights implications of the Summit far less substantially and less critically than the statement adopted by the November International Symposium. The latter refers to “the commodification of information and knowledge, and the growing concentration of ownership and control of the means of producing and dissemination information and knowledge” as well as to the “limitations, surveillance and censorship by the state or private parties, especially in the post September 11 environment” (paragraph 6). It is also more specific in emphasizing that “there must be no censorship and no arbitrary controls or constraints on participants in the information process, on the content of information or its transmission and dissemination” (paragraph 12).

As previously mentioned, the Declaration of Principles refers to “a rich public domain” as “an essential element for the growth of the information society”, but fails to assert the public service principle. The statement of the International Symposium does so; it also affirms that ”public service broadcasting is an essential means of counter-balancing the commercial motivation of the media and ensuring the enjoyment of the right of everyone to participate in cultural life and the right of political participation” (paragraph 24).

The language of the Geneva Summit texts is weak with regard to access to information produced or maintained by public authorities. Paragraph 12 b of the Plan of Action states:

“Governments are encouraged to provide adequate access through various communication resources, notably the Internet, to public official information. Establishing legislation on access to information and the preservation of public data, notably in the area of new technologies, is encouraged.”

This is a far cry from a human right to access to information held by public authorities.

One of the most striking lacunae in the Geneva Summit texts concerns the right freely to participate in cultural life. Contrary to other relevant provisions of the

Universal Declaration of Human Rights, Article 27, paragraph 1, which affirms this right, is not mentioned in the Geneva texts. However, they address intellectual property protection (paragraph 42 of the Declaration of Principles) which is referred to in paragraph 2 of Article 27 of the Universal Declaration.

The digital divide – a symptom

Nobody can deny the reality and depth of the digital divide. The figures are eloquent. To give only two examples, in Iceland 61% of the population are internet users; in the Democratic Republic of Congo 1 out of 8,774 inhabitants uses the internet. In the United States of America 62% of the population have a personal computer; in Niger 1 out of 1,958 inhabitants has one[70]. The digital divide is no more than a symptom of a far more serious and deep-seated evil, i.e. the unequal distribution of wealth among and within countries, the growing gap between the rich and the poor. Any serious effort to heal, remedy or alleviate must obviously address the disease and not simply the symptom. ICTs are not the panacea. It is certainly naïve to believe that giving people in the poor countries mobile phones or internet connections will in itself eradicate or reduce poverty. Is it necessary to recall that for internet one needs electricity and that the use of internet is difficult for people who are illiterate? True, there is a boom of cellular phones in many countries of the South, however essentially concentrated in the cities. This certainly serves the interest of the producers of cellular phones, but does it serve the interests of the poor in the South and will it reduce poverty? Is a (costly) cellular phone or an internet connection a priority need for people who lack nutrition, water and health? ICTs should not be seen as ends in themselves. Any serious policy of ICT development must be part and parcel of a global policy of human and sustainable development and poverty reduction.

Threats and challenges

The texts adopted by the Geneva Summit refer in euphoric terms to the potential and benefits of ICTs and the new opportunities they open up, but fail to address the threats and challenges they can bring with them. These are particularly apparent with regard to the right to privacy. True, ICTs can and should be used to protect the right to privacy, but they also provide unprecedented possibilities for massive violations of this right. The use of increasingly invasive means of surveillance and of interception of communications, of intrusive profiling and identification and of biometric identification technology, the development of communication technologies with built-in surveillance capacities, the collection and misuse of genetic data, genetic

[70] Global information Technology Report, published by the World Economic Forum, available at www.weforum.org

testing, the growing invasion of privacy at the workplace and the weakening of data protection regimes give rise to serious concerns from the point of view of respect for human rights. Contrary to the Summit, the International Symposium considered these issues. It emphasized that new means must be developed to protect the human right to privacy and the right to know about one's personal data held by public and private institutions and to have them deleted where not strictly necessary for a legitimate purpose in a democratic society. The Symposium also stated that the development, transfer and use of technology permitting illegitimate invasion of privacy must be controlled and curbed[71].

Contentious issues

In addition to the question of including human rights language in the Summit texts which has been referred to above, a number of other contentious issues divided delegations before and during the Summit.

One of these is Internet governance. The issuance of Internet domain names is presently administered by a private organization, ICANN (Internet Corporation for Assigned Names and Numbers) based in San Francisco. Many developing countries argued that the administration of domain names and other aspects of global Internet management should be entrusted to an intergovernmental body. However, this demand was strongly resisted by some developed countries. In the end, the Summit did not take a stand on the issue, but, as stated above, asked the Secretary-General of the United Nations to set up a working group on Internet governance.

Another hot issue was that of free software. It is obvious that free software can be an important instrument of digital inclusion, one of the declared objectives of the Summit. However, there are powerful interests trying to stop the spread of free software. The Summit texts refer to "different software models" and lump free software together with proprietary software without expressing any preference for one or the other (paragraph 27 of the Declaration of Principles and paragraph 9 e of the Plan of Action).

The shape of the present and future intellectual property rights regime gave rise to heated discussions before and during the Geneva Summit and will undoubtedly continue to do so in the years to come, not only in the WSIS context, but in a number of international fora. On this issue like on many others, the main dividing lines ran between countries of the South and most NGOs, on the one hand, and countries of the North, on the other. The former consider that the existing intellectual property rights

[71] Cf. paragraph 16 of the statement adopted by the International Symposium.

regime, including the Agreement on Trade-Related Intellectual Property Rights (TRIPS) and instruments of the World Intellectual Property Organization (WIPO), is unbalanced and should be reevaluated; the latter basically favor maintenance of the status quo. The United States strongly opposed discussion of these issues within the WSIS context, arguing that the proper fora for dealing with them were the World Trade Organization (WTO) and WIPO.

In fact, the intellectual property rights regime, as it emerges through WTO and WIPO, seems to contradict proclaimed goals of the WSIS such as sharing of knowledge and empowering the poor. It does not seem to foster the common good; it is not in the interest of the poor and clashes with internationally recognized human rights. In paragraph 2.3.3.2. of the Civil Society Declaration it is rightly stated:

"Today, the vast majority of humankind has no access to the public domain of global knowledge, a situation that is contributing to the growth of inequality and exploitation of the poorest peoples and communities. Yet instead of extending and strengthening the global domain, recent developments are restricting information more and more to private hands. Patents are being extended to software (and even to ideas), with the consequent effect of limiting innovation and reinforcing monopolies."

In paragraph 2.3.3.3. of the Civil Society Declaration it is recommended that "the UN should carry out a fundamental review of the impact on poverty and human rights of current arrangements for recognition and governance of monopolized knowledge and information, including the work of WIPO and the functioning of the TRIPS agreement".

Paragraph 42 of the Geneva Declaration of Principles unfortunately skirts these fundamental issues. They will have to be addressed seriously by the second phase of WSIS. The primary goal of the regime of knowledge ownership and management must be to strike a balance that will both maximize access to, and use of, knowledge and at the same time encourage creativity. That balance is at the heart of Article 27 of the Universal Declaration of Human Rights. It is sadly significant that, as stated above, in the Geneva Declaration of Principles there is no reference to the right freely to participate in the cultural life of the community, enshrined in paragraph 1 of Article 27. One of the big challenges of the years to come will be to elaborate a just intellectual property rights regime that contributes to human and sustainable development.

Finally, there has been strong disagreement on the financial means of bridging the digital divide, of moving from the digital divide to the so frequently evoked digital solidarity. The President of Senegal, strongly supported by other Third World leaders, proposed the creation of a Digital Solidarity Fund to finance the digital solidarity agenda. This proposal was opposed by developed countries, some of which claimed that existing amounts and channels of aid were enough and that the developing countries should commit their own funds. The solemnly conjured digital solidarity seems to stop at the purse. This issue nearly was to be the stumbling block of the Geneva phase of the Summit. At the last minute, the parties agreed to the above-mentioned compromise formula in paragraph 27 f of the Plan of Action. However, the negative attitude of countries from the North caused profound disappointment and frustration among delegations from the South.

The main merit of the Geneva Summit probably was to enhance awareness of the serious issues at stake in connection with the so-called information society. Many of these have been laid on the negotiating table. Progress towards their solution before and during the Tunis phase will require a strong political resolve and a genuine willingness, especially of the wealthy countries, to share knowledge and to overcome the digital divide and, even more, the deep-seated inequalities of which it is a symptom.

Critical Reflections On The Present State Of The International Community

The first phase of the WSIS gives rise to a number of critical reflections on the present state of the international community. Three points will be addressed below: the role of civil society, the growing penetration of corporate interests in the international arena and the lack or insufficiency of solidarity within the international community.

Civil society represented by numerous NGOs, including numerous community based organizations, had a considerable and highly positive impact on the first phase of WSIS and its results. NGOs have shown that, in spite of their great diversity, they are capable of getting their act together, to act responsibly and to present and defend serious and credible positions. It is by no means a coincidence that on most issues of substance they sided with the countries of the South.

The strong presence and influence of corporate interests at WSIS is a striking illustration of their growing penetration in the international arena. There seems to be a tendency towards "privatization" of the international community. Powerful multinational corporations exert a growing influence in international fora without undertaking corresponding responsibilities, particularly with regard to human rights. Against this background, the work carried out in various international organizations to hold multinational corporations accountable for human rights abuses takes on particular importance[72].

Finally, discussions before and during the first phase of WSIS, particularly on the financial means of bridging the digital divide, have shown that professions of faith in international solidarity remain essentially verbal. This is highly deplorable. Indeed, there cannot be an international community worthy of this name without a more than verbal recognition of a community interest, a common good of humanity that must prevail over particular interests, both national and corporate interests. An international community worthy of this name cannot exist without acting solidarity. As far as the subject of WSIS is concerned, it is obvious that public authorities, the private sector and civil society in the developed countries have a special responsibility to share the benefits of the information society with the peoples in the developing countries.

To be solid, the international community needs to be based on shared values, in particular those of respect for the human being and his or her dignity and human rights - all human rights, civil, political, economic, social and cultural rights. The information and communication society must be based on these values and contribute to the twofold liberation promised by the Preamble to the Universal Declaration of Human Rights, namely, liberation from fear and liberation from want.

[72] Cf. in particular the Draft Principles for transnational corporations and other business enterprises elaborated by a Working Group of the UN Sub-Commission on the Promotion and Protection of Human Rights, documents E.CN.4/Sub.2002/WP.1 (Draft Principles) and E.CN.4/Sub.2/2002/WG2/WP.1/Add 2 (Commentary on Draft Principles).

World Summit on the Information Society[73]

Richard Stallman

At WSIS, in a climate of suppression of dissent, the score is 0-0
-- Richard Stallman

The World Summit on the Information Society is supposed to formulate plans to end the "digital divide" and make the internet accessible to everyone on Earth. The negotiations were completed in November, so the big official meeting in Geneva last week was more of a trade show and conference than a real summit meeting.

The summit procedures were designed so that non-governmental organizations (mainly those that promote human rights and equality, and work to reduce poverty) could attend, see the discussions, and comment. However, the actual declaration paid little attention to the comments and recommendations that these organizations made. In effect, civil society was offered the chance to speak to a dead mike.

The summit's declaration includes little that is bold or new. When it comes to the question of what people will be free to *do* with the internet, it responds to demands made by various governments to impose restrictions on citizens of cyberspace.

Part of the digital divide comes from artificial obstacles to the sharing of information. This includes the licenses of non-free software, and harmfully restrictive copyright laws. The Brazilian declaration sought measures to promote free software, but the US delegation was firmly against it (remember that the Bush campaign got money from Microsoft). The outcome was a sort of draw, with the final declaration presenting free software, open source, and proprietary software as equally legitimate. The US also insisted on praising so-called "intellectual property rights". (That biased term promotes simplistic over-generalization; for the sake of clear thinking about the issues of copyright law, and about the very different issues of patent law, that term should always be avoided.)

---

[73] On the web at http://www.gnu.org/philosophy/wsis.html and originally published on Newsforge.

The declaration calls on governments to ensure unhindered access to the public domain, but says nothing about whether any additional works should ever enter the public domain.

Human rights were given lip service, but the proposal for a "right to communicate" (not merely to access information) using the internet was shot down by many of the countries. The summit has been criticized for situating its 2005 meeting in Tunisia, which is a prime example of what the information society must not do. People have been imprisoned in Tunisia for using the internet to criticize the government.

Suppression of criticism has been evident here at the summit too. A counter-summit, actually a series of talks and discussions, was planned for last Tuesday, but it was shut down by the Geneva police who clearly were searching for an excuse to do so. First they claimed that the landlord did not approve use of the space, but the tenant who has a long-term lease for the space then arrived and said he had authorized the event. So the police cited a fire code violation which I'm told is applicable to most buildings in Geneva--in effect, an all-purpose excuse to shut down anything. Press coverage of this maneuver eventually forced the city to allow the counter-summit to proceed on Wednesday in a different location.

In a more minor act of suppression, the moderator of the official round table in which I spoke told me "your time is up" well before the three minutes each participant was supposed to have. She later did the same thing to the EPIC representative. I later learned that she works for the International Chamber of Commerce--no wonder she silenced us. And how telling that the summit would put a representative of the ICC at the throttle when we spoke.

Suppression was also visible in the exclusion of certain NGOs from the summit because their focus on human rights might embarrass the governments that trample them. For instance, the summit refused to accredit Human Rights In China, a group that criticizes the Chinese government for (among other things) censorship of the internet.

Reporters Without Borders was also excluded from the summit. To raise awareness of their exclusion, and of the censorship of the internet in various countries, they set up an unauthorized radio station in nearby France and handed out mini-radios, so that summit attendees could hear what the organization had been blocked from saying at the summit itself.

The summit may have a few useful side effects. For instance, several people came together to plan an organization to help organizations in Africa switch to

GNU/Linux. But the summit did nothing to support this activity beyond providing an occasion for us to meet. Nor, I believe, was it intended to support any such thing. The overall attitude of the summit can be seen in its having invited Microsoft to speak alongside, and before, most of the various participating governments--as if to accord that criminal corporation the standing of a state.

Libraries@the Heart of the Information Society[74]

International Federation of Library Associations and Institutions

The Declaration of Principles and Action Plan were finally adopted on Friday evening after many hours of statements about the Information Society. Particularly strong statements were made about gender issues and the needs of people with disabilities.

Adoption was the culmination of eighteen months of consultations and negotiations and represented a major achievement for IFLA and its partners in lobbying the negotiators. The final versions were agreed at the eleventh hour, late on Tuesday 9 December, just before the opening of the Summit.

Unqualified acceptance of the fundamental importance of human rights, and especially of freedom of expression and information was obtained but two issues could not be resolved. The first was Internet governance which some nations wish to keep under the control of ICANN, supervised by the US Department of Commerce and with the involvement of major ICT operators, while others would prefer supervision by an INGO such as the ITU. The second was funding mechanisms to address the digital divide on which a split emerged between developed and developing nations. The Government of Senegal had proposed a Digital Solidarity Fund while the EU and other developed nations argued that existing funding mechanisms should be used. To secure endorsement of the documents, it was agreed to study both between the Geneva and Tunis phases of the Summit. Striking a positive note, the Mayors of Lyons in France and Geneva in Switzerland announced on Friday that they had added to the Senegal Government's contribution taking the fund to over €1 million.

As the civil society organisations have noted, the Declaration and Action Plan fall short of providing the means to implement fully a vision for an equitable and inclusive information society. The make a start but there is much to do.

---

[74] IFLA Issues from World Summit 10-12 December 2003 Nr. 4 www.ifla.org/III/wsis/wsis-1103.html
Marian Koren (Member of IFLA Governing Board, Netherlands Public Library Association), Winnie Vitzansky (Standing Committee Member of the IFLA Section on Management of Library Associations, Director of the Danish Library Association), Alex Byrne (IFLA President-elect, University of Technology, Sydney)

IFLA has signed the Civil Society Declaration and will be working with our partners in civil society to advance a shared vision.

Nevertheless, most of our concerns are included in the Declaration and Action Plan which offer a framework for action over the next 23 months to Tunis and beyond. It is now up to us to demonstrate to governments that we can turn the statements into reality, that the global library network provides the foundation for the information society.

This has been the most sustained and widespread advocacy campaign ever undertaken by IFLA. It has demonstrated that we can be successful but has taught us many lessons, including the need for the strong core support, provided this time by our Swiss colleagues. We need to learn for the experience as we engage with the Tunis phase of the Summit and for advocacy in other areas.

Many colleagues from national library associations, national libraries and other related organisations participated, presenting an alliance to promote the role of libraries in the information society. Right up to the end, IFLA representatives met with key players including government delegates and ministers, civil society members and HE Adama Samassékou, President of the preparatory process who spoke at WLIC 2003 in Berlin. Contacts made during the summit included funders and organisers of Telecentres in the developing world. IFLA considers this as a valuable contact and we are preparing a joint workshop during the World Library and Information Congress in Buenos Aires in August 2004.

The assistance of students and lecturers from the School of Library and Information Science in Geneva was particularly valuable because they willingly staffed our booth, which we shared with ICA, and distributed information while we met with the key players.

A commentary on the Declaration and Action Plan will be distributed shortly. It will show how IFLA, library associations and libraries are turning the ideas and actions into practice and how, with a little support, we can extend our work so that we will have many stories to tell in Tunis.

We will also work to strengthen the outcomes in those areas in which the Declaration and Action Plan could be improved including the deficiencies identified in the Civil Society Declaration.

The effectiveness of our advocacy campaign was demonstrated when an IFLA representative was told by a government delegate: *"I am sick of hearing about libraries and from you librarians ..."*

As IFLA President Kay Raseroka noted. *"This experience reminds us of the need to partner but also to remember our core values"*.

WSIS: Two Years' Work to Stay in the Same Place[75]

Ronald Koven, World Press Freedom Committee

Press freedom groups generally succeeded in holding the line on the international community's commitments to free speech and a free press during the UN-sponsored World Summit on the Information Society, Dec. 10-12 in Geneva, although there were some dents in that line.

It was a success for damage control that took two years of intensive lobbying efforts during a preparatory process that stretched across the globe, with meetings in Bamako (Mali), Bucharest, Beirut, Cairo, Tokyo, Dominican Republic, Geneva, Paris and elsewhere.

Groups in the Coordinating Committee of Press Freedom organizations were well represented at most of the preparatory meetings. Notably active among the groups were the International Association of Broadcasting, the Inter American Press Association and the World Press Freedom Committee.

Now there is the prospect of another two years' struggle leading to a follow-up summit in Tunis, Nov. 16-18, 2005. The Coordinating Committee, meeting Dec. 8-9 in Geneva on the eve of WSIS, adopted a resolution calling for either a change in venue of the next summit because of Tunisia's record of repressing its press, or cancellation of the second summit altogether.

A large corps of Tunisian representatives, both governmental and representing "GONGOs" (Governmental Non-Governmental Organizations), at the Geneva summit and in the preparatory meetings made it plain that they mean to fight hard against any effort to take a second summit away from them. During the Geneva summit, the Tunisians confiscated as many copies as they could of the summit newspaper, "Terra Viva" (published by the Third World activist Inter Press Service), containing critical comments on Tunisia's highly repressive free speech/press freedom record.

WPFC European Representative Ronald Koven read out the Coordinating Committee's resolution at a downtown meeting of Tunisian opposition journalists -- also addressed by the son of a journalist jailed for more than 11 years. Four Tunisian

---

[75] On the web at http://www.wpfc.org/

GONGO delegates accosted Koven the next day at WSIS to complain, and one of them said he could not wait for Koven to come to Tunis and be greeted by a special "welcoming committee."

The first preparatory meeting for the Tunis summit is tentatively scheduled for April or May, presumably in Tunis. A major difficulty with moving the summit away from Tunis is that the meeting was mandated in a UN General Assembly resolution, and changing that would require fancy footwork by the UN Secretariat in New York. One idea discussed in the corridors is moving the second summit to UN Headquarters in New York.

The Arab states' group can be expected to resist any change. The Arab League, with its score of member-state votes, got the summit for Tunisia by threatening Yoshio Utsumi, Secretary-General of the International Telecommunication Union, the WSIS organizing agency, that it would block consensus on his reelection at the ITU's biennial Plenipotentiary Assembly in Marrakech, Morocco in September 2002, unless he arranged for Tunis to win its bid against Geneva. His "Solomonic" solution was to propose that the summit be split into two phases, in Geneva and Tunis, two years apart. This was a first, for a UN summit.

Meanwhile, the ITU was totally overstretched by the Geneva summit. ITU officials admit that it created a huge deficit in the agency's finances, but they refuse to say how large it is. Other UN agencies have so far refused to fill the gap. The ITU had announced that it would dismiss140 staffers, nearly 15 per cent of its 1,0000 slots. After the staff threatened to strike and demonstrate at WSIS, Utsumi agreed to negotiations in view of averting staff reductions.

The ITU has, however, put the UN system on notice that it cannot accept the same responsibility for organizing Tunis that it had for Geneva. The ITU seeks to renegotiate its role with the rest of the UN system. Swiss government sources say that the financial problems are partly an excuse for ITU's desire to wiggle out of continuing to be the UN's lead agency for WSIS. The Swiss say the ITU simply did not realize at first what a political hot potato WSIS would be. The agency's leaders apparently thought that WSIS would be a purely technical conference to discuss the kinds of technology standards that it has been used to dealing with.

Utsumi had made plain that his ambition was to take over Internet governance from ICANN (Internet Corp. for Assigned Names and Numbers), a California company which runs the Internet under contract to the U.S. Commerce Department. Sentiment has grown in the current anti-American climate, including among West European governments that it is abnormal for management of the Internet to be in the hands of a private U.S. company. Countries that have explicitly called for a transfer from ICANN to an international agency include Brazil, China, India, Saudi Arabia and South Africa.

The ITU saw this as an opportunity for a major boost in its role, just as this was diminishing because of the worldwide trend toward telecommunications deregulation. And countries, led by China, saw it as an opening to seek international blessings for governmental control of its Internet Service Providers, which already prevent the unrestricted free flow on news and views over the Internet. ITU has also indicated that it had in mind content controls over the Internet -- a radically different approach from the merely technical facilitation role of ICANN.

Chinese diplomats are reliably understood to have offered to drop their opposition to incorporating Article 19 of the Universal Declaration of Human Rights into the WSIS final Declaration, in exchange for explicit international recognition of China's right to control Internet traffic. Getting China to drop its blocking of consensus on the WSIS texts involved a last-minute trip to Beijing by Pascal Couchepin, the president of host-country Switzerland, to see the top Chinese leaders.

The compromise that was hammered out involved an official call for UN Secretary General Kofi Annan to organize a two-year study, in time for the second summit, on the future of Internet governance. The panel he has been called upon to organize involves ICANN, industry, the UN system, key governments and civil society. This represents a major setback for the ITU, which is clearly not intended to emerge as the organizer of the new Internet management system.

But the compromise language adopted by WSIS Dec. 12 leaves much room for mischief. The Declaration of Principles adopted in Geneva notes that "policy authority for Internet-related public policy issues is the sovereign right of State. They have rights and responsibilities for international Internet-related public policy issues." (Para 49)

Another time bomb embedded in the compromise texts was a stricture against "illegal and harmful content" on Internet. This represented the adoption of heavily contested language that the Council of Europe has promulgated over protests from press freedom and human rights groups -- protests on grounds that content may be legal or illegal but that "harmful content" is a dangerously vague and subjective halfway house open to abuse by countries like China.

There are several references to the concept in the WSIS texts, the clearest of which reads: "Take appropriate measures -- consistent with freedom of expression -- to combat illegal and harmful content in media content." (Section C9, para 24 c) of the Plan of Action). Red-faced U.S. and some libertarian West European diplomats admitted that, even though they had been warned about the problem, they had let this slip by on Saturday Dec. 6, when the Swiss chairman was gaveling everything through in a closed-door intergovernmental meeting called in a last-minute effort to rescue the summit from failure.

The prospect of failure was so high that a large number of chiefs of state whose participation had been announced canceled at almost the last moment. Such no-shows included German Chancellor Gerhard Schroeder and Cuban leader Fidel Castro. There was never any question of U.S. President Bush attending, but U.S. Secretary of State Colin Powell was dissuaded from going by his own negotiators. Instead, the United States was represented by White House National Science Adviser John Marburger.

Chiefs of state notable for their suppression of press freedom who did come and speak at the WSIS Plenary included Zimbabwe's Robert Mugabe, Alexander Lukashenko of Belarus and Tunisia's Ben Ali, who stressed what a warm welcome WSIS II would receive in Tunis.

When it came to the explicit reference to and the language of Article 19 of the Universal Declaration of Human Rights -- the major feature that press freedom groups worked to preserve, there was a compromise in which both the advocates and adversaries of press freedom ambiguously get to crow victory. Efforts to chop up and/or alter the language of Article 19 were staved off. It was cited in full and by name as "an essential foundation of the Information Society" (Declaration of Principles, Para 4). But press freedom restrictionists were satisfied because Article 29, the loophole clause of the Universal Declaration of Human Rights, allowing limitations in the name of "morality, public order, and the general welfare," followed in the very next paragraph. Each side will undoubtedly stress the Article that is favorable to its argument.

The United States tried to get the reference to Article 29 moved elsewhere, so that it wouldn't butt up against the paragraph on Article 19, but the Americans didn't succeed in that. They did manage to get the full text of Article 29 reproduced, to include the passage that tries to restrict usage of the restrictions.

Press freedom advocates also expressed disappointment that their call for the Declaration to seek the actual implementation of Article 19 -- dating from 1948 -- was in the end ignored.

Yet, the restrictionists had to give up their attempts to include a controversial "Right to Communicate" to "improve" on Article 19. That victory was largely the work of Canadian Ambassador Isabelle Massip, who chaired a special negotiating group on the issue. She was struggling against the perhaps uninformed adoption by the ITU's Utsumi early on in the WSIS process of the "Right to Communicate" as a slogan.

Various civil society advocates of the "Right to Communicate" in the social activist CRIS (Communication Rights in the Information Society Campaign) nevertheless made it known that they would continue to press between now and Tunis for the "Right to Communicate" or for a new formulation they propose -- "communication rights." Yet, it was a major victory for press freedom groups lobbying within the official "Civil Society" caucuses during WSIS preparations that they got the radicals to adopt reaffirmation of Article 19 as a major joint goal. The CRIS-dominated Civil Society organs came invariably to cite the demand to honor Article 19 high up in every statement they issued.

Another major threat that went by the board in the WSIS final texts was the attempt by the Chinese-led bloc (Cuba, Vietnam, most of the Arab group, Pakistan and Iran, and, belatedly, South Africa) to stipulate that press freedom would be subject to the laws of each country -- rather than be a universally recognized right, as provided for in Article 19. Relatively early on, the U.S. delegation beat back attempts to water down Article 19 by having the Universal Declaration of Human Rights be flanked by the International Covenant on Political and Social Rights, which contains a very restrictive version of Article 19.

A major ally throughout the process was UNESCO, which responded consistently and without hesitation to WPFC appeals for help in the form of letters to national and UN system leaders, speeches, newspaper columns, personal meetings with ambassadors and ministers by Koichiro Matsuura and the dispatch of staffers to monitor, lobby and speak out at preparatory conferences.

The United Nations Secretariat itself also responded positively to appeals against backsliding that would be costly to the image of the UN system. But the responses of Secretary-General Kofi Annan and his Under-Secretary-General for Communications and Public Information, Shashi Tharoor, were somewhat more ambiguous and required more prodding than those of UNESCO.

Speaking to a dinner of the Coordinating Committee on the eve of WSIS, Tharoor insisted that press freedom must be non-negotiable and that any attempt to negotiate it away would represent a failure in the eyes of the press and public.

Yet, he insisted: "Some legal restrictions are reasonable. ... One of the conundrums that media professionals and governments face -- in a world where new information technologies have given us media without borders -- is to strike the right balance between legitimate freedom of the press -- an established right that must be upheld and is essential to any peoples' development -- and the legitimate concerns of governments about the misuse of media. ... Away from the rhetoric of the battleground, I think we need to acknowledge this conundrum, and work together to find solutions. ... We need to find a way to allow legitimate governments to impose legitimate checks on those who dominate, manipulate or abuse the media ..."

This, among other signs, promises that the standoff at WSIS -- in and of itself a victory of sorts for press freedom -- is only one battle in a continuing war.

Whose "information society"? Or: Was WSIS worth it?[76]

Anriette Esterhuysen[77]

Was WSIS worth it? The general verdict on the recent United Nations World Summit on the Information Society (WSIS) held in December 2003 was a thumbs-down. The Summit outcomes were limited after an arduous and expensive process. However, argues Anriette Esterhuysen, APC executive director, from the perspective of many civil society organisations that participated actively, the WSIS has created a new opportunity for solidarity across ideological, sectoral and geographical divides.

Many of us question the use of the term 'information society', which has the tendency to de-emphasise ongoing inequalities in access to resources.

Nevertheless, the term is here to stay, and the recent United Nations World Summit on the Information Society (WSIS), held in Geneva in December 2003, has popularised its use by governments and the media. A Declaration and Plan of Action which outline policy for global coordination of information and communications technologies (ICTs), and propose actions to "bridge the digital divide" were adopted by participating governments. Civil society organizations adopted their own Declaration, developed over the two preceding years, and expressing an alternative vision and proposals.

Since the completion of the first phase of WSIS academics and activists have been debating the event, the process, the outcomes and the prospects for the second phase, which, controversially, will be held in Tunis in 2005.

WSIS: was it worth the effort and the expense?

The common verdict is that the official outcomes are very limited, considering the time and expense. In their quest for consensus, governments opted for generalities: broad principles regarding the potential of ICTs for development characterise the Declaration, while the Action Plan focuses on connectivity and infrastructure. Often

---

[76] Captured from www.worldsummit2205.org. A shorter version of this article was first published in Alliance, Vol 9, No 1, March 2003. 2004. This version was originally published at the APC website at http://www.apc.org/english/about/history/english.shtml?cmd[384]=i-575-17983.

[77] Anriette Esterhuysen is the Executive Director of APC, the Association for Progressive Communications. Contact: <anriette(at)apc.org>

Declaration and Action Plan contradict one another: the principles expressed in the Declaration are not always carried through to the proposals in the Action Plan. As Sally Burch points out, "the first article of the Declaration affirms 'our common desire and commitment to build a people-centred, inclusive and development-oriented Information Society, where everyone can create, access, utilize and share information and knowledge, enabling individuals, communities and people to achieve their full potential in promoting their sustainable development and improving their quality of life…'. But in its first article, the Plan of Action limits this vision to 'promoting the use of ICT- based products, networks, services and applications' to achieve development goals." (Burch, Other News - Roberto Savio / IPS, 22 December 2003)

One of the key areas on which governments could not agree on was the financing of digital inclusion programmes. An initiative like the proposed 'digital solidarity fund' which could involve individual buyers of ICTs in rich countries paying a 'digital divide' levy will be discussed by a working group who will make recommendations to the Tunis Summit. Whether this potentially innovative initiative will survive in a form that promotes citizen engagement in development and disburses its funds transparently remains to be seen.

From the perspective of several civil society organisations that participated actively, the WSIS has been an extremely important process, creating a new platform of solidarity across ideological, sectoral and geographical divides.

How effective was civil society participation?

The convenor of the WSIS, the International Telecommunications Union (ITU), adopted a 'multi-stakeholder' approach, which included civil society and private sector groups as observers to the official process. Formal opportunities for making an impact were created through short speaker slots, where civil society and private sector representatives could address governments in the plenary, and more significantly, through submitting written proposals.

That looked good on the surface. In practice there were many barriers to the effective participation of civil society. The limited financial resources allocated to travel scholarships, and a hostile attitude on the part of several governments are particularly worth highlighting, e.g. civil society observers were asked to leave some of the government working groups that were set up to deal with controversial issues such as internet governance. A further obstacle was the well-intentioned but cumbersome bureaucracy established by the WSIS civil society secretariat, which resulted in organisations wasting valuable time in trying to sort themselves into 'families' or clusters according to their thematic activities or regions.

Nevertheless, due to the commitment, solidarity and hard work of many civil society participants, and possibly because of the degree of deadlock among governments, a fair amount of the proposals put forward by civil society made it into the final text. Notable examples are the references to the universal declaration of human rights, equality between men and women, and free and open source software.

A watershed in public participation

At the informal level the outcomes are more significant. I believe that the WSIS has been a watershed in the process of public participation in ICT policies. It has facilitated a shift from the world of obscure ICT policy jargon, engaged by a select group of NGOs, consultants, donor agencies, and governments, to a new context in which ICT policy has become firmly located in broader debates on development and society. Many more CSOs have entered the debate, lobbying for important and specific interests. For example, through WSIS new voices sounded in the ICT policy arena, such as those of people living with disabilities, the education and research sectors, the free software movement, children's rights advocates, campaigners for the global information commons and so on.

Civil society organisations that had engaged ICT policies before the WSIS process started, have tended to fall into four broad groups:

- community media, concerned with spectrum allocation and the regulation of community radio
- privacy and anti-censorship groups, concerned with online privacy, interception and monitoring of online communications, and censorship, for example through the filtering of web content
- working specifically in ICTs for sustainable development, lobbying for universal public access and affordable internet and telecommunications infrastructure, and
- those tracking the ICANN process, the process of assigning internet names and numbers.

These groups have tended to focus narrowly on specific areas of regulation. They have rarely engaged ICT policies in a holistic way, or dealt with issues of global ICT governance. They have been geographically divided between the 'development' groups based mostly in the south, and the 'privacy and civil liberty' groups mostly in the north. The community radio groups have tried to deal with policy and regulation, as well as freedom of information issues, but usually in relation to radio and media ownership and control. They have paid little attention to the specific regulation of the internet and the broader telecommunications sector.

The exception to this was found in groups such as the 'Platform of Action', which launched the Communication Rights in the Information Society (CRIS) campaign in 2001. While this campaign raised critical issues, it was primarily a platform for progressive organisations already working in the field. Through WSIS its membership has expanded and it became able to fill a gap in the process, as indicated by the very well attended World Forum on Communication Rights convened by CRIS during the WSIS in Geneva on 11 December 2003.

What has changed during WSIS?

Since WSIS, a much broader range of CSOs are tackling ICT policy issues. Experience, confidence and knowledge built during the relatively 'safe' spaces of the civil society plenary and caucuses in WSIS, are feeding directly into national advocacy campaigns. To tell just one story.... In November 2002, the internet activists Association for Progressive Communications (APC), the freedom of expression organisation Article 19, and the United Nations' Economic Commission for Africa, held an ICT policy workshop and WSIS orientation for African civil society in Addis Ababa. Kenyan participants, once back home, asked their national telecommunications regulator: 'What is Kenya doing about the WSIS?' At the time the answer was 'not very much', but at one of the WSIS preparatory meetings (prepcom) in Geneva, the Kenyan CSOs and government delegates got talking again, and the government delegates offered to table civil society proposals in the official forum. At the next prepcom, civil society was invited to join the Kenyan delegation.

The real gain is that these links continued beyond Geneva. Currently there is a national ICT policy process underway in Kenya and it is relatively inclusive, involving civil society and the private sector. In the Philippines, CSOs are measuring their government's national policy process against the principles agreed on by civil society in its declaration to the WSIS. In South Africa, SANGONeT, a progressive ICT service provider, is convening public consultations on ICT policy in small and medium-sized towns, far away from Johannesburg, where community organisers are able to confront government officials with questions such as 'Where are those phone lines we were promised in 1996'? In Senegal, ENDA Synfev, a women's networking initiative convened a WSIS report-back session attended by more than 75 women. Participants ranged from organisations for the disabled to IT entrepreneurs. In Brazil a civil society organisation, Rits (Third Sector Information Network) has launched an interactive online 'observatory' to facilitate public participation in 'info-inclusion' policy.

These examples show the potential for influencing policy outcomes and for creating a space for networking, from which collaborative implementation can flow. It creates awareness of policy promises and demand for transparent delivery; an important form of public participation absent in many countries. It locates ICT policy as social policy, not technical policy, and it keeps it in the public domain where it belongs.

Current ICT policy and regulation trends raise the danger that the freedoms needed for using ICTs for social justice and sustainable development would be limited. From treaties on cybercrime that can result in invasion of privacy, to the over-commercialisation of radio spectrum and restrictions placed on innovation by intellectual property regimes and telecommunications regulations (for example by limiting low cost options like internet telephony), civil society interests are threatened. We need to be out there protecting them.

ICT infrastructure and civil society

While policy debates rage on, fortunately more openly than before, how are civil society organisations engaging the technology itself?

The opportunities are there: working in a networked way has the potential for greater collaboration, exchange of information, sharing of learning and experiences, and linking the local to the global. But there appears to be a general consensus that the potential of using ICTs to increase the impact of civil society is not fully realised. Often this has been attributed to the poor quality and high cost of connectivity in much of the world. However, connectivity is increasingly more accessible, and often the most innovative uses of ICTs are found among organisations with poor access.

A recent study by Mark Surman and Katherine Reilly commissioned by the Social Science Research Council says that "This issue of appropriation – using networked technologies strategically, politically, creatively – is amongst the most pressing that civil society faces in the information society. The big question is: what should we do with these networked technologies now that we have access to them? ... By all accounts, the broad majority of civil society organizations are struggling with the issue of how to mold these tools to meet their needs – to increase the impact of campaigns, projects and programs using networked technologies. Or, in many cases, they are simply using them without any thought about where and how these technologies fit into the political work for which they feel so much passion. It is not that these organizations use networked technologies completely without question or critique, but rather that they don't take the time to consider how they can be using these technologies most strategically." (Surman and Reilly, *Appropriating the Internet for Social Change*, SSRC, November 2003)

I would argue that there are four dimensions to tackle: policy and regulation, at national and global levels, as discussed above; understanding the information technology market place, and how it tends to turn people into consumers rather than creative users of technology; capacity building so that people have the know-how to use the tools available to them, and; planning and thinking strategically about ICTs and networking.

The capacity issue

The thread that links the challenge of creatively using ICT to the involvement of civil society in the policy process is capacity. It is a very fragile thread. There is not enough investment in learning and capacity building, within individual institutions and more broadly in the sector.

APC used the WSIS as a springboard for building the capacity of civil society to engage in ICT policy advocacy. We developed a curriculum and manual of ICT 'for beginners', and a guide to conducting national policy consultations. Demand for the training has been overwhelming; donor support less so. If it were not for the networking opportunities presented by WSIS, the scale of formal capacity building and informal learning would have looked very different.

How do we build capacity for strategic appropriation of ICTs? We want to do this not for the sake of technology on its own, "but rather to enable civil society organizations to collaborate better, communicate more effectively and to have more social impact." Surman and Reilly outline several innovative recommendations in their paper, ranging from the need for building a "social tech movement" made up of organisations and individuals that provide support and training to CSOs, to "embracing the open source movement" and creating "better maps of civic cyberspace".

I would support their suggestions and, in summary, make the point that we need to enhance learning and capacity building, as well as engage actively in the political and policy processes that surround the technologies we use.

Learning how to use ICTs creatively can be both formal and informal and is one of the most enduring outcomes of online networking. We need to actively learn and share experiences of our use of ICTs in collaborative work. The unintended outcome of the WSIS process that will stay with many CSOs even once hopes for policy transformation have faded is the experience of using ICTs creatively. The many WSIS online forums and websites, committees and consultations are testimony to this.

In the ICT world, as in the rest of the world, it matters who owns what, who controls innovation, and who shapes policy and regulation. We need to take our passion and our policies to our PCs. Shifting from MS Office to a free software application like Openoffice.org may seem a low priority for CSOs, but it can save money and make a statement about the power of choice.

The slogan "Another world is possible", adopted by the global justice and solidarity movement, applies to the ICT world as well. It is up to us to make it concrete by thinking creatively and acting to appropriate technology. It is up to donors to continue to invest in networking and learning.[78]

---

[78] References
CRIS, http://www.crisinfo.org
APC News, December 2003, http://www.apc.org/english/news/index.shtml?x=15966
Rits is the APC member in Brazil, http://www.rits.br.
http://www.infoinclusao.org.br/
http://www.ssrc.org/programs/itic/publications/knowledge_report/final_entire_surman_reilly.pdf
http://www.apc.org/english/capacity/policy/index.shtml
Surman and Reilly 2003, p.74.
See Surman and Reilly 2003 pp. 71-74.

Failure and Success at the WSIS: Civil Society's Next Moves[79]

Sean O'Siochru, Spokesperon for the CRIS Campaign

The depth of disappointment with the formal outcome of the World Summit on the Information Society cannot be fully explained by reference to the usual process of Summit attrition, governments horse-trading down to the lowest common denominator.

Yes, a mutually convenient alliance of powerful and autocratic governments blocked action to tackle the erosion of civil and human rights in electronic space; the US watered down support for development-friendly free and open source software; and community-driven approaches got barely a mention. But other areas might in time yield modest results, such as the call to reroute huge volumes of southern internet traffic internally instead of via the US, the idea of an archive for scientific research setting, and even the review of internet governance.

What is difficult to explain is the failure of wealthy governments to act decisively on the primary motivation for the Summit – the fear that the 'digital divide' is reinforcing the 'education divide', the 'income divide', the 'health divide', instead of alleviating them. No new mechanisms were created; a decision on the Digital Solidarity Fund was pushed forward only to prevent a collapse of the Summit. A fuller answer emerges when the WSIS is viewed in its historical context, as the intersection of two global debates that for several decades have unfolded in parallel, seldom touching. The WSIS witnessed the dying moments of one, but the other raises hope for the future.

The 'official' debate on the 'information society' (then called the 'post-industrial society') dates to the early 1970s. Academics demonstrated that 'information workers' had become the largest block of workers in wealthy countries, that an 'intellectual technology' infrastructure was emerging alongside the industrial infrastructure, and that more and more goods were in fact packaged information. These insights predated the explosion in ICTs, and offered several different strategic models for society to take full advantage of the trend, from state-led investment through to market-led approaches. This is interesting for two reasons: It gives the lie to 'technology determinists' who argue that technological innovation drives what

[79] 23 February 2004. This version appeared first on the website of the "Communication Rights in the Information Society" (CRIS) campaign, see www.communicationrights.org. An edited version was published in UNRISD News No. 26, Spring/Summer 2004.

later became known as the 'information society', pointing to a more complex process of a growing role of information provoking the revolution in technology. More important, however, it reminds us that there are more ways to build an information society than the purely market-driven one – that there are many conceivable information societies and that the way we choose to construct it will leave a deep imprint on the kind that we end up with.

Only in the mid 1990s did the 'information society' agenda narrow to its current form, with the coining of the term by the European Union to launch its efforts to compete with the US' Global Information Infrastructure. In the political drive to privatise and liberalise, the corporate sector henceforth was to be the main actor with governments playing merely a facilitating role. The WSIS uncritically adopted this vision, the inherent limitations of which resulting in failure to inspire the innovation needed to achieve its goals.

For this model has reached its limits. The ITU in 2002 reported that the growth rate in new telephone lines (still the basic means for people to access the information society) had for the first time "plunged", and with half the world's telecom operators in private hands, that "...most 'easy' privatisations have already been carried out." (Telecoms Development Report 2002) Although partly cyclical, evidence is mounting that with pent-up demand among the middle classes and commercial entities largely satisfied, the market is incapable of delivering services to the mass of people outside. A narrow profit-driven agenda and the absence of effective universal services policies leave the majority of poorer people globally with little prospect of joining in this information society. The failure of the WSIS to set up, let alone finance, a 'Digital Solidarity Fund' demanded by poorer countries was down to the refusal of powerful governments to deviate from the prescribed model, which have served their corporations so well, and to consider alternative paradigms for development.

However, this information society agenda was met in Geneva by another, broader, agenda.

Also in the 1970s, the world for the first time debated the role of communication in society, embracing such matters as media governance, freedom of expression and human rights, spectrum and satellite use, journalism ethics and news, and cultural diversity. For a decade, the halls of UNESCO echoed with the heated arguments of governments trapped in a Cold War vocabulary, in the end achieving little. But concerns raised by this effort, however compromised, and the hopes raised by the idea of a right to communicate, did not disappear. In the two decades since, many in civil society have grown worried about the concentration of ownership of media and its focus on profits, the ever-growing duration of copyright and exceptionally powerful criminal laws to enforce it, the commercialisation of knowledge creation and a host of related issues.

Many among the thousands of NGOs converging on Geneva last December brought these issues to the WSIS, arguing that it is impossible to truly debate an ‘information society’ without considering who owns information, who controls its production and dissemination, and whose interests that information ultimately serves. At the WSIS, civil society demanded that these issues also be put on the table. When they were refused, they produced their own ‘Civil Society Declaration’, containing the bones of an alternative vision of an information society that truly puts people first, that holds the information and communication are inseparable, and that points to alternative ways of getting there.

Of course, it is perhaps unfair to criticise the WSIS for not tackling these issues. Neither governments nor the ITU ever intended it to address such broad concerns, no matter how genuine. The problem facing the CRIS campaign and others was that there is nowhere else to debate them at global level. Key changes to accessing knowledge, to the diversity of the audio-visual sector, or to cultural creativity are often wrought in the small print of WTO agreements, World Bank and IMF conditionality, the arcane language of WIPO, or endless technical meetings of the ITU. There exists no forum for all stakeholders to openly debate them, to fully explore their implications, to allow society as a whole into decisions that will deeply effect our future. Civil society had no choice but to bring them to the WSIS - a fact appreciated by many sympathetic governments - and the CRIS Campaign was always explicit concerning both the limitations of the formal WSIS process but and the opportunity offered by the informal process.

This ‘side-door’ entry into the WSIS raises the question of where this valuable debate can now reconvene, and is a key question for the CRIS Campaign and for many others.

The second phase of the WSIS is unlikely to offer an opportunity to rehearse the broader questions. But momentum gathered at the WSIS can be carried forward, apart from Tunis, towards other transnational governance fora and processes. The proposed UNESCO convention on cultural diversity might offer a useful platform to collaborate with like-minded governments; whilst the ongoing WTO negotiations around audio-visual sectors is an opportunity to articulate alternatives to the market approach. And there are many others, including at regional and bi-lateral levels.

On the other hand, at least equally important is to keep momentum going within the transnational processes of civil society itself, to deepen our understanding of the issues and build wider coalitions through for instance the World Social Forum and its regional counterparts. In the medium term, progress will depend largely on the capacity of civil society, working in collaboration others, to develop credible, realistic alternatives to the current paradigms to build the information and communication society.

Finally, organising and advocacy at the national and local levels, for the CRIS campaign as for others, is the key to long term sustainability and progress in communication rights. Despite all the talk and activity at global level, the national level is still where most people identify and feel the impact of change, the level at which they organise together, the level of most policy decision-making, and the level at which governments can be influenced and persuaded how to proceed in global and regional fora.

Indeed the importance of the national level is a lesson that the WSIS might usefully have been taken to heart, though there is little evidence that the Summit has created a momentum for that.

Next Steps

Arrangements for the Tunis Phase of the Summit

WSIS Secretary-General[80]

At its resumed third session, on 14 November 2003, the Preparatory Committee took note of the following proposal concerning the Tunis phase which would be submitted to the World Summit on Information Society in December for decision:

Arrangements for the Tunis phase of the Summit

We decide to hold a preparatory meeting in the first half of 2004 to review those issues of the information society which should form the focus of the Tunis phase of the WSIS and to agree on the structure of the process for the second phase on the basis of contributions from delegations. The Bureau of the Tunis phase of the WSIS under the leadership of its Chairman should commence preparation of this preparatory meeting.

[80] 10 December 2003, Document WSIS-03/GENEVA/DOC/8-E, Original: English, on the web at http://www.itu.int/wsis/documents/listing-all-en-s|1.asp

More Hypocrisy as Tunisia Hosts International Congress on Digital Divide[81]

Reporters sans Frontières

RSF has voiced outrage that an international congress on the digital divide is being held in Tunisia, a country that is assuming an increasingly important role within international bodies regulating the Internet despite the fact that it is one of the most repressive towards its own Internet users.

The congress is being held in Tunis from 14 to 16 October 2003. It was organised by the World Federation of Engineering Organizations (WFEO) and is viewed as a preparatory encounter for the next World Summit on the Information Society (WSIS), the second stage of which is scheduled to take place in Tunis in 2005.

"The WSIS is a major event for the Internet's development. The summit's member states must take action to prevent the Internet's future from being dictated by nations that repress freedom of expression," RSF Secretary-General Robert Ménard said.

The Tunisian authorities continue to detain a cyber-dissident, Zouhair Yahyaoui. Using the pseudonym "Ettounsi", which means "The Tunisian" in Arabic, Yahyaoui founded the online magazine "TUNeZINE" in July 2001 to distribute opposition documents and thereby provide information about the fight for democracy and freedom in Tunisia. He was one of the first persons to publish a letter to the president by Judge Mokhtar Yahyaoui criticising the judicial system.

Yahyaoui was arrested by plainclothes police in an Internet cafe on 4 June 2002. He was subjected to interrogation that included three sessions of "suspension", a form of torture in which the victim is suspended by the arms with his feet barely touching the ground. On 10 July 2002, the Tunis Appeals Court sentenced him to two years in prison for "distributing false news".

Further evidence of the Tunisian government's cynicism towards the WSIS has been President Ben Ali's decision to appoint Habib Ammar to head the preparatory committee for the summit's second stage. As a former national guard commander and

[81] 26.Oct.03: For further information, contact the RSF Internet Desk, rue Geoffroy Marie, Paris 75009, France, tel: +33 1 44 83 84 62, fax: +33 1 45 23 11 51, e-mail: internet@rsf.org, Internet: www.rsf.org

interior minister, Ammar actively participated in repression for many years. "During the period when he was interior minister, the ministry's facilities were transformed into a detention and torture centre," according to the organisations TRIAL and the World Organisation Against Torture (OMCT).

These two organisations recently lodged a criminal complaint against Ammar with the Canton of Geneva's general prosecutor, but the Prosecutor's Office shelved the complaint on the grounds that the Swiss Confederation gives immunity from arrest and detention to representatives of member states of the International Telecommunications Union (ITU), which is organising the WSIS.

The goal of the summit is to narrow the digital divide between rich and poor countries, but it is also supposed to adopt a declaration of principle on nations' policies towards the Internet. Many non-governmental organisations specialising in human rights issues are concerned about the current draft of the declaration, which has been heavily influenced by those countries that are the most repressive with regard to the Internet.

Tunisia and WSIS: Petition at the initiative of the WSIS Human Rights Caucus[82]

Human Rights Caucus

September 26, 2003

To the attention of the Press and civil society organizations

The WSIS Human Rights caucus publishes today a petition regarding the venue of the second phase of the World Summit on the Information Society in Tunis in 2005, and the nomination of a highly controversed personnality as president of the organizing committee.

The text of the petition reminds that "the two principal objectives of the Summit, that is to say the struggle to overcome the digital divide and the respect for human rights and fundamental freedoms in the information and communication society, cannot be dissociated from each other", and demands that "the holding of the second phase of the Summit in Tunis is subordinated to concrete signs by Tunisia that it respects human rights and fundamental freedoms, specially:

- the freeing of journalists and others held in prison for their opinions in Tunisia
- the appointment of a personality who is not the object of opprobrium at the head of the organizing committee of the second phase of the Summit
- the commitment to allow all civil society representatives from Tunisia and abroad to participate freely in the work of the Summit".

The WSIS Human Rights caucus has expressed its deep concerns with this regard during WSIS PrepCom3 in Geneva (15-26 September 2003) to many governmental delegations, including the group of European Union member States and accessing countries during a meeting organized with European civil society organizations.

This petition is published while the criminal complaint jointly lodged by the OMCT (World Organization Against Torture) and TRIAL (Track Impunity Always) has been shelved by the Canton of Geneva's General Prosecutor, with the motivation that "Article 12 of the headquarters agreement, which was signed in July 1971 by the

[82] Press Contact in Geneva: Christine Ferrier, OMCT, cf@omct.org, Tél: 00 41 22 809 49 39
Send signatures to Rikke Frank Jorgensen, DIHR, rfj@humanrights.dk
On the web at www.iris.sgdg.org/actions/smsi/hr-wsis

Swiss Confederation and the International Telecommunications Union (which is holding the summit), provides immunity from arrest and detention for state representatives to the ITU". See the joint communique on the website of OMCT, a member of the Human Rights caucus (http://www.omct.org).

The text of the petition, with the list of first signatory organizations, is available in English, French and Spanish on the Human Rights Caucus website: http://www.iris.sgdg.org/actions/smsi/hr-wsis

The WSIS Human Rights caucus is pursuing the collection of signatures, from all the organisations concerned with the respect of human rights and fundamental freedoms, and of their major importance in an information and communication society.

Positioning for second summit phase has begun: Tunisia meeting showed some directions[83]

Document of the Heinrich Boll Foundation

The structure as well as the struggles for the second phase of the WSIS summit process are slowy becoming clearer. One thing is clear: It will be more complex than the first round, as it has to deal with many more loose ends. WSIS 2003 only had to deliver two pieces of paper (the declaration of principles and the action plan). This left a lot of time for endless discussions, arm-twisting on wording, sorting out friends or foes in different arenas, and for civil society to start playing inside the official UN process. Now, the negotiators from Geneva will meet the real world. And as conflicts remain, the actors are positioning themselves for the second round.

Monitoring Implementation

In Tunisia in 2005, there will have to be a report on the implementation of the action plan and the principles from Geneva 2003 – so who is taking care of implemenation, by the way? And who is doing the benchmarking and reporting? A recent ITU proposal that was emphasized by ITU head Utsumi at an informal meeting in Tunisia earlier this month suggested a multistakeholder "coordination group". The UN ICT Task Force that is meeting in New York this week also is under discussion as an evaluator in fields where it has expertise. The ITU also regularly produces assessments of the world connectivity, and on 5 March, all the UN agencies that are involved in information society issues had a meeting in New York that mainly dealt with statistics. In other areas, there are useful annual reports done by NGOs, like the amnesty international yearbook or the privacy and human rights survey by EPIC and Privacy International. The reporting on implementation could therefore really become a multistakeholder exercise. But still, somebody has to take care that there will be any implementation in the first place. This is not about documents, it is about spending real money and sometimes making tough political decisions.

Implementation, part one: building infrastructures with no extra money

The conference "implementing the WSIS action plan" organized by the Commonwealth Telecommunications Organization this week in Nairobi will be a

[83] On the web at www.worldsummit2005.org 22 March 2004

good chance to discuss this and also present best practices and needed follow-up. It will especially deal with the situation in less developed countries and how to build up telecommunication infrastructures there. Therefore it will serve the interests of a broad range of diverse groups: The population and elites interested in getting more connectivity, the telecom companies interested in selling their services, the governments interested in positioning their contries as role models, the civil society organizations interested in linking the projects to their grassroots experience.

The major WSIS conflict on the financing of these activities will only sheepishly be adressed, though, according to the outline of the conference. The "digital solidarity fund" that was set up by Senegal and others after the summit is not eben mentioned. If delegates from richer governments will participate, they will mostly come from the development aid agencies and will not have any mandate to discuss fresh money or even structural reforms of bandwidth cost distrubution or even the global financial economic inequalities that are underlying the digital divide.

Implementation, part two: securing human rights? really?

This focus on infrastructures follows the technocratic approach that had been more prominent when the summit process started in 1998. But in the last year, civil society and some friendly governments have pushed the agenda from "information" (read: ICTs) to "society". This includes much more than infrastructures, and central for most other issues are human rights in the information society. There has been no initiative yet that looks into this direction for implementation. Regarding privacy for example, just a few days ago the Council of Europe's Cybercrime Convention has entered into force, which gives governments and law enforcement agencies broader powers of internet surveillance and sharing of personal information. In many parts of the world, censorship on- and offline is still prevailing. This is a clear contradiction to many principles of the WSIS summit declaration. Who is taking care of these implementation issues?

In this area, there are not so many overlapping interests. Some governments would officially like to strengthen human rights in the information age, and Brazil has even adopted the idea of communication rights. But many at the same time are extending surveillance at home, and few want to enter into open conflict with others. This is where civil society is already quite active, but many of these activities are not yet related directly to the WSIS follow-up process.

The problem will become very concrete when the first preparatory meetings start in Tunis. Pressure from the WSIS community on the repressive Tunisian regime has already built up considerably during phase one. The torture general responsible for organizing the summit on behalf of the Tunisian government (see more here) has been relegated to "logistics only", and rumours say he might be sent to another job soon. Still, the government's overall human rights record is not bettered through such symbolic acts. All incoming and outgoing internet traffic in Tunesia is still censored and monitored. As participants at the recent informal WSIS meeting in Tunis could experience, the Human Rights Watch and amnesty international websites could not be accessed from either Internet cafes in the city or at the cybercafe set up at the meeting by the conference organizers. People still are put into prison for accessing opposition websites. Use of cryptography is illegal.

The civil society organizations involved in the WSIS process will have to make sure that these problems are adressed clearly, but in close coordination and solidarity with local groups. But they also have to make sure that the focus is not on Tunisia alone, but on all human rights violations around the world. The implementation of this will have to include constructive dialogue, but also heavy public pressure and close coordination among diverse groups. Only slowly are the traditional human rights organizations approaching the new area of digital rights or civil liberties in the information age. The case of Tunisia can be helpful in getting them more involved in the WSIS process. At the same time, though, very governmental Tunisian NGOs are threatening to mess everything up.

Implementation, part three: extending global knowledge commons

While the 2003 summit declaration speaks about finding a balance between the interests of creators of knowledge and the public interest to use it widely, the intellectual property battle in the real world is going back and forth. A few examples: The European Union recently agreed on a strong enforcement policy that allows severe punishment of teenagers who share music online. Scientists are more and more publishing their research online and for free. The creative commons license is spreading all over the world. The U.S. music industry is filing thousands of lawsuits against users of filesharing networks. Free Software is being used in ever more public institutions.

This patchwork actually shows a true implementation of the summit decisions, as the governments in Geneva have not has been able to decide in favour of a true vision, but instead chose an unclear comprimise formula. The underlying conflicts and struggles are still going on, and so will the debate on this in the second WSIS phase.

The Latin America and Caribbean (LAC) regional meeting and the Global Knowledge Partnership (GKP) meeting in San Jose, Costa Rica in May will be the first major events where this is adressed again after the summit. Brazil as a major regional power has been heavily pressing for Free Software and the global knowledge commons in the WSIS process. If you look at the agenda of the GKP meeting, it sounds familiar: Free Software, Knowledge Sharing, Financing and Internet Governance will be debated there. Topics like "the way forward in ensuring sustainability, replication and upscaling of initiatives" do not sound very pro-monopoly or pro-proprietary. Brazil and others are clearly planning to put this issue on the agenda of the preparations for WSIS 2005, as will civil society. It is pretty open if there can be a coherent implementation in this field if the underlying conflics are still prevailing.

The ITU proposal for the second WSIS phase is suggesting thematic preparatory conferences that would be organized by international organizations with specific knowledge in the respective fields. In this case, it would be the World Intellectual Property Organization (WIPO). WIPO has showed some interesting movements during the last year, and it seems it is opening up towards open knowledge production models. But it still is a biased organization, as is the WTO with its TRIPS agreement on international trade in intellectual property. How can the WSIS implementation activities, the benchmarking and the follow-up discussions be managed and facilitated to ensure a balanced process? These questions have not yet been clearly adressed. Civil society has to make sure that it not only deals with WSIS, but also engages other relevant international organizations. Governments also have to take this into account. Brazil has already announced it will hold a WSIS thematic meeting in the second half of 2004 – let's see if they get the relevant players on board.

Unresolved conflicts, part one: Internet governance

The diplomats assigned to the WSIS are also forced to continue working on the major open conflicts: Finance and Internet Governance. The latter, too, brings them down to earth, or better: into the basement, to the technicians who run the internet (and who are missing the "Jedi Engineers"). The upcoming meeting of the UN ICT Task Force this week in New York is opened with a "nuts and bolds" lecture by ICANN president Vinton Cerf, who will attempt to explan to the politicians and global elites how the internet really works. Good luck, one is tempted to say.

The most tricky issue will be to define what "Internet governance" means. As became clear in the recent ITU workshop, it is not just technical coordination anymore, and ICANN will have to face a broad discussion over its legitimacy and its mandate. After the summit 2003, a number of governments announced more or less publicly that they don't want to go through the whole process again for phase two. They prefer to leave the summit declaration as it is, to not open any closed cases, and to just focus on the two controversial issues, namely Internet governance and finance. It might be the case that now that the discussion has broadened the term "internet governance" to encompass everything from the management of the name space to such complex and heterogenous matters as worldwide privacy legislation, licencing schemes or filtering, to name some examples, the "Internet governance" working group under the auspices of UN secretary general Kofi Annan will have to break down the matter into sub-groups anyway. These might easily mirror the different negotiating and drafting groups that were set up in preparing for the Geneva phase of the summit.

Swiss "e-envoy" Markus Kummer, who was picked by Kofi Annan as chairman of this working group, was not too happy about this task. "I was just a diplomat at the wrong time at the wrong place". But at least Kummer has announced that "the WSIS format based on its past record would not have satisfied those who wanted a truly open process with the full and active participation of private sector and other stakeholders." It is not yet clear, though, if the different stakeholders will really have the same or even more participation rights as they had in the WSIS prepcoms before December 2003. The UN ICT Task Force meeting in New York for example seems to be "invitation only", though a number of key WSIS participants are willing to participate. If they again are locked out, the second phase of WSIS will already have its first little scandal.

Unresolved conflicts, part two: finance

The other working group set up by the Geneva phase of the summit is on finance. Though it has not started working yet, as for internet governence it is at least clear who will chair it. Kofi Annan has reportedly picked Mark Malloch Brown, administrator of the UN Development Programme UNDP.

Though this sounds good at first sight, there might be a problem with this. UNDP recently shut down the ICT4D ("D" for development) programme area. It has mainstreamed it into the existing programmes, a maneuver that normally is linked to budget cuts. Even worse, the "finance" and "donations" this issue might get from big Western ICT corporations can mean a backlash for the global knowledge commons and here especially for the Free Software movement. At the World Economic Forum in Davos in January this year, Bill Gates announced that Microsoft would bring cash and software to a computer training programme it has set up with UNDP, as part of a $1 billion company investment to bring computers to developing countries. UNDP will work with the Microsoft "Unlimited Potential" programme to invest in community centres in poor regions, following a pilot project in Afghanistan where the two organisations set up 16 centres. UNDP administrator Mark Malloch Brown - the same one that now will lead the finance issue for the WSIS - said the ambition of this project was "to hook up the world to the Internet". (see here for more)

Well, this hook will certainly turn into an addiction and lessen the freedom of the information society in developing countries if it is implemented 1:1. Microsoft's "embrace and extend" strategy has long been critizised, because it is like a drug dealer who looks nice and altruistic by giving you the first shot for free. And by the way, "a billion dollars worth" of Microsoft software costs the company only a small fraction if this sum – it is essentially only shipping cheap CDs to customers who would normally never buy them anyway. This is not what "bridging the digital divide" – the original motto of WSIS – was intended to mean.

The stronger governments of the south are already preparing for the follow-up and show a strong will to not let this issue be buried and forgotten in a working group. The heads of state and ministers particpating in the G-15 summit in Venezuela in late February "particularly support the initiative aimed at the creation and mobilization of a digital solidarity fund", as the final declaration states. But this is easily done when you are among peers and do not have to negotiate and argue with the ones whose money you are asking for.

As said above, the upcoming Nairobi conference on implementation later this week will neither generate fresh money nor even sustainable economic models for North-South relations. The more fundamental question – how to tackle the global economic divide – will also not be adressed here. The WSIS might not be the perfect place for this anyway, but just ignoring it here does not lead any further. Quite to the contrary, a summit with the task of producing a global vision for society will have to adress underlying unequalities. But who is going to do this in a way that can build pressure on the rich and powerful North?

Civil society will have to build much stronger links to the critics of neoliberal globalization and the wider social movements – like the world and regional social forums - if it wants to maintain its legitimacy as the defendor of equality and freedom for WSIS two.

Anything else?

Barcelona is planning a thematic meeting on cultural diversity, as is Lyon on the role of cities and local authorities in the information society. And Italy reportedly also wants to take care of the financing issue.

Ah, yes: The United States government has reportedly announced it wants to hold a meeting on security. Did anybody say "surprise"?

The big picture

So, looking at the mosaic that slowly is forming into a bigger picture: The next phase could be a patchwork show of pet projects, where everybody holds meetings of differing relevance but still somewhat connected to the summit, in his area of interest and political preference. Getting these together into a unified vision will be a tough task.

If WSIS I had only reached an agreement on the last day before the summit itself, it seems that phase two might overstretch the ability of negotiators to deal with complexity. Let's see if civil society with its more fluid structures is better suited for this task.

Of course the really big picture would be on another level. It would adress the global power shifts, the information revolution in general, its impact for global governance and the fact that visions are not invented but grow slowly but constantly. But for this task, even we feel a bit too overwhelmed by the complexity at the moment.

And don't believe all the "experts" who gather in New York and Nairobi this week know better. They may have some smart ideas, but they also can only make educated guesses.

Excerpt from Pole Star: Human Rights in the Information Society[84]

Deborah Hurley

Key Recommendations

This section articulates five sets of key recommendations to define the way forward and to muster scattered forces to renew the effort to embed the development of the information society securely in the ground of human rights. The goal is to stimulate dialogue at national and international levels to create concentric rings of action, agreement, and adoption that ripple out across the globe.

All stakeholders in the information society must contribute to its development, with a common, explicit vision to implant it firmly in the foundation of human rights. Governments, the private sector, international organizations, civil society, researchers, and individuals must contribute their authority, competence, expertise, and commitment. Indeed, the first article of the Charter of the United Nations states that the purpose of the United Nations is "to achieve international cooperation _ in promoting and encouraging respect for human rights and fundamental freedoms for all."

World Summit on the Information Society

The Declaration of the World Summit on the Information Society should record the commitment of states to establish human rights as the platform on which the information society will be constructed. In the interim between the 2003 WSIS and the 2005 WSIS, activities to this end should be undertaken that are high-visibility, low-cost, short-term, and that catalyze or facilitate ongoing activities and other actors in measurable ways. Specifically, in fulfillment of these goals, three to five concrete projects should be identified to provide a quick launch, boost, and public statement of increased investment in human rights in the information society.

These efforts should feed into a larger work program for the period after 2005, which can be developed in parallel and adopted at the 2005 WSIS. The work program should be of three to four years' duration, with phases of activity and different timeframes for specific projects, producing a stream of outputs throughout the life of

[84] On the web at www.ichrdd.ca/english/commdoc/publications/ globalization/wsis/polestar.pdf

the program. Substantive, crosscutting issues might be chosen for maximum impact. Some of the projects should address the most dispossessed, such as Africa, least developed countries, and failed states, and the most critical policy issues, among them security of the global networks, basic ICT infrastructure, and use of ICT for literacy, food and water safety, and health. All stakeholders must be called on to contribute. The goal for 2010 will be to document specific measures and their outcomes that have raised the human condition, especially in the areas of greatest need, by the use of ICT and human rights.

World Commission on the Information Society

Similar to the Brundtland Commission(29) of the 1980s, a World Commission on the Information Society should be formed to articulate and establish, based on human rights, the necessary norms and institu-tions for the information society.

Presently, information policy issues are addressed in several international fora, including the International Telecommunication Union, the World Trade Organization (WTO), the Organization for Economic Cooperation and Development (OECD), the United Nations Educational, Scientific and Cultural Organization (UNESCO), and the Asia-Pacific Economic Coope-ration forum (APEC). No one organization has responsibility, competence and expertise across the full range of information policy issues and a solid grasp of their inter-relationships. In light of the partial coverage of information policy issues among these institutions, the meagre expertise that does exist is scattered.

Specific Information Society Initiatives

1. Governments should abolish the principle of governmental ownership of copyright, such as Crown Copyright, in information produced by the government. This step would immediately inject vast quantities of information into the public domain, making it freely available for use and increasing access to information.

2. Assistance should be provided to developing countries to make the transition to reasonable flat-rate subscriber charges in order to increase access to and use of communication technologies, including the Internet.

3. Governments and the relevant international organizations should review the international instruments adopted to date, which relate specifically to the information society, to assess their compliance with human rights instruments and principles.(30) This review should be conducted under the auspices of the Secretary General of the

United Nations, in collaboration with the United Nations Commission on Human Rights and the Office of the High Commissioner for Human Rights. The review should recommend, as necessary to bring these documents into compliance with human rights obligations, any needed amendments and additions to the accords, as well as specific, concrete implementation and enforcement measures and mechanisms. Such instruments include the WTO's *Agreement on Trade-related Aspects of Intellectual Property Rights, Information Technology Agreement, Agreement on Basic Telecommunications Services*, the Council of Europe's *Convention on Cybercrime*, and the OECD's *Guidelines for the Security of Information Systems and Networks: Towards a Culture of Security*, as well as other regional security arrangements under development.

4. Similarly, all governments should review legislation adopted to date, which relate specifically to the information society, to assess their compliance with human rights instruments and principles and revise these documents, as necessary to bring them into compliance. This review should include recent counter-terrorism and national security proposals and legislation by states, such as the 2001 Patriot Act of the United States, Canada's 2001 *Anti-Terrorism Act* and similar initiatives and laws in many other countries.

5. States, especially the United States, as a leading producer, user and exporter of ICT and information services, should join the international trend to protect privacy and personal information and adopt national legislation, covering both the public and private sectors, based upon the OECD Privacy Guidelines and the Council of Europe Convention.

6. In order to build human capacity and improve conditions in the developing world, governments should undertake specific measures to increase ICT technical, legal, business, and educational infrastructure and indigenous expertise. Researchers, academics, and experts, including graduate students, in developed countries should be given incentives to become more involved in collaboration with developing countries. Governments in developing countries should be assisted to concentrate their precious intellectual capital on local needs in economic and social development in their own countries and regions, to convene experts from developing countries to collaborate on common problems, and to connect them with developed country counterparts with relevant expertise and interests. This work must be undertaken with care, so as to enhance, rather than overwhelm, local activities and indigenous capacity in developing countries.

Strengthening Human Rights Implementation and Enforcement

The principles of human rights are well-known and recognized and the governing instruments widely adopted and ratified, but compliance and human rights protection are still insufficient. Ratification of applicable human rights accords is the necessary first step. Approximately three-quarters of nations have ratified the two treaties that, along with the UDHR, comprise the *International Bill of Rights*, namely the *International Covenant on Civil and Political Rights*, and the *International Covenant on Economic, Social and Cultural Rights*.(31) Significantly, China has not yet ratified the *International Covenant on Civil and Political Rights*, while United States has not ratified the *International Covenant on Economic, Social and Cultural Rights.* Similarly, states should accept the jurisdiction of relevant human rights bodies, such as the Inter-American Commission and Court, the African Commission on Human and People's Rights, and the Council of Europe.

States should identify specific, concrete measures that they will take to implement and enforce human rights instruments, especially with reference to issues of the information society. Finally, the United Nations Commission on Human Rights should appoint a Special Rapporteur on the Information Society to complete a study of human rights and the information society, as an input to the 2005 WSIS and the World Commission on the Information Society.

Additional Research

Since the information policy field is still developing, there are many potential areas of additional research. A few of the most critical are listed here. As the information society evolves, the economics of information must be better understood. Similarly, it would be useful to develop and disseminate further economic theories and studies that include non-economic, social goals, such as environmental protection and labour rules. There should be further mapping of the life cycle of information, through creation, access, distribution, use and destruction.(32) As yet, there has been little assessment of the impact of ICT on human rights and of the manner in which human rights laws and policies apply in the information society. Furthermore, there is limited methodology for making these assessments.

Specific, acute issues of the information society, especially for developing countries, should be identi-fied, highlighted, targeted and ameliorated, similar to the manner in which the international community has tackled certain diseases and other human health issues and brought about real improvement.

At Issue in the World Summit: Internet Governance

WSIS Agreement on Internet Governance: convene a working group to report back in 2005.

Document of the ITU

Text of the Declaration

44. The Internet has evolved into a global facility available to the public and its governance should constitute a core issue of the Information Society agenda. The international management of the Internet should be multilateral, transparent and democratic, with the full involvement of governments, the private sector, civil society and international organizations. It should ensure an equitable distribution of resources, facilitate access for all and ensure a stable and secure functioning of the Internet, taking into account multilingualism.

45.The management of the Internet encompasses both technical and public policy issues and should involve all stakeholders and relevant intergovernmental and international organizations. In this respect it is recognized that:

a) policy authority for Internet-related public policy issues is the sovereign right of States. They have rights and responsibilities for international Internet-related public policy issues; b) the private sector has had and should continue to have an important role in the development of the Internet, both in the technical and economic fields; c) civil society has also played an important role on Internet matters especially at community level and should continue to play such a role; d) intergovernmental organizations have had and should continue to have a facilitating role in the coordination of the Internet related public policy issues; e) international organizations have also had and should continue to have a important role in the development of Internet-related technical standards and relevant policies.

46. International Internet governance issues should be addressed in a coordination manner. We ask the Secretary General of the United Nations to set up a working group on Internet governance, in an open and inclusive process that ensures a mechanism for the full and active participation of governments, the private sector and

civil society from both developing and developed countries, involving relevant intergovernmental and international organizations and forums, to investigate and make proposals for action, as appropriate, on the governance of Internet by 2005.

Text of the Action Plan

4e) We ask the Secretary General of the United Nations to set up a working group on Internet governance, in an open and inclusive process that ensures a mechanism for the full and active participation of governments, the private sector and civil society from both developing and developed countries, involving relevant intergovernmental and international organizations and forums, to investigate and make proposals for action, as appropriate, on the governance of Internet by 2005. The group should, inter alia:

i) develop a working definition of Internet governance;

ii) identify the public policy issues that are relevant to Internet governance;

iii) develop a common understanding of the respective roles and responsibilities of governments, existing intergovernmental and international organisations and other forums as well as the private sector and civil society from both developing and developed countries;

iv) prepare a report on the results of this activity to be presented for consideration and appropriate action for the second phase of WSIS in Tunis in 2005.

f) Governments are invited to:

i) facilitate the establishment of national and regional Internet Exchange Centres;

ii) manage or supervise, as appropriate, their respective country code top-level domain name (ccTLD);

iii) promote awareness of the Internet.

ICANN or ITU? Civil Society debates Internet Governance

Document of the Heinrich Böll Foundation[85]

In the run-up to the Intersessional Meeting which is currently taking place in Paris, controversial debates broke out between civil society members around the theme of internet governance. While some criticised the business-based approach of ICANN, a largely corporate body which currently regulates most of the basic rules of the internet, others feared a government-led take-over of the net through ITU.

The first version of the Civil Society Priorities document stated that the current management of internet names and numbers as well as other regulations "should be re-examined with the full participation of all stakeholders...."

Stick with ICANN?

Several participants of Civil Society discussions felt that such a statement could be interpreted as support for a shift in internet governance from ICANN to the ITU. Many governments had previously expressed their wish to give an intergovernmental body more control in regulating the net, often enough for dubious reasons. One member of the Civil Society organisation involved in governance issues said that this statement "can only serve to support the arguments of governments that wish to gain control over Internet resource allocation, and others hoping to see the ITU or some other inter-governmental organization take control of Internet naming and addressing." It would be seen as a call for governments to take over the internet management system. And as another observer stated, "unless there was simultaneously some fundamental changes in the ITU's membership and procedures, this would be a disaster for civil society organizations (which are unable to participate there, unlike in ICANN) and probably for the Internet more generally." While everyone regarded ICANN as far from perfect, its policy making processes were seen as far more open to Civil Society than those of any possible alternatives.

---

[85] Document of the Heinrich-Böll-Foundation. On the web at http://www.worldsummit2003.de/en/web/401.htm 16 July 2003.

Or support ITU?

Opponents argued that "ICANN has been and still is in the hands of the corporate interests, and that ICANN final decisions are in the hands of the US Department of Commerce, to which ICANN reports and without which it doesn't make any important decision." A "byzantine structure" like ICANN would essentially be geared towards corporate needs and would therefore not be an appropriate system for allocating a global commons. As for government control of the net, one observer stated: "When governments are in, we favour multilateralism among unilateralism (i.e. in this case the sole US government decision)."

Another rationale for supporting change towards ITU participation in internet management was seen in encouraging competition between the two institutions. Internet governance split between ICANN and the ITU, and thereby a separation of powers, was regarded as a promising path towards keeping the dangers of internet control at a minimum.

State control vs. Corporate influence

Essentially, the debate was about choosing the lesser evil – corporate regulation with some Civil Society input, leaning towards neoliberalism, or government-based regulation, implying the danger of repressive abuse by states. A "third way", calling for complete reexamination and discussion on new bases, and to work out models for alternative regulation, was seen by many as the most desirable option – in the words of one discussant: "taking stands on behalf of the non-state, non-corporate public interest" – but also as unrealistic at the present state of negotiations.

A compromise

The final version of the Priorities document offered a compromise, referring to "the values of participation, inclusiveness, transparency and accountability", calling for "the democratic management of international bodies dealing with ICTs", and stressing "public interests and compatibility with human rights standards."

In the first plenary session of the Intersessional Meeting, Wolfgang Kleinwaechter from the Internet Governance Caucus elaborated on this approach, calling for an inclusion of all stakeholders – civil society, private industry and governments – and noting that "no single body and no single stakeholder group is able to manage these challenges alone". Internet management should be a bottom-up process, "as inclusive as possible, transparent and open for participation by all interested parties, in particular for civil society and individual Internet users." But, referring to the first of the above positions, he also made clear that the Caucus saw "no need for any intergovernmental organization to take responsibility for management of the domain names and the IP addresses," but that rather "we see a need for ongoing improvement of the existing structures and mechanisms."

ICANN Statement to the World Summit on the Information Society Plenary[86]

Speech by Dr Paul Twomey, President and CEO, ICANN

Your Excellency President
Your Excellencies, Heads of States and Governments
Ministers
Ladies and Gentlemen:

Thank you for the opportunity to speak to such a distinguished audience at an historical Summit. I am the President and CEO of ICANN, the organization that is responsible for the coordination of the Internet's domain name system. This public-private partnership based on a NGO model designed to encapsulate the mechanism by which the Internet functions. It has responsibility for the coordination of the management of Internet's system of unique identifiers including Internet Protocols (IP) address space allocation, protocol identifier assignment, Domain name system management, and root server system management functions. Its structure reflects the global Internet community (governments, the technical community, registries, the business community, academia and non-commercial communities and representatives of consumer interests) working together to promote the stability and integrity of the Internet.

We are very committed to achieving the Secretary General's goals for the Information Society, and his objectives for the Summit. We are pleased with the level of knowledge about the Internet that this Summit has generated. And we are pleased with the Summit's call for a Working Group under the guidance of the Secretary General to further discuss and define these important issues. We think that the fully inclusive nature of such an approach, involving governments, the private sector, civil society and international governmental organisations and International organisations reflects the general partnership approach which has helped build the Internet over the past 35 years. We look forward to sharing our experiences and learning from the perspectives of others as part of these discussions.

---

[86] On the web at http://www.icann.org/correspondence/twomey-to-wsis-11dec03.htm
Plenary of the World Summit for the Information Society
Geneva, Switzerland
11 December 2003

The Information Society is everyone's future - partly thanks to the Internet and its rapid development. Why do we have an Internet today? Because the technical community, academia, and governments started something and private sector (business, civil society, investments) academia, governments, technical community, kept building it.

In following the WSIS process, and discussions to date, many issues have been raised. These issues fall within four general layers - these being socio-cultural, economic and development, jurisdictional and legal, and technical coordination.

We do not stand in the way of governments and others feeling that they want to establish a mechanism to discuss issues in the area. And our experience suggests that equal participation of all sectors is essential to any discussions surrounding any Internet issues.

The impacts of the limited technical functions ICANN helps coordinate and manage have different aspects in different parts of the world. As someone from the Asia Pacific I am very conscious that the Internet and its surrounding issues look different according to where one sits. ICANN looks forward to further discussing and learning from both its global and regional governmental, private sector, technical and civil society partners. As the Internet continues to evolve we are committed to continuing to evolve. We must take both a global and a local perspective. As part of our commitment to this vision, ICANN is expanding its physical office presence over the next six months to having offices in all the regions of the world. And our virtual global presence will be increasingly multi-lingual.

As we discuss the issues of Internet governance and of the need to keep growing the Information Society, let us also be conscious of what we have built in the technical field and how well it does work. The bottom-up, inclusive model for technical coordination - built over the last 35 years - involves tens of thousands of practitioners on a daily basis. Their results are impressive:

On a global level, there are an estimated 55 million domain names that are registered. The Regional Internet Registries and ICANN, working together, have allocated approximately 313 million IP v4 addresses since 1999. And some experts think there is sufficient spare IP v4 address space for allocation to meet demand for another 20 years or so. Further, the new generation of IP v6 addresses contains 3.4 by 1038 addresses. Many billions for every person alive today. Approximately an IP address for each atom of the known Universe.

Every day 750 millions users use the Internet to achieve approximately 18 billion resolutions per day. That is more than five times the number of phone calls in the North America per day. The system works. It works in the same way for all users of the Internet.

Let us build on it for the benefit of all.

Thank you.

News from the Internet Society: Developing the Potential of the Internet through Coordination, not Governance[87]

The Internet Society

The Internet Society (ISOC) is a global not-for-profit membership organisation founded in 1991 to provide leadership in Internet-related standards, education, and policy issues. We are dedicated to ensuring the open development, evolution and use of the Internet for the benefit of people throughout the world. Our education initiatives, for example, have helped bring Internet connectivity to virtually all developing countries over the last 12 years. ISOC is the organisational home of the Internet Engineering Task Force (IETF) - an open consensus-based group responsible for defining Internet protocols and standards.

Through our participation in WSIS 2003 we aim to increase understanding and awareness of what is important in order to develop and maintain the Internet's stability, open nature and global reach.

The Internet has come of age

In many countries, the Internet has become a mass medium. This has brought with it reflexive pressure on policy makers to regulate it as if it were radio, television, or other mass media. While Governments naturally seek to address their citizens' interests regarding online privacy, spam, Internet security, intellectual property protection, the price of Internet access, and the digital divide, our position is that better use of technology, and broad participation in today's Internet coordination processes, not Government regulation, are the most effective and appropriate ways to satisfy these concerns.

The biggest barrier to the Internet fulfilling its immense potential could turn out to be misinformed and inappropriate intervention in the way in which the Internet's technologies, resources and policies are developed, deployed and coordinated. The Internet Society can help provide guidance here.

---

[87] The Internet Society at the 'World Summit on the Information Society' (WSIS 2003) http://www.isoc.org/news/7.shtml

What is the nature of the Internet?

The Internet is a modern distributed communications medium. No one is in charge of the Internet and yet everyone is in charge. Unlike the antiquated system of national telephone network monopolies, the global Internet consists of tens of thousands of interconnected networks run by Internet Service Providers, individual companies, universities, Governments, and other institutions. Some of these are global in scope, others regional or local. Hundreds of different organisations and thousands of different companies make decisions every year that contribute to how the Internet develops.

These varied entities, together with the users of the Internet and the developers of Internet technologies and applications, have specific needs for coordination. Collaborative processes that are critical for the future stability and evolution of the Internet, and which should not be modified arbitrarily or abruptly, satisfy these needs.

Coordination, not Governance

It is misleading to use the term 'Internet Governance' when the Internet is clearly not a single entity to govern. It is more useful to refer to 'Internet Coordination'. The multiple facets of the Internet require different types of coordination, each calling for specific competences and sensitivities to balance the needs of the Internet user community globally and locally.

Specific Internet Coordination activities are taking place globally at three levels:

- Coordination of the definition of Internet standards
- Coordination of the availability and assignment of Internet resources
- Coordination of the policies preventing misuse of the Internet

This coordination is best performed by the existing set of organisations using proven processes. Because of the diverse nature of these activities, it is unrealistic to expect a single body - Government or otherwise - to take on all these roles effectively.

Coordinating Internet standards

The Internet Engineering Task Force (IETF) under the umbrella of the Internet Society, is one of the oldest and most successful Internet coordination processes.

Other organisations are also involved in Internet-related standards, including the IEEE, the W3C and the ITU.

Many of the protocols at the heart of today's Internet (e.g. TCP, IP, HTTP, FTP, SMTP, Telnet, PPP, POP3, the DNS protocol etc.) were developed through IETF standards activities. The results of the IETF are well engineered and practical open protocol standards that are trusted and open to global implementation with little or no licensing restrictions - they are freely available on the Internet, without cost, to everyone.

The strength of the IETF process lies in its unique culture and talented global community of network designers, network operators, service providers, equipment vendors, and researchers. They all openly contribute their individual technical experience and engineering wisdom in an environment that fosters innovation and the open exchange of ideas.

This process, which is open to anyone, helps quickly identify and articulate problems of common interest. It also helps build the trust required to make the further investments necessary for a protocol to be usefully implemented and deployed. Ultimately, however, it is the Internet users themselves that determine whether or not a protocol is valuable and useful enough for widespread use. Here the IETF track record of producing useful, widely deployed protocols is unrivalled.

Coordinating Internet resources: The Internet registry system

There has always been a need to manage the allocation of Internet resources such as the unique addresses that identify devices connected to the Internet (IP addresses), generic top-level domain names (e.g. .org), country code top-level domain names (e.g. .ch), domain names (such as www.isoc.org), and the systems that translate domain names into IP addresses (e.g. the Domain Name System or DNS).

This coordination activity has been handled by long-standing, not-for-profit membership organisations such as the Regional Internet Registries (RIRs) and top-level domain (TLD) registries.

More recently, coordination at a global level has been supported by ICANN (the Internet Corporation for Assigned Names and Numbers). Established in 1998, ICANN is also a not-for-profit organisation. Business, technical, non-commercial, academic, governmental and end-user communities participate in ICANN.

These organisations are a meeting point for bottom-up, consensual, industrial self-regulation by the groups and individuals that use their services and resources.

Coordinating policies preventing misuse of the Internet

As we have seen, organisations such as the RIRs, TLD registries, ICANN and the IETF all have very specific roles. It is neither within their charters, nor within their capabilities, to take on responsibility for all areas of Internet Coordination - particularly that of preventing inappropriate use of the Internet. For example, areas such as 'cyber crime' (e.g. fraud and child pornography) require coordinated global attention by lawmakers - and not by those responsible for the equitable coordination of the underlying Internet infrastructure. Security matters also need to be addressed by organisations providing Internet access (not only by standards developers), and intellectual property issues may best be handled by organisations such as WIPO.

In discussions about these broader Internet policy issues there is cooperation between all the organisations mentioned above. ICANN for example works with WIPO to implement its Uniform Domain Name Dispute Resolution Policy (UDRP). And the Internet Society, with technical advice from the IETF, works with Governments and policy makers to explain the effects and possibilities of new Internet technologies.

The way forward - Make your voice heard

Existing consensus-based processes have given us the Internet and have successfully coordinated its phenomenal growth: thousands of new networks, new policy procedures, new top-level domain names, new protocols etc. All of them constantly balance the needs and stability of today's Internet with future demands.

An open debate is now needed to move towards common, globally acceptable policies, processes and technologies to prevent misuse of the Internet. Governments have a vital role to play here as a concerted effort on the part of the Internet community, non-governmental organisations and Governments can help strengthen and extend today's successful coordination processes.

The successful continued development of the Internet for the benefit of everyone can be ensured by participation in these proven processes rather than by attempting to create new untested mechanisms that are inappropriate to the unique characteristics of the Internet

The Internet Society remains dedicated to providing information and orientation about Internet structures and processes. We encourage broad participation in the activities of each of the organisations involved in Internet coordination.

At Issue in the World Summit: Media

Statement of the WSIS Civil Society Media Caucus at PrepCom 3: Proposal for Text to be included in the WSIS Declaration[88]

Tracey Naughton, Chair, WSIS Civil Society Media Caucus

Freedom of expression, media freedom and editorial independence are central to any conception of an information society.

The guiding overriding principle of WSIS on freedom of expression and media freedom should be Article 19 of the universal declaration of human rights:

"Everyone has the right to freedom of thought; this right includes freedom to hold opinions without interference and to seek, receive and impart information and ideas through any media and regardless of frontiers"

Article 19 needs to be implemented, for all media regardless of the technologies used.

Security and other considerations should not be allowed to compromise freedom of expression and media freedom.

New information and communication technologies will strengthen the important role of traditional media, such as broadcasting and print press.

Legislation to ensure the participation of all in the information society should:

1. Promote and defend the existence and development of free and independent media,
2. Encourage pluralism and diversity of media ownership and avoid excessive media concentration,
3. Recognize the specific and crucial role of public service broadcasting and community media,
4. Transform state-controlled media into editorially independent organizations.

International standards of labour rights and social protections must apply to all media workers.

---

[88] On the web at lists.sn.apc.org/pipermail/wsis/ 2003-September/000020.html

Formulation of professional and ethical standards in journalism is the responsibility of media professionals themselves.

Media: The Step-Child of WSIS?[89]

Nalaka Gunawardene[90]

In his 1992 book, *How the World Was One*, Sir Arthur C Clarke described a bizarre vision of the near future: Ted Turner is offered the post of World President, but he rejects it – because he didn't want to give up power!

Well, the founder of CNN no longer runs the network and spends time popularising bison burghers and supporting the United Nations. But Clarke was once again uncannily perceptive when he prophesied the emergence of media moguls whose power far exceeds that of nation states or political leaders.

The media has always been a manipulator of power, in both politics and commerce. But it is only in the past two decades that this power has been amplified by new information and communications technologies – ICTs for short. These, and deregulation policies that opened by many national markets, enabled a handful of trans-national corporations to build truly global electronic empires that press barons of the past could only dream about.

Ted Turner and Rupert Murdoch are only the best known faces of this industry that runs wide and deep. And it is no longer a western monopoly either: countries like India, Thailand and Mexico have produced their own mini-Murdochs.

The implications of this have been slow to sink in, and not surprisingly, these issues are hardly discussed in the media itself. We in the media love to turn the spotlight on everyone else – except ourselves.

Take television, for example. Viewers across developing Asia were euphoric when, in the early 1990s, trans-boundary satellite television ended the monopoly of dull and propagandistic state owned television. Not even the Great Wall of China could stop satellite television transmissions from 36,000 kilometres above the Earth, cooed one advertisement for STAR which ushered in this change. (China found ways of coercing STAR, but that's another story.)

---

[89] On the web at http://www.oneworld.net/article/view/72686/1/
OneWorld Guest Editorials represent the viewpoint of the authors and not necessarily that of the OneWorld Network.
[90] Nalaka Gunawardene worked in print and broadcast media in his native Sri Lanka before pursuing a career in non-profit media organisations in the region. He is a director of Panos South Asia and heads TVE Asia Pacific.

Shortly afterwards, many of our countries allowed private sector participation in the media – which transformed the entire mass media landscape in a very short time. Most parts of Asia moved rapidly from an average of 2.4 television channels in 1990 to several dozen by the decade's end.

A similar proliferation has happened in radio, where a cacophony of FM channels now crowds the airwaves.

Good news and bad news

A decade on, there is good news and bad news.
As the 2002 Global Civil Society Yearbook, published by the London School of Economics and Political Science, noted: "Liberalisation and diversification, particularly in Africa and Asia, have transformed both print and broadcast media from a largely government-owned, monopolistic and uncreative media environment to a more dynamic, popular, democratic, creative, commercial and complex one."

That good news is also bad news - for some. Media liberalisation has not been matched by a corresponding increase in the public sphere - the area that accommodates and nurtures wide ranging discussion and debate on matters of public interest.

Commercial media tend to ignore both poor people and those living in rural areas. Broadcasting has become a market-based activity where profits are being made - mostly in cities, attracting advertisers and audiences with a mixture of music and light entertainment catering to lifestyle needs of the middle class. Even in South Asian countries with widespread malnutrition, such channels would much rather talk about how to lose weight.

News has taken a particular beating in the business plans of media empires run at a profit. "Infotainment is a commodity and today's news coverage reflects market forces and the desire of media moguls to rule the airwaves," says Kunda Dixit, editor of the Nepali Times and leading media commentator. "The public service role of media is being usurped by businesses for whom the definition of news is very simple: news has to sell, otherwise it is not news."

Meanwhile, the former monopolies have fallen on hard times and completely lost their way. State-run broadcasting systems have found their audiences migrating to newer channels and government subsidies reduced or withdrawn.

Struggling to survive, they have abandoned their earlier remit for public interest broadcasting, and are trying to outdo private competitors in their own game. If they have to reduce transmission capacity in rural areas or cut down on programmes on health, education, environment or agricultural topics, so be it.

Media ignored by WSIS?

For many who are poor or living away from cities, there is now less information, fewer programmes on their concerns, and less chance to make their voices heard. As the Panos Institute has warned, without the capacity to seek information, to debate issues, and to make their voices heard, poor and rural people risk becoming more and more marginalised from their nation's and the world's economies. The 'dot com' has not come to them – and is unlikely to arrive anytime soon either.

The World Summit on the Information Society (WSIS) provides an important opportunity to raise these critical issues about North-South and rich-poor gaps in media ownership, content and access. Unfortunately, the official preparatory processes – and even civil society consultations – have focused too much on computers and Internet, ignoring the fact that the mass media have far greater outreach and power over people's lives and choices.

In fact, the widely accepted definition of ICTs – also used by the United Nations – covers the conventional communications technologies of telephone, radio and television as well as the newer ones - personal computers, mobile phones, satellite and wireless technologies and the Internet.

The reality is that we have far more radio and television sets on the planet than computers. The electronic media still provide the most effective - and often the only way - that people can access information to make sense of their lives, livelihoods and the choices they have to make in the complex and globalised society.

The crux of the matter is not technology but information itself - how much of information is available, in what relevant and timely manner to how many people at any given time. Immersed in digital hype, governmental and civil society participants at WSIS risk missing this crucial point.

They cannot afford to do so. The media are likely to remain the principal source of outside information for a majority of humanity for years to come. Media are also a critical way through which the people can, in turn, express their views and concerns in national discussion and debate. Consequently, the current status and on-going changes in the structure, content, ownership and access within these media is of equal, if not greater, importance in any discussion on how the Information Society affects the majority world.

Media pluralism in the globalised world

A key concern of the 'Information Society' is media pluralism – a situation where all people in society have access to information on issues that affect their lives and have a way of making their voices heard in national public debate.

Genuine media pluralism implies: diversity of ownership, including media which explicitly serve a public or community interest; media that are accessible and intelligible to all citizens, particularly in relation to literacy and language; and media that reflect diversity of public opinion, particularly of the marginalised in society.

When these criteria are applied, the global trend is that we are moving away from, not towards, real media pluralism. Media freedom is necessary, but not sufficient, for media pluralism. While the past decade has witnessed many advances in media freedom and a growth in the number of radio and television outlets, they have not necessarily enhanced media pluralism.

This is because media ownership - at the global, regional and national levels – has been concentrating in fewer hands, squeezing out independent players. This now threatens to replace the earlier governmentally controlled concentration of media with an increasingly narrow commercial and political one. This has serious implications for the diversity and accountability in the media.

WSIS is not going to resolve these major concerns, but it can draw attention to them. Media globalisation is not just fodder for academics to churn out papers – it affects us all, every minute of the day. We ignore these issues at our peril. One day soon we might wake up to find – on the morning news, where else? – that we do have a World President whose arrival we never noticed.

At Issue in the World Summit: Digital Solidarity Fund

Digital Solidarity and the Digital Gap[91]

Abdoulaye Wade[92]

Question: "How will developing countries join developed countries into the information society?"

Answer: "By simply jumping into the snake's belly !" Abdoulaye WADE, President of Senegal, says.

The digital gap which dangerously separates the countries of the North from those of the South has led the United Nations Secretary General to ask the ITU to prepare a World Summit on the Information Society, to be held in Geneva in December 2003. But even if this issue is keeping experts awake at night and many concerned people very active on the ground, no viable and definitive solution has yet been found.

Now, because of this, a voice comes from the South, proposing a solution which has surprised the experts with its conceptual relevance and its viability.

We have asked the author, Abdoulaye Wade, to explain to our readers his idea of digital solidarity.

> Now the serpent was more crafty than any of the wild animals the LORD God had made. He said to the woman, "Did God really say, 'You must not eat from any tree in the garden'?"
> The woman said to the serpent, "We may eat fruit from the trees in the garden, but God did say, 'You must not eat fruit from the tree that is in the middle of the garden, and you must not touch it, or you will die.' "
> "You will not surely die," the serpent said to the woman. "For God knows that when you eat of it your eyes will be opened, and you will be like God, knowing good and evil." - Old Testament

---

[91] http://www.unicttaskforce.org/news/digitalsolidarity.html

[92] President of Senegal, Former Dean of the Dakar University School of Economics, Associate (Agregation) Professor of Law and Economics, CES (Certificate of Advanced Studies) in General Mathematics, CES in Mathematics, Physics and Chemistry, CES in Rational Mechanics.

I do not know if Adam and Eve arrived in this world as babies or as adults as the story was told to us, but I am sure that their first achievement was to communicate. Perhaps with a look, then a gesture, then--or at the same time--the spoken word.

As a result, communications was born within the group, starting with two people. Then groups created ways and means of communication: words with their different inflections, body language, conventional language, a hollowed out log, music made with a wide variety of instruments. This is *intra-group* communications.

Then someone in one group noticed that in order to communicate with someone in another group, one has to learn the language of the other.

As long as these systems governed relations between people "speaking the same language"[93], as they say, people could easily communicate because the means of communications of some people were accessible to others.

Thus over time, persons and peoples have sent messages, some of which have never been decoded, because of a lack of communications. This is the case with cave paintings, megaliths, the pyramids, and more recently, Mona Lisa's smile. The message has always been the means for transmission of knowledge. This is the communications/knowledge link.

But then groups invented new ways to transmit messages over long distances: the stagecoach, the postal service, and the train. Then with the use of electricity, which gave birth to even quicker ways to transmit messages: wireless telegraphy, the telephone, followed by electronic mail which introduced the digital age. And now hard drives look down from the height of their megabits on the largest libraries, the voluminous contents of which they can send over long distances at the speed of light. Digital technology is creating a new man in a new civilization--the information society--in which not just anyone can enter, like in the early days of humankind. Now one needs to pay to use complicated and expensive equipment, or remain isolated.

I believe the great magic about information and communication technologies has been to suggest the measurement of distances in megabit per second instead of miles. Our journey in the quest for the other and for knowledge now comes down to our capacity in acquiring these technologies.

Because of the large time lag between economic and technological evolution, society has begun to divide into two groups, the North and the South, separated by an

[93] Languages, Binary or Cobol languages, for example.

electronic gap. In the North, people have the equipment and the money to pay for access. If one does not own the equipment, then one can pay the price of renting, access and use. In the South, are those who are excluded. The North and South communicate less and less, with a risk of no longer being able to communicate at all.

The opulence of technologies in many northern countries has favored the emergence of the fascinating e-economy. The latter has lately accepted to submit itself to the rigor of scientific analysis therefore leading to the end of the internet bubble. This warning is quite interesting for the economist that I am : the principle of a bursting volume relates to an excessive quantity of gas in a given quantified volume. If the volume had been made larger, the bursting would not have occurred. This very simple economic principle is mentioned in the Old Testament : *"And the land was insufficient for them to stay together, because they had so much wealth that they couldn't remain together".* This perspective is in line with Bill Gates' premonition that Africa will be the next technology market.

The digital gap brings with it a danger of isolating certain peoples, those in Africa in particular. It is paradoxical and ironical that the continent which invented writing would--at the end of a process which it initiated--be excluded from universal knowledge.

The concept of *digital solidarity* is proposed as a strategy with the goal of closing the digital gap through *"painless" individual contributions.*

Two lines can be defined as the *digital margins.*[94] Societies which are de facto excluded from information, e.g. the South, fall below the lower margin. The upper margin would ideally be found at the level of countries which have reached or are on the verge of reaching saturation, such as the United States, although it is preferable to set this upper margin at a realistic level. Between these margins lies a band defined as the *standard information society,* which could be reasonably accessible to all societies, if the most developed countries are motivated by a spirit of solidarity.

The goal is to lift up those at the bottom *toward and into* the information society, which is defined in the communications space by the presence of a certain number of measurable quantitative indicators, as well as qualitative indicators, which are the attributes of the information society.

[94] Inspired by the concept of monetary fluctuation margins, and the monetary snake agreed upon between two or several countries which seek to bring about a relatively stable convergence of currency exchange rates.

The band between the margins is called the *digital snake*[95]. It is called a snake because this band grows and changes scale over time and with progress in accessibility to communications.

These indicators could be the number of computers per inhabitant, number of websites, the cost of Internet access, the penetration rate of telecommunications in a society, etc.

The digital solidarity actors are the civil society, the international private sector and governments. They would act within a framework of a *Digital Solidarity Charter.*[96]

As for *Financing,* a *Digital Solidarity Fund*[97] would be created from voluntary contributions through yet to be established procedures.

For illustrative purposes, and given the above caveats, the following contributions could be considered:

- 1 U.S. penny per international communication,
- $1 per purchase of a personal computer,
- $1 per purchase of a software
- $1 per piece of network equipment, etc.
- Voluntary contributions from the private sector.

Digital Solidarity could thus be achieved by raising large amounts of money collected painlessly because the contributions are so small. They would be used to finance the entry and maintenance of a large number of nations from the South in the digital snake. This is how the *digital gap* gradually would be closed, on the road to *e-civilization.*

In closing, one notes that the societal division which is occurring is the fault of mankind's lack of wisdom. Mankind is too proud of its scientific achievements but it is totally ignorant of their larger consequences, even though world religions have already warned us of the dangers of societal divisions. So much the better if--conscious of the dangers of the digital gap--mankind would feel committed to digital solidarity. Then, soon the bytes would laugh at distance, leaving Mombasa[98] at the speed of light to travel to Paris, Oslo, London or New York, full of sound, color,

[95] Same reference as Footnote 3.
[96] To be written, perhaps by the United Nations, which would propose it to the actors.
[97] Note that these painlessly raised funds would go primarily to buy ITC equipment from the North.
[98] City in Kenya, the termination point for a proposed railroad called the Horizontal, which is planned for NEPAD, and which crosses Africa from Dakar in the west to Mombasa on the shores of the Indian Ocean.

knowledge, wisdom and joy. And society will have rewarded the patience of great libraries of the world, which have waited patiently over 2000 years for digital technology to send their immense wealth, saved from the vagaries of history, to every corner of the earth, in the North as well as in the South.

Digital Solidarity and the Idea of a Digital Solidarity Fund[99]

Civil Society Theme: Volunteers[100]

The developed and developing worlds seem to be looking in opposite directions concerning the issue of financing ICTs and practices in the developing countries, as demonstrated by the recent working group on Financing.

The Swedish Minister and Special ICT (Information and Communication Technologies) Advisor who chaired the meeting put the issue from the very start of the session in its right terms: 'What are we really talking about?' she asked, 'utilization of or creation of funding mechanisms?' The suggestion by many African countries to establish a Digital Solidarity Fund to replace existing funding mechanisms has met with considerable opposition. The purpose of the group on financing is to bridge the gap between the developed and the developing worlds, while being as open to suggestions as possible.

More analytically, most of the African countries support the establishment of a Digital Solidarity Fund that will finance the development and application of ICTs in the developing world. The delegation from Senegal, speaking on behalf of many developed countries, elaborated on the idea of the Digital Solidarity Fund, first suggested by Senegalese President Abdoulaye Wade. He justified the need for its creation on the basis that the existing funding mechanisms are 'heavy and time-consuming' as well as bureaucratic and complicated; hence merely improving them would prove insufficient. What is needed is their replacement. The fact that despite the existing mechanisms the digital gap between the developed and the developing world still exists is evidence, according to the Senegalese delegation, of the ineffectiveness of the current status of funding.

Moreover, what is important is that in the African countries people find it difficult to familiarize themselves with the new technologies and more importantly realize the utility of the ICT. For them this is not a priority and other issues such as education or agriculture rest high on the agenda. 'We can't eat computers' is the answer of the African people that do not see the link between ICTs and development. In order to fight this feeling it is necessary, according to Senegal, to finance ICTs in the schools, in agriculture etc. and also to ensure that for each of the actions mentioned in the Plan of Action, specific funding will be found. Another aspect that the Senegalese

[99] http://www.prepcom.net/wsis/1063970609430

[100] From: Melina Skouroliakou, Sep. 19, 2003 1:23 pm

underlined is that the first and most important step is the existence of the political will to confront the issue and discuss it openly.

Some representatives from developed countries (Italy on behalf of the European Union, Switzerland, the USA) expressed the idea that actions have to be taken on the basis of the existing funding mechanisms that might need reconsideration and improvement, but they were very hesitant in adopting the idea of a new fund as proposed by the developing countries.

Notwithstanding the different views, all countries present at the meeting reached a consensus on accepting the concept of digital solidarity and the need to address it in the Summit. A platform for a discussion on the idea and the meaning of digital solidarity and an inclusion in the text of the Declaration was set for the group to discuss again in the evening.

The importance given to separating the issues of the concept of digital solidarity and the idea of the Fund were evident at the session. All countries expressed their support to the former issue, but the establishment of a Fund is still open to debate. The developing countries seemed ready to move forward more quickly by establishing the Fund, whereas developed countries insisted on working on and through the existing funding channels. Either with or without a new Fund, however, it is equally necessary to empower people in the developing countries and integrate in their lives the idea that the ICTs can truly, besides agriculture and education, improve their lives.

Civil Society Statement on Information and Communication Solidarity Funding Mechanisms[101]

Civil Society Content and Themes Subcommittee, with input from those present at the South-South and Friends of the South Meeting

Civil Society from the North joins Civil Society from the South in supporting a solidarity approach to the overall discussion of information society. For purposes of this statement, we addressed ICT actions and initiatives for global development.

We believe that an appropriate funding approach is one that links social solidarity to digital solidarity, both for existing as well as new funding mechanisms.

For both new and existing mechanisms, we believe that serious consideration should be given to the following concerns:

1. Mechanisms for the distribution and implementation of such funds must be fully transparent and accountable, and ensure that the funds will reach the people who need them. The cost of administering the fund needs to be kept to a minimum.

2. Fair rules for distributing international telecom charges based on solidarity must be re-established.

3. Funding must not lead to further indebtedness and dependency to unequal trade relations, nor to privatization and deregulation. Funding must not to further reinforcing private and public monopolies.

4. Contributions to any newly established fund must reflect a multi-stakeholder participation, providing contributions from governments and the private and commercial sector as well as from citizens.

5. Funds must be managed and administered by people of the South.

6. Gender parity must exist in all such mechanisms and all spheres and in all levels of decision-making and implementation.

7. Funding mechanisms

[101] WSIS Prep Com 3, 25 September 2003, www.worldsummit2003.de/en/web/472.htm

- Should not be established under the simplistic notion that digital divides can be redressed mainly by addressing issues of infrastructure or connectivity. They must be accompanied by funding for education, applications, content, and dissemination.
- In order to ensure that the funds actually reach the most marginalized, mechanisms need to be set up to ensure distribution of these funds take into account intersectionality of race, class gender, ethnicity and other lines of discrimination.
- Must address traditional and community media, not only the Internet. It should take into full account low-end but appropriate technology, including indigenous knowledges.
- Must also be used to promote cultural and linguistic diversity.
- Must support technological sustainability, including the use and production of free software and the fostering of user-centered technology development practices.

At Issue in the World Summit: Public Domain/Intellectual Property

Free Software (a.k.a. ``Libre Software" or ``Open Source")[102]

Georg C. F. Greve, Co-ordinator of Patents, Copyrights, Trademarks (PCT) working group[103]

During PrepCom3, a regular request was for a reference document on Free Software and its role in the World Summit on the Information Society (WSIS). This document seeks to provide such reference.

Free in Free Software is referring to freedom, not price. Having been used in this meaning since the 80s, the first documented complete definition appears to be the GNU's Bulletin, vol. 1 no. 61,[104] published January 1989. In particular, four freedoms define[105] Free Software:

- The freedom to run the program, for any purpose. Placing restrictions on the use of Free Software, such as time (``30 days trial period", ``license expires January 1st, 2004") purpose (``permission granted for research and non-commercial use") or geographic area (``must not be used in country X") makes a program non-free.

- The freedom to study how the program works, and adapt it to your needs. Placing legal or practical restrictions on the comprehension or modification of a program, such as mandatory purchase of special licenses, signing of a Non-Disclosure-Agreement (NDA) or - for programming languages that have multiple forms or representation - making the preferred human way of comprehending and editing a program (``source code") inaccessible also makes it proprietary (non-free). Without the freedom to modify a program, people will remain at the mercy of a single vendor.

---

[102] Permanent URL: http://fsfeurope.org/projects/wsis/fs.html
Date: 2003/10/29 11:56:29 Revision: 1.6

[103] Georg C. F. Greve is the Chair of the European Caucus of Civil Society@WSIS, Chair; Coordinator of the Patents, Copyrights, Trademarks (PCT) working group of Civil Society@WSIS; Delegate of German Civil Society@WSIS coordination circle in German governmental delegation: and President of FSF Europe
[104] http://www.gnu.org/bulletins/bull6.html
[105] For the full definition, please see http://www.gnu.org/philosophy/free-sw.html

- The freedom to redistribute copies so you can help your neighbor. Software can be copied/distributed at virtually no cost. If you are not allowed to give a program to a person in need, that makes a program non-free. This can be done for a charge, if you so choose.

- The freedom to improve the program, and release your improvements to the public, so that the whole community benefits. Not everyone is an equally good programmer in all fields. Some people don't know how to program at all. This freedom allows those who do not have the time or skills to solve a problem to indirectly access the freedom to modify. This can be done for a charge.

These freedoms are rights, not obligations, although respecting these freedoms for society may at times oblige the individual. Any person can choose to not make use of them, but may also choose to make use of all of them. In particular, it should be understood that Free Software does not exclude commercial use. If a program fails to allow commercial use and commercial distribution, it is not Free Software. Indeed a growing number of companies base their business model completely or at least partially on Free Software, including some of the largest proprietary software vendors. Free Software makes it legal to provide help and assistance, it does not make it mandatory.

Terminology

English seems to be the only language in which such a strong ambiguity exists between freedom and price. When translated into other languages, Free Software becomes ``logiciels libre" in French, ``software libre" in Spanish, ``software libero" in Portugese, ``Fri Software" in Danish or whatever is the equivalent term in the local language referring to freedom.

Open Source

On February 3rd 1998, in the wake of Netscapes announcement to release their browser as Free Software, a group of people met in Palo Alto in the Silicon Valley and proposed to start a marketing campaign for Free Software using the term ``Open Source." The goal was to seek fast commercialization of Free Software and acceptance of Free Software by the companies and venture capitalists of the booming new economy. As a means to this end, they made a conscious decision toleave aside all long-term issues (such as philosophy, ethics and social effects) related to Free

Software, feeling these posed obstacles in the way of rapid acceptance by economy. They proposed to focus on technical advantages only.[106]

Often used in good faith by people who refer to what Free Software stands for, the term ``Open Source" - originally defined to mean the same thing as Free Software in terms of licenses and implementation - has seen inflationary usage. Nowadays, it is regularly used for everything between Free Software and the highly proprietary ``Governmental Security Program" (GSP) by Microsoft.[107]

Libre Software

When the European Commission started dealing with Free Software on a regular basis, they sought to avoid the ambiguity of the English word ``Free Software" and the misunderstandings of ``Open Source" alike, which led to the creation of a new term: ``Libre Software." This term has proven resistant to inflationary usage and is still used in an identical way to Free Software. So it may pose a solution for those who fear being misunderstood when speaking English.

Development

When thinking about Free Software, it should be seen as an encompassing concept for a reliable, sustainable and dependable information and knowledge society involving all stakeholders.

The price we are paying for the predominance of the proprietary software approach is high. Because the proprietary software paradigm has a strong, system-inherent monopolizing tendency[108] and software permeates all areas of economy, northern economies suffer and southern countries are giventhe choice between exclusion or co-suffering in total dependence. That is why breaking up Microsoft without a change in paradigm would not improve the situation significantly. Free Software, on the other hand, brings back competition while allowing cooperation among companies, people, and governments. All of these equally available and empowering to all the peoples.

---

[106] For reference, see http://www.opensource.org/advocacy/faq.html: How is "open source" related to "free software"? The Open Source Initiative is a marketing program for free software. It's a pitch for "free software" on solid pragmatic grounds rather than ideological tub-thumping. The winning substance has not changed, the losing attitude and symbolism have.

[107] In this program governments and intergovernmental organizations pay substantial fees for a superficial look at some parts of Windows sourcecode in special Microsoft facilities. This may increase``felt security" but is essentially useless - especially since they do not even know whether what they looked at is what they have on their computers. And of course it does not give them freedom.

[108] Explanation of these mechanisms will gladly be provided, if of interest.

While minorities remain at the mercy of large multinational companies regarding support for their culture and language when using proprietary software, Free Software gives them freedom to modify all software according to their needs. Thus, Free Software also allows building a sustainable local hard- and software industry independent from monopolies and large multinationals. Of course cooperation with large companies is possible and may be useful, but while dependency is the price to pay for such cooperation in proprietary software, Free Software provides independence.

Equality

The design, development and use of software is increasing in all societies. Increasingly, access to software is largely determining our capabilities for education, communication, work and even social networking. This includes building social movements, promoting citizenship and transparent democracy as well as general governmental and health services.

Software in general has grown into northern societies to a very large extent and if development policies are successful, this will also be true for southern societies at some point in time. Therefore software must be considered a cultural technique, sometimes even a cultural good.

For all central cultural techniques, we have to ask who should be put in control of it. Proprietary software puts large northern multinationals in control.[109] Free Software makes this cultural technique equally available to all the peoples.

Human Rights

For those who are connected - and we surely hope this will mean all the peoples at some point - human rights of participation in culture, freedom of speech and opinion are influenced to a large extent by their control over the software they use, as are freedom of association and movement. Software forms the medium. Unlike the proprietary approach, Free Software gives each person full control about their personal information space. Although this alone is not sufficient to grant privacy and security, it is a necessary prerequisite.

---

[109] Side note: Which should not be understood as a good thing for people in the northern countries. It is not.

Preventing Technocracy - upholding democracy

Legislation should be developed by democratically elected representatives in a transparent way. Even in situations where this is true, rights that cannot be exercised remain empty. Granting rights on paper does not mean people will have the means of exercising them.

The complexity of modern systems alone makes it a difficult task to uphold democracy in the digital domain, but the overall intransparency of proprietary software makes it impossible. Unless you are using Free Software, the rights you can or cannot exercise are determined by the proprietary software vendor - it is the vendors decision alone, a decision that nowadays is often given precendence over the democratic legislative process.

Good examples are the European Copyright Directive (EUCD) and Digital Millennium Copyright Act (DMCA), both implementations of the `The World Intellectual Property Organization (WIPO) CopyrightTreaty" (December 1996). While the DMCA already gained notoriety for enabling censorship of Scientology-critical sites in the United States,[110] the German implementation of the EUCD is silently making the right to fair use inaccessible. Although laws clearly state that customers have the right to copy a CD for their car stereo or even a friend, those who exercise this right on so-called ``copy protected" CDs or on any DVD now risk punishment. And if you think this is where it ends, feel free to read the EFF paper on so-called ``Trusted Computing" (TC).[111]

Proprietary software effectively puts an area that was previously governed by democratically elected representatives into the hand of corporations, therefore establishing technocracy.[112]

Summary

All of our hard work to defend and promote human rights, gender equality, rights of the disadvantaged, a free media, privacy and security, digital solidarity and other issues is in danger of having been for naught if the information age is based on proprietary software.

---

[110] For reference, see http://www-camlaw.rutgers.edu/publications/law-religion/scientology.htm

[111] http://www.eff.org/Infra/trusted_computing/20031001_tc.php

[112] Technocracy: ``Government by technicians or management of society by technical experts." (Merriam Webster Dictionary)

Free Software alone is certainly not enough to overcome all problems - but it is a necessity to empower people to exercise the rights we are fighting for in the information societies.

Debriefing on World Summit on the Information Society: Patents, Copyrights and Trademarks [113]

Georg C. F. Greve, Co-ordinator of Patents, Copyrights, Trademarks (PCT) working group [114]

PCT perspectives

The multitude of interesting Civil Society side events was another positive part of the summit. Personally, I enjoyed very much the opportunity to speak at the APC event on Free Software for women in Africa. Just afterwards, also on wednesday, Dec 10th, the Patents, Copyrights, Trademarks (PCT) working group of Civil Society held its "Free Software, Free Society" event.

After Prof. Lawrence Lessig, who shared his visions for a Free Society, the speakers shed light on their experience on building Free Societies with the help of Free Software in South America and Africa. This experience was complimented by the experience of the Swiss NGO Ynternet.org.

Surprising special guests were Sergio Amadeu Da Silveira and Rogerio Santanna of the Brazilian government, who told the audience about their experience building the Free Software policy for Brazil. And as the final speaker, just after his appearence at the governmental high-level round table, Richard Stallman, founding father of the GNU Project, vividly expressed the freedoms of Free Software.

Assessment of the documents

Leaving aside all problems, frustrations and obstacles that Civil Society faced, some positive influence on the governmental documents *Declaration of Principles* and *Plan of Action* adopted during the World Summit on the Information Society (WSIS) seems evident. This is my first personal assessment for the areas that I have been following most closely.

---

[113] Geneva Phase / Part I, Geneva, December 10-12.
http://www.wsis-pct.org/

[114] Georg C. F. Greve is the Chair of the European Caucus of Civil Society@WSIS, Chair; Coordinator of the Patents, Copyrights, Trademarks (PCT) working group of Civil Society@WSIS; Delegate of German Civil Society@WSIS coordination circle in German governmental delegation: and President of FSF Europe.

Access to public domain of global knowledge

It is self-awareness, the possibility to reflect and our ability to develop and communicate abstract concepts that make humankind different from any other species on our planet. As a result of that process, including concepts, thoughts and experiences from all people alive and dead, we create the public domain of global knowledge. From this reservoir we learn, improve ourselves and build new knowledge.

This makes the question of access to the reservoir that is the public domain of global knowledge central to humankind in general, but information societies in particular.

Central paragraphs dealing with access to the public domain of global knowledge adopted on Dec 12th, 2003 are

Declaration of Principles §24: *"The ability for all to access and contribute information, ideas and knowledge is essential in an inclusive Information Society."*

Declaration of Principles §25: *"The sharing and strengthening of global knowledge for development can be enhanced by removing barriers to equitable access to information for economic, social, political, health, cultural, educational, and scientific activities and by facilitating access to public domain information, including by universal design and the use of assistive technologies."*

Declaration of Principles §26: *"A rich public domain is an essential element for the growth of the Information Society, creating multiple benefits such as an educated public, new jobs, innovation, business opportunities, and the advancement of sciences. Information in the public domain should be easily accessible to support the Information Society, and protected from misappropriation. Public institutions such as libraries and archives, museums, cultural collections and other community-based access points should be strengthened so as to promote the preservation of documentary records and free and equitable access to information."*

The weakness of these paragraphs is their emphasis on the economic and development related aspects, which somewhat neglect the social and political issues. Also they put most of their attention on the past, not the future extension of human knowledge. But despite these weaknesses, the thrust is good. Most particular, they come before the paragraph on Patents, Copyrights, Trademarks (PCTs) in the declaration, emphasizing early on the significance of the public domain of global knowledge and of access to it.

Patents, Copyrights, Trademarks (PCT) (a.k.a. Limited Intellectual Monopolies (LIM))

Patents, Copyright and Trademarks (PCTs) centrally regulate access to the public domain of global knowledge, the reservoir of all human knowledge, from which new knowledge is in turn created. As an effect of the current system, some Northern companies have become immensely rich while the vast majority of humankind is excluded from access to that knowledge.

The lines of conflict in this area ran between the Southern and Northern countries, most particular United States, European Union and Japan. While Northern countries wish to see international treaties and organizations -- most notably the "World Intellectual Property Organization" (WIPO) -- accepted as they stand, Southern countries question the balance of the current system and wish to see the system reevaluated.

The PCT working group of Civil Society, which is working on these issues, has been giving support to the Southern countries in this area and supported them through statements (in plenary and beyond), personal discussions and drafts for compromise text.

The paragraphs dealing with the issue as they have been adopted on December 12th are:

Declaration of Principles §42: *"Intellectual Property protection is important to encourage innovation and creativity in the Information Society; similarly, the wide dissemination, diffusion, and sharing of knowledge is important to encourage innovation and creativity. Facilitating meaningful participation by all in intellectual property issues and knowledge sharing through full awareness and capacity building is a fundamental part of an inclusive Information Society."*

Plan of Action C3, 10, d): *"Governments, and other stakeholders, should establish sustainable multi- purpose community public access points, providing affordable or free-of- charge access for their citizens to the various communication resources, notably the Internet. These access points should, to the extent possible, have sufficient capacity to provide assistance to users, in libraries, educational institutions, public administrations, post offices or other public places, with special emphasis on rural and underserved areas, while respecting intellectual property rights (IPRs) and encouraging the use of information and sharing of knowledge."*

While it can and should be criticised that the paragraphs are using the ideologically charged and misleading terminology of "intellectual property" and contain a good load of fuzzyness, it should be realized that they are a step forward, albeit a small one.

As they stand, they still neglect that all monopolization of knowledge draws its sole justification from increasing the dissemination, diffusion and sharing of knowledge, as adequately stated in Article 1 of the United States constitution: "*To promote the progress of science and useful arts, by securing for limited times to authors and inventors the exclusive right to their respective writings and discoveries;*"

But unlike other statements (and what the Northern countries were also trying to achieve in the scope of WSIS), it does not put forward the notion that ultimate monopolization of knowledge should be the goal of humankind. Instead, it gives monopolization, dissemination, diffusion and sharing of knowledge equal weight.

Also, it does not mention the international treaties in the area, therefore not reinforcing them. In particular, it does not mention WIPO, in essence leaving room for the interpretation that it is not the Information Society that should serve WIPO, but rather WIPO which should serve the Information Society.

This is of critical importance. Earlier in 2003, WIPO cancelled a conference on knowledge sharing because of heavy opposition by the United States. When asked why the United States had opposed the WIPO meeting, Lois Boland, director of international relations for the U.S. Patent and Trademark Office, told the Washington Post, "*Open-source software runs counter to the mission of WIPO, which is to promote intellectual property rights.*" She added: "*To hold a meeting, which has as its purpose to disclaim or waive such rights, seems to us to be contrary to the goals of WIPO.*"

In short: WIPO has in the past years understood its mission as seeking ultimate monopolization of knowledge. Every aspect of society had to serve that goal. Thanks to WSIS, there is now room to reevaluate the role of WIPO into one of readjustment instead of single-minded expansion.

It is not enough to stop here, but a door has been opened that remained closed before.

Free Software

Software shapes the digital age and access to it determines who may participate in a digital world. That is why Free Software with its freedoms of use for any purpose, studying, modification and redistribution is an essential building block for an empowering, sustainable and inclusive information society.

The paragraphs adopted for this on December 12th were

Declaration of Principles §27: *"Access to information and knowledge can be promoted by increasing awareness among all stakeholders of the possibilities offered by different software models, including proprietary, open-source and free software, in order to increase competition, access by users, diversity of choice, and to enable all users to develop solutions which best meet their requirements. Affordable access to software should be considered as an important component of a truly inclusive Information Society."*

Plan of Action C3, 10, e): *"Encourage research and promote awareness among all stakeholders of the possibilities offered by different software models, and the means of their creation, including proprietary, open-source and free software, in order to increase competition, freedom of choice and affordability, and to enable all stakeholders to evaluate which solution best meets their requirements."*

One might have hoped that governments were already more advanced in their understanding of the digital society, but these paragraphs are going further than it may seem at first glance; especially given their development over time.

During the work on the documents, especially the United States tried to declassify Free Software by means of referring to it as the "open source software development model," pretending it was a foremost technical issue, which could later disappear from the documents entirely, as there is no need to talk about all the technical models in a political document. This was stopped around the Intersessional Meeting in Paris, when Civil Society managed to get Free Software into the official documents.

Although the official documents pose the risk of further spreading the notion of "open source" as "any software with (partially) visible source code," they do avoid the most severe misunderstanding by not confusing proprietary (non-Free) and commercial software, as both Free and proprietary software can be both commercial or non-commercial.

More importantly, instead of talking about software development models, the documents speak of "software models." For the first time, a formal United Nations level takes steps to acknowledge that the choice between proprietary and Free Software is not a mainly technical issue, but a political, economical and social choice of paradigm.

One of the most fundamental tasks of the Free Software Foundation has always been to build awareness, because ubiquitous understanding of the different software paradigms and their effects is the most effective way of establishing Free Software; someone who has understood the full consequences of that choice will not freely choose proprietary software.

So while encouraging research and promoting awareness may not seem like much, it is all that is needed for Free Software to be understood and prevail as the most favorable paradigm.

In essence: on Dec 12th, 2003, all governments represented in the United Nations have committed to encourage research and promotion of awareness for the different paradigms of software and their effects, something we can support entirely, even if we hoped that the governments had understood these issues better already.

Open Standards

Open standards are the equivalent of well documented and accessible languages in a digital world, allowing communication and cooperation.

Unfortunately, the paragraphs adopted for standardization adopted on Dec 12th were insufficient:

Declaration of Principles §44: *"Standardization is one of the essential building blocks of the Information Society. There should be particular emphasis on the development and adoption of international standards. The development and use of open, interoperable, non-discriminatory and demand-driven standards that take into account needs of users and consumers is a basic element for the development and greater diffusion of ICTs and more affordable access to them, particularly in developing countries. International standards aim to create an environment where consumers can access services worldwide regardless of underlying technology."*

Plan of Action C6, 13, p):*"Governments, in cooperation with other stakeholders, should promote the development and use of open, interoperable, non-discriminatory and demand- driven standards."*

While "open" and "interoperable" are important adjectives and "demand-driven" is uncritical, it is not enough to ensure open standards. Especially "non-discriminatory" has acquired sad notoriety in the standardization discussions by at times being used in ways to make Free Software implementations impossible.

As the PCT working group has repeatedly pointed out, no standard will ever qualify as a truly open standard unless it is *freely implementable* and *publicly documented.*

In essence, the paragraphs fall short of what they seek to accomplish.

Open Access

Science is the source of the technological development that empowers the Information Society, including the World Wide Web. In the best tradition of science, scientific authors donate their work to humankind and access to that information is crucial.

The paragraphs mention this explicitly in

Declaration of Principles §28: *"We strive to promote universal access with equal opportunities for all to scientific knowledge and the creation and dissemination of scientific and technical information, including open access initiatives for scientific publishing."*

Plan of Action C3, 10, i):*"Encourage initiatives to facilitate access, including free and affordable access to open access journals and books, and open archives for scientific information."*

While "encourage initatives" is not very binding, these paragraphs do mention in particular the significance of Open Access to scientific information, a part that had disappeared for a while in all documents throughout the process.

Since Francis Muguet, co-coordinator of the PCT working group and coordinator of Scientific Information (SI) working group, was most active in this part, I'm going to leave the full assessment of this up to him.

Summary

One can say that the governmental documents fall short of the essential benchmarks of Civil Society in all considered aspects. But one can also say that they have in most cases made progress and moved in the right direction.

A fair evaluation of both the process and the adopted documents might be that they have moved into the right direction, but that we cannot be satisfied yet and will have to keep working on all aspects. Given that Civil Society has networked itself better than ever before throughout the summit, my personal outlook is positive.

So my conclusion would be that we haven't arrived and will probably not do so in Tunis, but we've made progress and now are finding ourselves in a solid starting position for the years to come.

Useful Websites

Official WSIS Sites

- Official WSIS Site: http://www.wsis.org
- ITU WSIS web site: http://www.itu.int/wsis/geneva/index.html
- Official Civil Society site: http://www.geneva2003.org/wsis/indexa01.htm
- Civil Society meeting site: http://www.wsis-cs.org/
- Civil Society Caucuses: http://www.wsis-cs.org/caucuses.html
- Swiss Executive Secretariat: http://www.wsisgeneva2003.org/
- WSIS Civil Society Bureau: http://cms.privaterra.org/WSIS_CS_Bureau
- WSIS Events: http://www.geneva2003.org/wsis/index_c01_2_11.htm
- WSIS Tunis 2005: http://www.smsitunis2005.org/plateforme/index.php?lang=en

Regional Conferences Prior to WSIS Phase 1

- African Conference: http://www.geneva2003.org/bamako2002/
- Asian Conference: http://www.wsis-japan.jp/
- Latin American Conference: http://www.indotel.org.do/wsis/
- Pan Arab Conference: http://www.wsis-egypt.gov.eg/
- Pan European Conference: http://www.wsis-romania.ro/
- Western Asia Conference: http://www.escwa.org.lb/wsis/

Civil Society Caucuses

- WSIS Civil Society Caucuses: http://www.wsis-cs.org/caucuses.html
- African Caucus: http://www.wsis-cs.org/africa/
- Asian Caucus: http://www.wsisasia.org/
- Latin American Caucus: http://lac.derechos.apc.org/wsis/
- W Asia & M East Caucus: http://www.irancsos.net/
- Environment & ICT Caucus: http://www.wsis.ethz.ch/
- Gender Caucus: http://www.wougnet.org/WSIS/wsisgc.html
- Human Rights Caucus: http://www.iris.sgdg.org/actions/smsi/hr-wsis/
- Youth Caucus: http://ycdo.net/wsis

Handful of CS organizations and campaigns involved

- APC: http://www.apc.org/english/wsis/index.shtml

- Asia-Pacific Development: http://www.apdip.net/news/wsis-debate/default.asp
- CPSR: http://cpsr.org/wsis/
- CRIS Campaign: http://www.crisinfo.org/live/index.php
- Free Software Foundation: http://www.fsfeurope.org/index.en.html
- EPIC: http://www.epic.org
- German WSIS Forum: http://www.governet.de/themen/1_wsis/
- Global Information IC: http://www.giic.org/
- Global Knowledge: http://www.globalknowledge.org/gkps_portal/index.cfm?menuid=57&parentid=78
- Global Unions: http://www.global-unions.org/wsis.asp
- Harvard Law School: http://blogs.law.harvard.edu/wsis/
- Heinrich Boll Foundation: http://www.worldsummit2003.de/en/nav/14.htm and http://www.worldsummit2005.org
- Hello World Project: http://www.helloworldproject.com/
- HubProject: http://www.hubproject.org/en/?l=en
- I3C: http://www.i3c-asso.org/rubrique.php3?id_rubrique=8
- ICANN: http://www.icann.org
- ICC: http://www.iccwbo.org/home/e_business/wsis.asp
- ICTDAR: http://www.ictdar.org/index.html
- IFLANET: http://www.ifla.org/III/wsis.html
- Intl Council for Science: http://www.icsu.org/index2.htm?http&&&www.icsu.org/events/WSIS/
- International Trade Centre: http://www.intracen.org/wsis/
- Internet Rights: http://www.internetrights.org.uk/wsis.shtml
- Internet Society: http://www.isoc.org/isoc/conferences/wsis/
- IRIS: http://www.iris.sgdg.org/
- Italian Open Source Site: http://linfe.it/events/wsis-dec03-nov05
- IT4all: http://www.it4all-regions.org/wsis/what
- ITU: http://www.itu.int/osg/cec/wsis2003/
- Privaterra: http://www.privaterra.org
- The Public Voice: http://www.thepublicvoice.org
- Rights and Democracy: http://www.ichrdd.ca/english/about/about.html
- United States of Earth: http://united-states-of-earth.com/opinions.asp?MenuID=37
- US CRIS: http://www.worldwidewiki.net/wiki/CommRightsUSA
- WFEO: http://www.coi-tn.org/wfeo-cic/world_summit.htm
- Women's NGO site: http://www.isiswomen.org/onsite/wsis/
- World Forum on IS: http://www.irfd.org/events/wf2003/intro2.html
- WITFOR: http://www.witfor.lt/
- World-Information.Org: http://www.world-information.org/wio/wsis

- World Internet Security: http://www.wisekey.ch/pages/wsis.htm
- WSIS? We seize: http://www.geneva03.org/

News

- WSIS Civil Society News Centre: http://wsis-online.org/csnews/news/
- http://www.worldsummit2005.org
- Terra Viva on WSIS: http://www.ipsnews.net/focus/tv_society/index.asp
- Women Journalists Cover the WSIS: http://www.enawa.org/
- Association for Progressive Communications: http://www.apc.org/english/wsis/index.shtml
- German Civil Society Coverage in English and German: http://www.worldsummit2003.de/en/web/112.htm
- Blog by German NGO Contingent at WSIS:.http://wsis.infopeace.de/
- Swiss Civil Society Coalition: http://www.wsis.ethz.ch/
- Free Software Foundation Europe Coverage: http://www.fsfeurope.org/projects/wsis/wsis.en.html
- Digital Opportunity Channel: http://www.digitalopportunity.org/section/dochannel/wsis
- Unlocking WSIS for the World: http://www.dailysummit.net
- Daily Summit: http:///www.dailysummit.net
- African Civil Society: http://www.wsis-cs.org/africa/news.shtml
- ITU Newslog: http://www.itu.int/osg/spu/newslog/categories/worldSummitOnTheInformationSociety/
- One World South Asia: http://southasia.oneworld.net
- Reporters Without Borders: http://www.rsf.org/rubrique.php3?id_rubrique=43
- Tunisian Journalist Centre: http://www.capjc.nat.tn/fr/default.asp
- WSIS News: http://wsisnews.org
- WSIS Newsfeed: http://wsis.ashst.com
- Civil Society News Center: http://www.prepcom.net/wsis

E-mail Lists

An Extensive Directory of Listservs: http://www.wsis-cs.org/caucuses.html

Photographs

WSIS Photo Gallery: http://gallery.privaterra.org/

Getting Involved

The Public Voice project has compiled the documents in this Sourcebook in order to facilitate understanding of the World Summit on the Information Society and encourage greater civil society participation in the process. We hope the Sourcebook will also help to further productive interaction between civil society in general, across diverse issues and across regions. Finally, while the Sourcebook focuses intensively on this particular United Nations Summit, we hope the information in the Sourcebook will lead groups and individuals to collectively examine other spaces where Information and Communication Technologies may be shaped by civil society involvement.

The United States civil society lacked involved in the first phase, particularly in the preparatory process which was most significant. We hope this Sourcebook provides US civil society with an understanding and a motivation to get involved as their experience and perspective, as well as their interaction with the US government delegation could be quite useful in this process. European civil society was better organized and involved and had an impressive impact on the process and the construction of a very thoughtful civil society declaration. Other regions such as Latin America and Africa were arguably also more involved than United States civil society, however, their participation was impeded by funding and translation difficulties. Documents written and published in English need to be translated into many different languages to enable a truly global participation. It is already the case that groups from the South have less resources to travel to wsis meetings. These groups not only need funding for travel, which is often prohibitively expensive, but also need the ability to read, respond to and shape wsis documents and discussions. This is just one area where stronger and more broad civil society connections could impact the process.

As we move into this next phase of the World Summit on the Information Society, it becomes increasingly important to grow and improve civil society participation. There is less funding in this phase than in the first phase which makes coordination even more important. In addition, the official Summit documents were disappointing to many in civil society, and the implementation of the action plan must be monitored and shaped with all voices heard. Finally, this phase involves a new issue, the decision to hold a Summit touting freedom of speech in Tunisia, a country well known for human rights abuses and oppression of speech. This next phase could improve significantly if it is increasingly shaped by groups and individuals from a variety of related interests and fields, from those concerning Information and Communication Technologies directly, as well as anyone across the globe whose work and livelihood may be affected by Information and Communication Technologies. This includes human rights organizations, consumer advocacy groups, social justice organizations, educators, small business owners, etc.

Those who are interested can get further involved by using the sourcebook and the web sites listed above to understand the issues and processes and various civil society positions. There are many simple ways to begin interacting with others involved in the process such as by contacting any of the bureau members or caucus members listed in this Sourcebook, by joining one or some of the many listservs and caucuses (footnote to site), or by getting involved in the Public Voice meetings. Information about The Public Voice is available at http://www.thepublicvoice.orgg/. There are also campaigns such as the Communication Rights in the Information Society (CRIS) Campaign[115] including a newly formed US CRIS chapter for those in the United States who are interested in getting involved.[116] For reference materials on civil society organizing, see APC's manual, "Involving Civil Society in ICT Policy."[117]

The WSIS calendar currently suggests this work ends in November 2005, but the benefits of civil society networking around the World Summit on the Information Society extend far beyond the wsis itself and far beyond 2005. A stronger civil society network can push us further towards the millennium development goals of 2015.[118] A more concrete network will help formalize and legitimize our involvement with governments and intergovernmental organizations and promote our role and our voice in policy decisions. The focus of this work can extend beyond the UN wsis process and into free trade agreements that increasingly shape information and communication technology development, deployment, access and policy. We do not need to speak in the same voice, nor would it ever be possible to agree on everything. It is important, however, to have the opportunity to raise our diverse voices in diverse languages and be heard. We can and should debate various points, but we can only make an impact if we have a voice. We must work collectively to promote a global public voice.

[115] http://www.crisinfo.org
[116] http://alt.org/wiki/index.php/CommRightsUSA
[117] http://www.apc.org/english/news/index.shtml?x=14223
[118] http://www.un.org/millenniumgoals/

Contact Information for Civil Society Bureau[119]

Alan G. Alegre
Asia Pacific Region, Focal Point
email: alalegre@fma.ph

Neil Anderson
Trade Unions Family, Alternate Focal Point
Contact Organization: Union Network International (UNI)
email:neil.anderson@union-network.org
http://www.union-network.org

Kamel Ayadi
Science and Technology Community, Focal Point
email: cic@coi-tn.org

Amir Barmaki
Middle East & Western Asia Region, Focal Point
Email: westasiaregion@hotmail.com

Renate Bloem
Non Governmental Organizations (NGOs) Family, Focal Point
email: rbloem@ngocongo.org

Alke Boessiger
Trade Unions Family, Focal Point
Contact Organization: Union Network International (UNI)
UNI Campaigns&Organising and UNI Youth Co-ordinator
Tel: 0041 22 3652138
Fax: 0041 22 3652121
email: alke.boessiger@union-network.org
http://www.union-network.org

Beatriz Busaniche
Education and Academia Family, Focal Point
email: busaniche@caminandoutopias.org.ar

[119] Contact Information compiled by Privaterra, available at http://cms.privaterra.org/tiki-index.php?page=WSIS_FP_ContactList and updated by Robert Guerra

Sally Burch
Content & Themes Focal Point
Directora Ejecutiva, Agencia Latinomericana de Informacion
Direccion: Casilla 17-12-877, Quito-Ecuador?
Telefono: (593 2) 250 5074 / 222 1570 / 252 8716
Fax: (593 2) 250 5073
WWW: http://alainet.or
Email: sburch@alainet.org

Kenneth Deer
Indigenous Peoples Family, Focal Point
email: kend@easterndoor.com

Bineta Diop
Non Governmental Organizations (NGOs) Family, Alternate Focal Point

Adel El Zaim
Multi-Stakeholder Family, Focal Point
Address:
Bureau régional du Moyen-Orient? et de l'Afrique du Nord
CP 14 Orman, Giza, Le Caire, Égypte
Adresse municipale: 8 Ahmed Niseem Street, 8e étage
Dokki, Le Caire, Égypte
Tél. : (+20-2) 336-7051/52/53/54/57
Téléc. : (+20-2) 336-7056
Web : www.idrc.ca/cairo
email: adel.elzaim@canti.com (preferred), adel@elzaim.net

Frithjof Finkbeiner
Philanthropic Institutions Family, Alternate Focal Point
Email: frithjof.finkbeiws@f-online.de

Divina Frau Meigs
Education and Academia Family, Focal Point (Alternate)
International Association for Media and Communication Research (IAMCR)
email: neigs@wanadoo.fr

John R. Gagain Jr.
Think Tanks Family, Focal Point
Address:

Calle Capitán Eugenio de Marchena, No. 26
Ensanche La Esperilla
Santo Domingo, República Dominicana
Tel.: 809.685.9966 Ext. 2201
Fax: 212-898-1115
Email: j.gagain@funglode.org
Web: http://www.funglode.org

Georg Greve
North America & Europe Region, Alternate Focal Point
email: greve@gnu.org
website: http://www.gnuhh.org/

Robert Guerra
North America & Europe Region, Focal Point
Address:
131 Beecroft Road, Suite 2109
Toronto, Ontario
Canada M2N 6G9
tel: +1 416 893 0377
Click here to send him an email
Web: http://www.takingitglobal.org/community/profile.html?memberid=6958

Ann-Kristin Håkansson
Indigenous Peoples Family, Alternate Focal Point
email: akigua@telia.com

Hiroshi Kawamura
Disabilities Family, Focal Point
email: hkawa@attglobal.net
website: http://www.daisy.org/

Veronique Kleck
Cities and Local Authorities Family, Focal Point
email: info@cities-lyon.org

Wolfgang Kleinwaechter
Philanthropic Institutions Family, Focal Point
email: wolfgang@imv.au.dk

Viola Krebs

Volunteers Family, Focal Point
Address:
International Conference Volunteers (ICVolunteers)
P.O. Box 755, 1211 Geneva 4, Switzerland
Phone: +41 22 800 1436
Fax: +41 22 800 1437
Email: viola@icvolunteers.org
Web: http://www.icvolunteers.org
http://www.worldwidevolunteer.org

Alexis Krikorian
Creators and Promoters of Culture Family, Focal Point
email: krikorian@ipa-uie.org

Ron Koven
Media Family, Alternate Focal Point
email: rkoven@compuserve.com
Time Zone: GMT+1

Angela Kuga
Asia and Pacific Region, Alternate Focal Point
email: amkt@apcwomen.org

Olinca Marino
Latin America and the Caribbean Region, Focal Point
email: info@laneta.apc.org
website: http://www.wsis-cs.org/lac/

Nick Moraitis
Youth Family, Focal Point
Email: nick@takingitglobal.org
web: http://profiles.takingitglobal.org/nick

Pierre Alain Muet
Cities and Local Authorities Family, Alternate Focal Point

Alice Munyua
African Region, Alternate Focal Point
email: munyua@femnet.or.ke

Olivier Nana Nzepa

African Region, Focal Point
email: anais_ac@yahoo.fr

Tracey Naughton
Media Family, Focal Point
Nyaka - Communication & Development
201 Somerset Hall
239 Oxford Road
Illovo 2196
South Africa
Phone/fax: +27 (0) 11 880 5030
cell: +27 (0) 82 821 1771
Email: t.naughton@iafrica.com
Time Zone: GMT+1

YJ Park
Networks and Coalitions Family, Alternate Focal Point
email: yjpark@myepark.com

Adam Peake
Think Tanks Family, Alternate Focal Point
email: ajp@glocom.ac.jp
Website: http://www.glocom.ac.jp/users/ajp/ajp.e.html

Ross Shimmon
Creators and Promoters of Culture Family, Alternate Focal Point
email: ross.shimmon@ifla.nl

Seán Ó Siochrú
Networks and Coalitions Family, Focal point
NEXUS Research
14 Eaton Brae, Shankill, Co. Dublin, Ireland
Central office: tel: +353 1 473 0599, Direct office tel: +353 1 272 0739
fax: +353 1 473 0597, Mobile: +353 87 20 48 150
e-mail: sean@nexus.ie
Web site: http://www.iol.ie/nexus

Berni Vigano
Gender Family, Focal Point
email: bvigano@genderwsis.org

Contact Information for Focal Points[120]

Family Focal Points

Education, Academia and Research

Contact organization: Centro de Teletrabajo y Teleformación de la Universidad de Buenos Aires
Focal Point: Beatriz Busaniche (busaniche@caminandoutopias.org.ar)
Alternate: Divina Frau Meigs (meigs@wanadoo.fr)
2nd Alternate: Francis Muguet (muguet@mdpi.org)
Website: www.caminandoutopias.org.ar

Science and technology community

Contact organisation: WFEO;
Focal Point: WFEO, Mr. Kamel Ayadi (cic@coi-tn.org)
Alternate:
Website: http://www.wfeo.org

Media

Contact organization:
Focal Point: Tracey Naughton (t.naughton@iafrica.com)
Alternate: Rony Koven (rkoven@compuserve.com)
Third contact point: Jacques Briquemont (briquemont@ebu.ch)
Wbsite: http://www.wpfc.org

Creators and promoters of culture

Contact organization: International Federation of Library Associations (IFLA), International Publishers Association (IPA)
Focal Point: IPA, Alexis Krikorian (krikorian@ipa-uie.org)
Alternate: IFLA, Ross Shimmon (ross.shimmon@ifla.nl)

---

[120] Contact Point Information is from http://cms.privaterra.org/WSIS_CS_Bureau updated by Robert Guerra.

Website: http://www.ifla.org, http://www.ipa-uie.org

Cities and Local Authorities

Contact organization: World Summit of Cities and Local Authorities on the Information Society
Focal Point: Veronique Kleck (info@cities-lyon.org)
Alternate: Pierre Alain Muet
Website: http://www.cities-lyon.org

Trade Unions

Contact Organization: Union Network International (UNI)
Focal Point: Mrs. Alke Boessiger (alke.boessiger@union-network.org)
Alternate: Mr. Neil Anderson (neil.anderson@union-network.org)
Website: http://www.union-network.org

NGOs

Contact organization: Conference Of Non-Governmental Organizations (CONGO)
Focal Point: Renate Bloem (rbloem@ngocongo.org, congo@ngocongo.org)
Alternate: Bineta Diop (Femme Africa Solidarite)- (info@fas.org)
Website: http://www.ngocongo.org, http://www.prepcom.net/wsis

Youth

Contact organization: TakingITglobal
Focal Points: Nick Moraitis (nick@takingitglobal.org)
Alternate: Alex Fielding (alex@takingitglobal.org)
Website: http://www.ycdo.net/wsis

Gender

Contact organization: WSIS Gender Caucus
Focal Point: Berni Vigano (bvigano@genderwsis.org)
Alternate: Nish Matenjwa

Website: http://www.genderwsis.org

Volunteers

Contact organization: International Conference Volunteers
Focal Point: Viola Krebs (viola@icvolunteers.org)
Alternate:
Website: http://www.worldwidevolunteer.org, http://www.icvolunteers.org, http://www.cev.be

Indigenous Peoples

Contact organization: Indigenous Media Network
Focal Point: Kenneth Deer (kend@easterndoor.com)
Alternate: Ann-Kristin Håkansson (akigua@telia.com)
Website: www.indigenousmedia.org/

Networks and Coalitions

Contact organization: Communications Rights in the Information Society (CRIS Campaign)
Focal Point: Seán Ó Siochrú (sean@nexus.ie)
Alternate: YJPark (Yjpark@myepark.com)
Website: http://www.crisinfo.org

Multi-stakeholders Partnerships

Contact organisation: Association ISOC-Québec, Secrétariat d'ÍSOC- Francophonie,
Focal Point: M. Adel El Zaim (adel.elzaim@canti.com, info@isoc.qc.ca)
Website:

Philanthropic Institutions

Contact organization: Global Contract Foundation
Focal Point: Wolfgang Kleinwaechter (kleinwaechter@wsis-philantropic.org)
Alternate: Frithjof Finkbeiner (finkbeiner@wsis-philantropic.org)

Website: http://www.globalcontract.de/

Think Tanks

Contact organization: FUNGLODE Global Foundation for Democracy and Development
Focal Point: Mr. John R. Gagain Jr. (j.gagain@funglode.org)
Alternate: GLOCOM, Mr. Adam Peake (ajp@glocom.ac.jp)
Website:

People with Disabilities

Contact organization: DAISY Consortium
Focal Point: Hiroshi Kawamura (hkawa@attglobal.net)
Alternate:
Website: http://www.daisy.org

Regional Groups

Africa
Coordinating organization: Africa Civil Society Bureau; African Women's Development and Communications Network
Focal Point: Olivier Nana Nzepa (anais_ac@yahoo.fr)
Alternate: Alice Munyua (munyua@femnet.or.ke)

Latin America and the Caribbean
Coordinating organization: La Neta/APC La Neta; Association for Progressive Communications (APC).
Focal Point: Olinca Marino (info@laneta.apc.org)
Alternate:
Website: http://www.wsis-cs.org/lac/

Asia and Pacific?
Coordinating organization: Foundation for Media Alternatives (FMA); Association for Progressive Communications (APC)
Focal Point: Alan Alegre (alalegre@fma.ph)
Alternate: Angela Kuga Thas (amkt@apcwomen.org)

Europe, CIS and North America
Coordinating organizations: Computer Professional for Social Responsibility, Free Software Foundation Europe
Focal Point: Robert Guerra <rguerra@cpsr.org>
Alternate: Georg C. F. Greve <greve@gnu.org>
Website: http://cms.privaterra.org/WSIS_CSB_EUN

Middle East and Western Asia
Coordinating organization: Iranian Civil Society Training and Research Center (ICTRCT) ex-ICSORC
Focal Point: "Amir Barmaki" <abarmaki@irancsos.net>
Alternate: westasiaregion@hotmail.com
Website: http://www.irancsos.net/english/index.htm

Secretariat:[121]
Coordinating organization: Fondation du Devenir (Interim)
Focal Point: Alain Clerc (alain.clerc@fdd.org)
Alternate: Louise Lassonde (louise.lassonde@fdd.org)
Website: http://www.geneva2003.org, http://www.fdd.org/

- Alain Clerc <alain.clerc@fdd.org>
- Louise Lassonde <louise.lassonde@fdd.org>
- Liliane Ursache <liliane.ursache@fdd.org>
- Claire Chombeau <claire.chombeau@fdd.org>

Each family has a contact person. Do not hesitate to contact them for additional information. The civil society division of the Executive Secretariat is the Secretariat of the Bureau.

[121] Note: The civil society division of the Executive Secretariat ceased to exist as of February 2004. The Executive Secretariat (ES) has assumed the registration of civil society for the summit. Further details will be posted on the news sites as they become available.